ESSAY

ON THE

PRODUCTIVE RESOURCES

OF

INDIA

ESSAY

ON THE

PRODUCTIVE RESOURCES

OF

INDIA.

J. F. ROYLE, M.D., F.R.S., L.S., & G.S.

GYAN

Published by

Gyan Publishing House
5, Ansari Road
Daryaganj, New Delhi-110002
Phone: 011-47034999, 9811692060
E-mail: books@gyanbooks.com

Distribution Network
gyanbooks.com
India, USA, Canada, UK, Australia, France

ISBN: 978-81-212-9302-0 (PB)
First Published, 1840

2nd Impression 2023

Printed at: Gyan Press, Delhi.

ESSAY ON THE PRODUCTIVE RESOURCES OF INDIA

Author: J. F. ROYLE

ESSAY

ON THE

PRODUCTIVE RESOURCES

OF

INDIA.

BY

J. F. ROYLE, M.D., F.R.S., L.S., & G.S.,

Late of the Medical Staff of the Bengal Army, and late Superintendent of the Hon. E. I. C.'s Botanic Garden at Saharunpore; Fellow of the Imperial Society Naturæ Curiosorum; of the Asiatic Societies of Calcutta and London; of the Agricultural and Horticultural Society of India; of the Horticultural Society of London; and of the English Agricultural Society.

PROFESSOR OF MATERIA MEDICA AND THERAPEUTICS, KING'S COLL., LONDON.

LONDON:

WM. H. ALLEN AND CO.,

LEADENHALL STREET.

1840.

PREFACE.

As the Title-page and Table of Contents will inform the reader of the nature of the work he is about to peruse, the Author might refrain from engaging his attention with a Preface, if it did not seem advisable to explain one or two points respecting the nature of the work.

Having long paid attention, both in India and in this country, to the productions of the former, whether the spontaneous gift of Nature or the produce of Agriculture, the Author observed that they were both varied and abundant, and fitted for every purpose, whether for affording food, for contributing to the comfort of the inhabitants, or for yielding materials for Manufactures and Commerce. The country being fruitful in soil and rich in climate, he noticed, however, an unaccountable discrepancy between its natural riches and the quality of the different productions, when compared with similar products from other countries. Observation and consideration, combined with an examination of the modes of culture and manufacture in other parts of the world, enabled him to perceive, that many of the causes of failure were purely of a Physical nature, some, dependent on the Soil, a few, on the Climate, and others, on the processes of Agriculture. The defects seeming as often to be those of redundancy as of deficiency of growth, it appeared feasible so to modify the operations of Agriculture, as to subject the plants under cultivation to the influence (in different degrees) of the several physical agents which controul vegetation, such as Light, Heat, Air, and Moisture, and thus produce different and the desired results.

Being anxious to contribute to the improvement of the Agriculture of India, and hoping that some of his suggestions would have that tendency, the Author might have commenced his work by giving, in the first instance, a general view of the influence of Physical Agents on the functions of Vegetation, more especially in connection with the soil and climate of India. This, from the general neglect of the Natural Sciences in English education, appeared to him the most important, as few writers, in their experiments or their descriptions, refer to the true causes of the results which are obtained. Such a plan would have given cultivators principles for general culture, instead of empirical rules for routine practice, and, at all events, would have enabled experimentalists more easily to detect errors, and at the same time more readily to adopt improvements in their own practice. Or instead of treating, in the first instance, of general principles, he might have taken up any of the principal objects of Indian Agriculture, and exemplified in the culture of these the operation of the different physical agents, or the Physiology of Vegetation.

But before proceeding to adopt either course, it was necessary to become acquainted with the attempts which already had been made. In doing this the Author found that many experiments had been instituted, and much had been done for the improvement of many Indian staple products; but that the generality of modern experimentalists seemed to be unacquainted with the labours of their predecessors; many of them commencing improvement by repeating experiments which had already been made, and announcing results as new, which had long previously been ascertained.

The Author has, therefore, thought it preferable, on the present occasion, to take a general view of the principal objects of Indian Culture, of the course which has been followed in attempting to improve them, and of the results, often successful, which have been obtained. He has interspersed these with explanations of, what appear to be, the physical causes of the successful or unsuccessful culture, and the obvious methods of improvement. For the purposes of comparison, he has commenced, however, with a brief history of the Arts of Culture in other parts of the world. This is instructive, as showing that, in all, difficulties have at first been encountered, which have, on the increase of experience and skill, disappeared; and soils and climates which at one time were pronounced unsuitable for the culture of particular plants, have been afterwards found to produce them of the finest quality.

By this method, the Author hopes he has been able to prove to a greater number in this country the capability of India for all kinds of culture, and the probability of the almost indefinite extension of these, with increased improvement in most of the principal staples of Indian Commerce. While Cultivators in India will see the number of interesting and important subjects to which they may attend with profit to themselves, and if they undertake experiments with due attention to all the circumstances which controul the results, his object will be equally gained, whether his opinions be refuted or confirmed. He hopes he may be able, on future occasions, to take up more in detail both the General and the Specific subjects to which he has alluded.

That the information on the subjects treated

of in this work is varied and authentic, will appear from the references to the works which are quoted in the text: that it is not better known must be ascribed to its being scattered about in publications not easily accessible, even to those desirous of information, as the large works are only found in extensive libraries, and the small ones rapidly disappear from circulation.

He cannot conclude without rectifying an omission, in not having mentioned, when treating of Wool, that the Right Honourable Holt Mackenzie had placed in his hands the materials for a paper on this subject, which the Author hopes he may yet be induced to complete; but having only referred to the same official documents, and not quoted from the paper, the omission is accounted for. The Author has also to acknowledge the receipt of a paper from Dr. Falconer, on Putchuk or Koot, the Costus of the ancients, mentioned at p. 223 of this work. Dr. F. finds that this belongs to a new genus, which he has "named 'Aucklandia,' in honour of George, Earl Auckland, Governor-general of India, not in compliment to his rank, but as a distinction well merited by his Lordship's services in the cause of Indian Botany."

CONTENTS.

ON THE

PRODUCTIVE RESOURCES

OF

INDIA.

In contemplating the sources, and examining the various substances which constitute the wealth of nations, whether these be the necessaries, the conveniences, or the luxuries of life, we observe that the greater number have been derived from the Earth. So much, indeed, is this the case, that some have argued that the earth is the only source of wealth, and have proceeded to propose, that all taxes should be levied on the land alone, as the productiveness of Agriculture is so greatly promoted by the vegetating powers of Nature. Labour, however, is as requisite for working the soil, as for enabling us to modify the properties of material substances to fit them for our comfort or enjoyment; so that labour in a mixed society, and in an advanced state of civilization, must be equally valuable, whether employed on the production of the raw material, in preparing it for our use, or in transporting it from one place to another.

Sources of the wealth of nations.

The Earth.

Agriculture.

Labour.

Products of the earth,

But the Merchant cannot transport, nor the Manufacturer prepare, except what has in the first instance been the result of the labours of the Agriculturist, or is the spontaneous produce of the earth, whether obtained on its surface or from its interior, or procured from the waters of the ocean or of rivers. Therefore, to give an impulse to Commerce, and to obtain materials for Manufactures, it is necessary to investigate both the natural productions of the earth, and the fruitfulness of the soil; not only as fitted for a variety of products, but also with reference to its ability to produce more than what is sufficient for the use or sustenance of its inhabitants. As the earth yields the various mineral, vegetable, or animal substances which form our food, or the materials of our clothing, of our dwellings, or of the different implements necessary for the various arts of life, so it is the chief source of wealth from Agricultural, Commercial, and Manufacturing labours.

require investigation,

as employing the Agriculturist, Merchant, and Manufacturer.

Connection of Arts and Manufactures with Natural Products.

But linked as are the several Arts and Manufactures one with another, and all with Agriculture and the Products of the earth, it is difficult, if not impossible, to determine which is the most important in an advanced state of civilization, or which kingdom of Nature is the most indispensable to man.

Mineral kingdom. Chemical arts.

Deprived of the multiplied treasures of the Mineral Kingdom, most of the arts called Chemical would never have been known, and others would have languished without the aid of their most efficient agents; even Agriculture itself would have laboured with inferior, instead of the best, materials for its implements. Metals, moreover, are required to give strength to Shipping, and facility of movement to Machinery, while those called Precious give us the most convenient medium of Exchange. Coal, though derived from the accumulation of vegetable matter in former periods of the world, is yet dug out of the interior of the earth, and now forms so excellent a fuel that it has given a superiority to the manufactures of England, with which the natural advantages of other countries have hitherto been unable to compete. Iron, as abundantly diffused as it is useful, has so surprisingly assisted man in the career of improvement, that Mr. Locke has said that the discoverer of its uses may be truly styled the "father of arts and author of plenty."

MINERAL PRODUCTS.

Metals.

Coal.

Iron.

Animal substances are, however, equally valuable; for man, in the early periods of society, depended as much upon the skins of animals for clothing as he relied upon their flesh for subsistence. Nations, even in the most advanced stages of civilization, derive a great portion of their food from animals, at the same time that they employ their skins, wool, and silk, for parts of their clothing. These, therefore, form extensive articles of commerce, from the nearer as well as from the most distant parts of the world; as Wool from Germany, Spain, the North of India, and New Holland; Silk from the South of Europe, China, and Bengal; Hides

ANIMAL PRODUCTS.

Flesh for food.

Skins for clothing.

Wool.

Silk.

Hides.

Animal Products. Furs. from the North of Europe and South America, as well as from India; Furs and Skins from Canada and Russia; while, to dye these of colours more convenient or agreeable than those afforded *Cochineal.* by Nature, Cochineal is imported from Mexico, *Lac.* and the Lac from India. In late, as in early *Fat and oil.* civilization, the fatty portions of animals are employed for affording light; hence fleets are despatched into polar regions in pursuit of the Whale, and Tallow is imported in large quantities *Horns.* from Russia, and even from India. Horns are manufactured into various sorts of implements, and are obtained from different parts of the world. The clippings of horns and of skins are *Bones.* boiled down into glue, and the bones and offal of *Draught cattle.* animals are employed as manure. Several kinds of cattle, moreover, aid by their labour the processes of Agriculture; some are employed in transporting the produce of the soil, or the treasures of the mine, and others in giving motion to the machinery of many manufactories.

Vegetable kingdom necessary to animals. But still, whether required for food or for its spoils, or for employment as a beast of draught or of burden, the animal cannot subsist in the air or in the water, on the barren soil or arid rock, but must derive its sustenance from the Vegetable kingdom. Plants, therefore, are necessary to all, for not even could the Bee collect its honey, unless this were first secreted by the flower; nor the Silk-worm spin its silk, if deprived of the sustenance of the leaf: neither could the

Cochineal, nor the Lac insects, elaborate their dyes without their vegetable food. Skin even cannot be converted into leather, and rendered fit for the purposes of man, without the astringent tanning principle yielded by the bark, the wood, the leaf, or the fruit of different Plants.

Vegetable kingdom necessary to animals.

Commencement of civilization.

In tracing the progress of civilization, it has every where been observed, that in the earliest stage of society man is found with imperfect weapons, depending for his subsistence on the precarious, long-continued, and fatiguing labours of the chase, assisted by a scanty and uncertain supply of the wild fruits of the forest. In this state a small number of men require for their support a large extent of territory. From pursuing animals, man proceeds to attempt their domestication, and the Pastoral state succeeds to that of the Hunter. Population still is much scattered, as every tribe has to travel in quest of fresh pastures, and each family has to provide itself not only with food, but also with whatever it requires for its clothing, as well as with the necessary arms and implements. In favourable situations, Tillage, or the preparation of the soil, and the cultivation of useful plants, is next discovered, and then the habits of the settled Agriculturist succeed to those of the wandering Shepherd. A comparatively small space of cultivated ground is then sufficient for the maintenance of a large number of individuals, as the ground may be tilled and the fruit of the favourite

The Hunter.

Pastoral state.

Tillage.

Agriculture.

Abundance of food.

Abundance of Food.

tree continue to be collected, while the flocks at the same time are driven to pasture.

Division of labour.

Commencement of manufactures.

A superabundance of food allows larger numbers of men to congregate together, and settled habits afford them leisure for other pursuits. The first division of labour then takes place, when men finding, that by giving their undivided attention to any one pursuit, they are enabled to prepare much more of the manufacture on which they are engaged, than is required for their own consumption, they are ready to barter it for the produce of the labour of others. This exchange, though at first taking place only between the members of their own tribe, is soon extended to those of others, and Commerce, in the full sense of the term, is established. This progressive advancement in occupation marks the stages of society. Some peculiarity of country or of climate, however, often renders one pursuit more advantageous than another, this, therefore, is followed in preference, and continues to characterize particular people. Hence we find some nations addict themselves principally to Pasturage, and others to Agriculture; some chiefly to Manufactures, and others again, who possess but limited territories, or are deficient in produce, employ themselves almost entirely in transporting from one country to another the products of different parts of the globe. Great Britain happily unites with extensive Pasturage the most advanced Agriculture, and great perfection of Manufactures,

Commerce established.

Occupations of different nations.

Great Britain.

with unbounded Commerce.* India, early celebrated for the richness and variety of its Products, as well as for the Manufacturing skill of its inhabitants, may in the present day rather be considered as a great Agricultural country. India. Agricultural.

It is sometimes made a subject of discussion, what parts of the world were first peopled, and became great agricultural and commercial nations; and it is generally supposed that the exchange of commodities first became considerable in Mesopotamia, Egypt, and on the coasts of Arabia. We now know, that Arabia produces none of those valuable products for which, in ancient times, it was so celebrated; the Arabians must therefore have obtained them from the regions where they were produced. The nearest of these are the peninsula of India and the island of Ceylon; and as we learn from history that caravans entered into and departed from the north-western parts of India, it is evident that its COMMERCE. Early history of. Indian.

* Dr. Buckland, in his Bridgewater Treatise—Geology and Mineralogy, has happily observed, vol. i. p. 2, that if three foreigners were to land at separate points and travel over different parts of Great Britain, which he points out, "One would represent it as a thinly-peopled region of barren mountains; another, as a land of rich pastures, crowded with a flourishing population of manufacturers; the third, as a great corn-field, occupied by persons exclusively engaged in the pursuits of husbandry." These dissimilar conditions," Dr. B. observes, "of three great divisions of our country, result from differences in the geological structure of the districts, through which our three travellers have been conducted."

ANCIENT INDIA. Commerce of. products must have been objects of desire to the nations of antiquity. From these facts it is highly probable that the Manufactures, and necessarily the Agriculture, of ancient India were contemporary with those of the far-famed, but probably not earlier civilized, Egypt. Indeed, the extensive and fruitful plains of India, intersected by magnificent rivers, and having a favourable climate, must early and easily have supplied a super-

Fruitfulness of. abundance of food to its inhabitants; and thus have allowed some the leisure necessary for those other pursuits in which they early excelled contemporary nations. Their country, moreover, must have produced then, as now, a great variety

Natural products of. of natural products, which when known, must in those days have been objects of desire, as they are to distant nations at the present time. It is in consequence of this that we find so many of them noticed and described in the earliest records which we possess in the ancient literture of the West.

Chiefly vegeble. The articles of commerce for which India was so early famed having been chiefly the products of plants, and as the culture of plants, from affording abundance of food, and thus leading to settled

Importance of these. habits, and to the establishment of property in land, forms the most important step in the progress of civilization; so this subject necessarily claims the first consideration in the economic history of a country, and in the development and improvement of its resources.

The vegetable world, though constantly before our eyes, is seldom thought of by the generality of people, except as varying the appearance of a country, as producing vegetables or flowers, or as being the source of some of the products useful or agreeable to man; and therefore, in the ordinary attempts to cultivate plants for our use or amusement, especially in new situations, every thing, except the desire to possess them, seems to be forgotten. **Plants, general ideas of.**

Notwithstanding this, almost every one knows, however, that plants, like animals, are living bodies, and that they require nourishment for their support, which must be procured by them from the world without. Animals, from their locomotive habits, are enabled to go in search of food, which having obtained, they convey into their interior. During the process of digestion, the nutritive particles are separated and absorbed into the system, along the *internal* surface of the alimentary canal. Plants, on the contrary, being stationary in nature, depend for their subsistence on the soil in which they are placed, or on the atmosphere by which they are surrounded. The particles adapted to their growth being in the one case suspended in the air, and, in the other being intermixed with, or forming a part of, the soil, are dissolved in water, and in this state are absorbed by the *external* surface into their interior, where, by peculiar processes, they are assimilated to the purposes of the individual. Both animals **Plants. Living bodies. Distinction between them and animals.**

PLANTS. and plants, though acting in conjunction with, are yet able, by the influence of their living principle, to control the powers of attraction and affinity to which, being without life, mineral substances are alone subjected.

Derive sustenance from inorganic matter. Plants, unlike animals, are able to derive sustenance from inorganic matter, such as air, water, carbon, and carbonic acid; but they flourish most on that which has been already organized, though it is in a state of decomposition. Hence, in the

Position in scale of nature. scale of nature they hold an intermediate position between animals and minerals. No animal derives its food immediately from unorganized matter, but many prey upon other animals, which have, in the first instance, been nourished by vegetable matter. It has therefore been well said, that "if plants ceased to grow, animals would cease to exist."

Influence of. The influence of Plants, therefore, even of those of the lowest grade, is much greater than what would at first appear to an unreflecting observer; for even the jelly-like forms of vegetation seen floating on stagnant water, afford nourishment to animalculæ, which are themselves to serve as food

Food for animals. to more highly-developed animals. Sea-weeds afford sustenance to many fish, and even to the Dugong and Lamantine of the tropical seas, as well as to the huge Hippopotamus. Lichens and Mosses are among the first plants to grow upon newly-formed lands, and may be seen vegetating even upon the barren rock. These, insignificant as they may appear, afford by their decay a portion of organized matter to barren soil, and allow of the vegetation of grasses and other small herbaceous plants, which decaying in their turn, give additional organized matter to enrich the soil, and thus prevent that which has been long in cultivation from becoming sterile. PLANTS. Enrich soil.

Myriads, also, of the minutest as well as of the largest living beings feed upon vegetable matter; even the insignificant rock-moss serves as food for the rein-deer, the pasture grasses for herds of ruminating cattle, and the leaves of trees for the largest quadrupeds now seen upon the surface of the earth. From the great similarity in nature of the different pasture grasses, in every part of the world, man has been able to transport cattle into the various countries of the earth which he has chosen to colonize. Some fruits afford nutriment to birds and small quadrupeds; while others, employed as such by man, form, with vegetables, the chief objects of attention to the Gardener, and the principles of their culture the science of Horticulture; while the Cereal grasses, as yielding the greater portion of the food of man, form the principal objects of Agriculture. Uses of. Food for animals. Gardening. Agriculture.

But it is not only as leading to settled habits in the early ages of the world, and giving an interest to property in land, or as continuing to afford a great portion of the food of man, and pasturage for his cattle, that plants claim prominent consideration. For we find that the various PRODUCTS OF PLANTS. Their uses.

PRODUCTS OF PLANTS. principles which compose the organs of plants, or which are stored up within their structure, serve man for many useful and important purposes. The flower he may admire for its colour, or value for its scent; but the leaf he uses as a thatch for his habitation; the bamboo serves him for arms and implements, and with the reed he forms arrows. Hollowed trunks of trees no doubt early afforded him the means of crossing rivers; while the wood serves all the purposes to

Timber.

which timber is applied; and these are so varied that it is difficult to say whether they be more important previous or subsequent to the discovery

Cotton.

of metals. The cottony covering of the seed must early have been converted into clothing, and may have led to the discovery of the applicability of vegetable fibre to the same purposes, when existing in situations where it is less obvious, as in the Flax and Hemp.

Flax. Hemp. Starch.

Besides the Fecula, or starch, which is stored up in the Corn-grasses, we find a similar substance, and nearly as well fitted for food, in such seeds as the Chestnut, and in tubers of various kinds, as in those of the Potatoe and of the Yam; in the Arrow-root of the West, as in that of the East-Indies, as well as in the Cassava and the Sweet Potatoe; and in the Arums, the taccas, and eddoes of the islands of the Pacific Ocean,

Salep.

with an analogous substance in the Salep, which has long been famed for its nourishing properties.

Woody fibre.

Even the woody fibre, from the similarity in constituent principles, may, when reduced to the state of saw-dust, by the slow application of heat, be converted into a kind of gummy substance, which has been proposed as a substitute for bread in times of scarcity. Other plants secrete Saccharine principle, as the Sugar-cane and several of the Palms, as well as the Sugar-maple of North America, and the Beet-root of European countries. PRODUCTS OF PLANTS. Sugar.

Some plants are remarkable for the Mucilage which they contain, or the Gum, soluble in water, which they exude. Others, again, yield Resins, which, unlike these, are dissolved by oils and spirit, and are therefore employed for making Varnishes, to defend various substances from the influences of air and moisture. Nature herself presents to us some of these, fitted for such purposes, as the Piney Varnish tree of the Peninsula of India, as well as that of Burma. Gum. Resin. Varnish.

The natural mixtures of Gums with Resins are employed chiefly as medicines, as are also the Volatile Oils, though many of these give the agreeable flavour to our most valued Spices and Aromatics. Volatile oils. Spices.

The Fatty Oils are expressed from the Cocoa-nut, Olive, Sesamum, Rape, Linseed, and from many other plants; or they are found in the form of Butter, as in the Ghee tree of Almora, the Tallow tree of Canara and of China, all employed either in cookery, for anointing the body, or for affording light. Other plants are remarkable for Fatty oils. Butter.

PRODUCTS OF PLANTS. Dyes. secreting Colouring matter, which may be employed as a Dye, or for the astringent principle, Tannin. which is indispensable to the art of Tanning.

Some substances which are very peculiar in Caoutchouc. their nature, as the Caoutchouc, or Indian-rubber, take long before their applications are discovered, but when time and science have effected this, they are found to be not less important than others of which the uses are Acids. more obvious. The several vegetable Acids are chiefly useful as articles of diet or as medicines; but are also necessary in a variety of arts, like Alkalis. the alkalis obtained from the incineration of vegetables. Wood serves every where as fuel, except where Coal is abundant, which, though more valuable, is also of vegetable origin.

As articles of commerce. As Plants and their products may be applied to such a variety of purposes, and as most countries have some which are peculiar to themselves, or to which their soil and climate are best adapted; so it is found that different countries produce very different products, or, if the same, then of very different degrees of goodness. Hence these become objects of desire to other nations, and thus form a very large proportion of the Commerce of the world, as we may observe in the Corn, Hemp, and Flax of the North of Europe; the Timber of Norway and of Canada; the Gin of Holland; and the Oil, the Fruits, and the Wine and Brandy of the South of Europe; the Cotton and Tobacco, the Rice and Flour of the United

States of America; the Logwood and Mahogany of Honduras; the Caoutchouc of Para; and the Bark of Peru; the Sugar and Rum, Cocoa and Coffee, Tobacco, Allspice, and Arrow Root of the West-Indies; the Gum, Myrrh, and Aloes of Africa; the Dates, the Coffee, and Senna of Arabia; the Saffron and Gum Resins of Persia; the Rhubarb of Tibet; the Tea of China; the Rice and Indigo, Spices and Sugar, Opium and Teak of India; with a variety of Medicines from all parts of the world; and Barilla from the South of Europe; with Potash, Pitch and Tar, from the North of Europe, as well as from North America.

PRODUCTS OF PLANTS.

Articles of Commerce.

Many Manufacturers, moreover, are engaged entirely on the products of Plants, as those who use Timber for carpentering, mill-work, and house or ship-building; or such as make use of vegetable fibre, as Flax and Hemp, or Cotton, for spinning and weaving into cloth for domestic purposes, or into sails for shipping, or for manufacturing into ropes and cables. Others, again, are employed in Bleaching the cloth, or in Dyeing it of various colours, or in Calico-printing; and in this also employ vegetable substances to effect their purpose. Some occupy themselves in grinding the corn into Flour, or in converting this into Starch, or in Malting, Brewing, or in Distilling, and in some countries in making Wine or Vinegar; in manufacturing or refining Sugar, in expressing Oils, or in extracting Tannin, or in

Employed in manufactures.

PRODUCT OF PLANTS.

dissolving Gum or Resin, for the various purposes to which these substances are applied. Even the destruction of vegetables affords useful products, as Charcoal, Pitch and Tar, Potash and Barilla; finally, vegetable matter is required for making paper in all its varieties.

Employed in manufactures.

Relative importance of products of Nature.

The relative importance of these, as compared with one another, or with the other products of Nature or of Art, which contribute to the wealth and resources of a country, it is not easy to determine, as they must vary in different parts of the world, and in the several states of society, as well as at different times in the same country. But their value as objects of commerce, or as contributing to the revenues of a country, may be seen by the quantities in which they form its Exports or Imports; and also in a great measure, by the amount of the Taxes collected on each. This is likewise an interesting subject of investigation, as giving us some means of ascertaining the nature of the products of a country, as well as the occupations of a people.

Great Britain.

The result in Great Britain, we observe, is that a very large proportion of the Imports consists of raw produce obtained from the vegetable kingdom. Thus, in the year 1836, the net produce of the Custom-house duties amounted to £22,774,991. Of this large sum, 98¼ per cent. of the whole, or £22,376,869, was collected upon forty-five articles; that is, no less than £21,127,455 upon Vegetable, £1,177,091 upon Animal, and

Imports.

only £72,323 upon Mineral Substances.* These sums are certainly not in proportion, to the importance to the country, of the three kingdoms of Nature, as the Exports consist chiefly of Manufactured articles, both of Mineral and Animal products, as well as of the Vegetable Substances previously imported; but they very strikingly confirm the importance of the Vegetable Kingdom.

In India, however, the Exports, (amounting in 1837-38, in value to Co. Rs. 6,14,79,472,)† consist chiefly of Vegetable Products, as of Opium and Indigo, Sugar, Rice, and Cotton, Wheat, Flour, and Pulses; with Ginger, Safflower, Vegetable Oils, Indian Hemp and Jute, also Cotton Piece Goods and Coarse Cloths. The Animal substances, of Raw Silk and Piece Goods, Lac, Hides, Horns, and Elephants' Teeth; with Saltpetre, Borax, and Sal Ammoniac from the Mineral Kingdom. The Imports, on the contrary, consist principally of the Manufactured produce of Europe, as of Cotton and Silk Piece Goods, chiefly the former, with Wines and Spirits, and the various articles required for the use of the European inhabitants. Betel-nuts, Pepper, Cloves, Spices, and Teak from the

* The Progress of the Nation, by G. Porter, Esq. F.R.S. Interchange, Revenue, and Expenditure, p. 323.

† A comparative view of the External Commerce of Bengal during the years 1836-37, and 1837-38, by John Bell, Superintendent of the Preventive Service in the Calcutta Custom-house.

countries to the southward and eastward; Coffee and Dates from Arabia, Tea from China, large quantities of Metals from Europe, and Salt from the Sunderbunds; with Coral, Chanks, Cowries, Horns, Hides, &c., many of which are again re-exported.

These Imports, contributing to the comforts of the inhabitants, are evidently bought with the raw produce of the soil, which, as we have seen, is exported in such large quantities. The culture of the land, therefore, is of proportionate importance, as it not only affords abundance of food, and employment for the great agricultural population, but also materials for manufactures, and likewise for both external and internal commerce.

Tabular View of the Value of Exports and Imports from the Port of Calcutta, in 1837-38, arranged according to the Kingdoms of Nature by which they are produced.

	1837-38. Imports—Value.	1837-38. Re-Exports—Value.	1837-38. Exports—Value.
VEGETABLE.	35,53,799	3,95,524	4,54,21,074
Manufactured:—			
Cloth, Rope, &c.	1,15,82,859	12,51,640	13,59,261
Wines, &c.	14,55,963	——	75,284
ANIMAL.	6,22,104	69,931	67,56,613
Manufactured	10,76,139	1,93,037	43,88,497
MINERAL.	61,12,436	3,14,164	27,48,980
Manufactured	24,60,446	——	——
MISCELLANEOUS.	29,94,149	10,25,303	7,29,763
TOTAL..	2,98,57,895	32,49,599	6,14,79,472

CULTURE OF VEGETABLES.

Vegetables and their products being thus necessary for the food of man, and the maintenance of his cattle, forming a great part of his clothing, and furnishing materials for his habitation, affording medicines to relieve him when sick, and products necessary for the various arts and manufactures; their culture has from the earliest times, and in all civilized nations, been favoured by the people, and patronised by sovereigns. An art which leads to settled habits, affords employment to a large portion of the population, as well as food for the whole, materials for the arts and manufactures, as well as for internal trade and external commerce, must necessarily command the favourable consideration of every Government. Besides its obvious utility, the culture of Vegetables, moreover, affords much pleasing employment even to those who do not follow it as an occupation. Hence it has been observed to have a civilizing effect on the passions, and to lead to orderly habits, ever since the first great advance was made in civilization by the transition of the nomade shepherd into the settled cultivator of the soil. Therefore not only did those nations become first civilized who had the greatest facilities for pursuing the Arts of Culture, or were the most determined to overcome by labour the difficulties opposed by nature; but even in the present day those who are the most

CULTURE OF VEGETABLES.

Connected with Civilization.

CULTURE OF VEGETABLES.

civilized in other respects, are observed to pay the greatest attention to the Arts which improve the fruitfulness, or increase the variety of the Products of the Soil.

In early times.

The Arts of Culture were probably, in the first instance, restricted to Fruit-trees and the Cereal grains, and must then have been limited in degree; but in progress of time they came to be distinguished by different names, either according to the kinds of Plants, or the extent in which these were cultivated. This is evident if we observe that the culture of the same plant is considered in different countries as belonging to different departments. Employed upon plants required for the food of man, or for producing materials fitted for arts and manufactures and extended into the open culture of a country, it is denominated Farming or Agriculture. In the present day, this also includes the rearing of Stock, whether required as labouring cattle, or as food for man. When this culture is moderate in degree, or carried on in enclosed spaces, and chiefly by manual labour, it is called Gardening or Horticulture. This is usually engaged upon plants yielding fruit, or such as are required in their vegetable state, or as condiments, or which are agreeable for their appearance, or grateful for their odour. The culture of Plants is sometimes more minutely divided, as into that of Corn, Hay, and Pasture Grasses, or into that of Timber or of Fruit-trees, or such as are suited

Agriculture.

Horticulture.

to the Shrubbery or Flower Garden, or into that of Medicinal plants. Such as are too delicate for our climate are protected from its severity in the Green House, while those which have been procured from the hottest regions of the globe have their climates imitated by the artificial heat and moisture of the Hot-house. Culture is often still more divided, as into that of particular plants, as of the Hop, Hemp, Flax, and Cotton; Sugar, Tea, Coffee, Tobacco, Opium, and Indigo.

CULTURE OF VEGETABLES.

Culture must at first be limited in extent.

Culture of every kind must necessarily, in the first instance, be limited in extent, as it is only by the multiplication of the seed, or offsets from the plant first cultivated, that means are obtained for extending the cultivation even of one that is indigenous in a country. This must be still more the case with such as are foreign to the soil. It is evidently impracticable, except at unnecessary expense, to introduce new plants, or their seeds, in large enough quantities to suffice for the culture of a country; and, at all events, it is premature to do so, before the question of their success or failure in a new locality has been carefully determined by experiment. Then their peculiarities of habit in the new situation will have been ascertained, as well as the modifications required in culture, to compensate for differences of soil or of climate.

Therefore of the nature of Gardens.

It is evident, therefore, that as culture must be, in the first instance, limited in extent, it will partake, more or less, of the nature of garden

Institution of Gardens.

culture. Institutions of this kind, by whatever name distinguished, may be traced from very early to the present times, whether simply denominated a Garden, an Experimental Farm, a Nursery, a Horticultural, or a Botanic Garden. The earliest we find described as agreeable, from affording shade or from coolness, or from containing an assemblage of plants, pleasing for their appearance or grateful for their odour, or such as were celebrated for yielding delicious fruits.

Gardens first established in the East.

The East having been the first peopled, and the earliest civilized, it is not surprizing that to its nations we are able to trace the origin of many of the arts, and among the rest that of Gardening. This, not only because in these countries the arts of culture had been discovered, and the transition first made from the wandering shepherd to the settled cultivator of the soil, but also because these regions present the greatest contrasts of climate, at different seasons of the year, as well as very dissimilar products in different parts of the country. The mountains under the influence of a cool and refreshing temperature, afford verdant pastures, beautiful flowers, and well-flavoured fruits; while the plains, like the summers, being hot and dry, present only a brownish, stunted, and thorny vegetation, except in the immediate neighbourhood of the streamlets which descend from the mountains. The earliest accounts of gardens we read of are in Syria, Palestine, Mesopotamia, and Persia; and in the almost imperishable paintings of the Egyptians we observe the attention which they paid to the culture of vegetables, as well as to all the other arts of Peace.

Gardens in ancient Europe.

The Greeks.

The Greeks have described the Gardens of Cyrus; and it is more than probable, that from their intercourse with Persia and Egypt, they may have learned to value their uses. Thence also they may have acquired their love for and employment of flowers, as offerings at the altars of their gods, as well as for adorning the persons of their priests, philosophers, and warriors, as has always been the custom in Eastern countries.

The Romans.

The Romans, though so warlike a people, paid great attention to all the arts of culture; indeed we are indebted to them for many of the vegetables and fruits at present so common in Europe. They took great pains not only in introducing the useful plants of the countries they conquered into those which they already possessed, but also in inculcating the practice of their own improved agriculture throughout their widely-spread territories.

Gardening in modern Persia.

Granting the origin of civilization and of the arts of culture in those regions described in the earliest works of Western writers, it is not probable that they would cease to be esteemed in the countries where they originated, or that they would not, like civilization, spread to the south and east as well as to the north and west. Gardens, therefore, have continued to be cultivated by the

Gardens in the East. Persia.

modern as by the ancient Persians; but there is a remarkable difference between those of Ancient and Modern Europe and the gardens of the East. In the former every year has seen numerous accessions to their riches, and an increase in their uses and applications, while the latter remain the same in appearance, and without much increase of the objects of cultivation; as the same plants continue to be cultivated now as in ancient times, with but few additions to their number. Persian gardens, in modern times, are described as having a reservoir of water in the centre, with a broad and straight avenue, planted on either side with poplars, cypresses, and the Oriental plane, the latter especially valued for the shade it affords. The fruits cultivated are the melon, apple, apricot, peach, and grape-vine: also a few flowers, conspicuous for their odour or appearance, as the rose, jessamine, narcissus, hyacinth, and tulip, all of which are however indigenous in the plains or mountains of the country; and for the love of which the Persians have always been distinguished as a nation.

India.

The arts of culture were not long confined to the Persians, or to the ancient Egyptians, for contemporary with them the Hindoos excelled in all the arts of Peace; and no doubt originated many of them, as they early practised improved

Fruitfulness of.

processes of Agriculture. India, rich in natural products, and easily cultivated, having water near the surface, and its plains intersected by magnificent rivers, with a climate in which wheat and barley probably introduced from the north, could be cultivated at one season, and at another the rice and joar, indigenous in the country, must easily have furnished superabundance of food, and thus have afforded facilities for some of the inhabitants to follow arts, pursue commerce, and give themselves up to literature and science, for which they were so early celebrated. India, Fruitfulness of.

The Hindoo modes of Culture are in many respects peculiar, as in sowing several kinds of seed together, and collecting the different crops as they successively come to perfection. Though their Rice is collected year after year, and often twice in the same year in the same field without manure, they are well acquainted with the improving effects on land, of the culture of leguminous plants; and also that the corn grasses, rice excepted, impoverish it: whence Dr. Roxburgh was of opinion, that "the western parts of the old world first learned the art of changing their crops." They have, besides, employed the Drill plough from time immemorial, though this is considered a modern European invention. The native peasant, according to Mr. Colebrooke, "feels a superstitious predeliction for the trees planted by his ancestors, and derives comfort, and even profit from their fruit," while "the clumps of bamboos which, when once planted, continue to flourish as long as they are not too abruptly thinned," supply him materials for Indian Agriculture.

Gardens in Bengal.

the construction of his cottage, at the same time that they are sources of profit.

The Hindoos also grow useful plants near their houses, and are attached to the culture of flowers, for offerings at the shrines of their gods, or for throwing into their sacred streams, as well as for adorning their persons, as in the form of necklaces of jessamine and of the night-blowing nyctanthes. Yet Gardening seems never to have made much progress, as Dr. Wallich describes the gardens of the natives in Bengal, and many will recognize the truth of the description, as consisting of an assemblage of straight and narrow rows of arecas, planted at right angles; beds of endless tagetes, and a few others of the most common flowers; with wildernesses of inferior sorts of plantains and some other ordinary fruits; also the mangoe in its natural state, the guava, and custard-apple.

Gardens in N. India.

In the north-west of India, where the customs of the Mahomedan conquerors chiefly prevail, the gardens partake of the Persian character, but with the intermixture of the usual Indian with some northern plants. The gardens are generally laid out in squares, divided by imperfectly kept roads, which are bordered with water-courses for irrigation. These are also agreeable for the coolness they create; and are sometimes formed of stone, and at others, as in the palaces, of marble. The trees often consist of rows of cypress, or of oranges and limes, with fine peaches, the pomegranate, apple, grape-vine, and mulberry; in- different mangoes, plantains, with the guava and custard-apple, Indian jujube, and curounda. The Melon tribe is extensively cultivated, and also some of the more ordinary vegetables. The usual flowers consist of the rose, jessamine, and tuberose, with the hyacinth, narcissus, crinum, some flowering arborescent bauhinias and cassias, with a few trees, such as the neem and bukayun, with the simbhaloo, used like the others medicinally.

Gardens in N. India.

Vegetables.

Flowers.

The gardens of India usually disappoint a European, accustomed to the rich variety of English gardens, yet that the natives are much attached to such institutions, is evident by their having been established, and also villages assigned for their maintenance, by the native governments at Agra, Secundra, and Saharunpore. The gardens at Delhi, especially that called Shalimar, were formerly of great repute; but that of the palace of the king is alone kept up with any care. Here the shady trees, surrounded by the lofty palace wall, and constant irrigation from a branch of the Canal flowing through the garden, produce an artificial climate, which is cooler, moister, and more equable than that of the surrounding country. This accounts for the existence there in the open air, of a tree, found only in the southern parts of India, and which is allied in nature to, and requires a similar climate with the tropical Mangosteen.

Delhi.

THE ARTS OF CULTURE IN EUROPE.

Progress of Agriculture in Europe.

The Romans, who practised successfully the arts of culture in their own country, also introduced them perseveringly into those which they conquered, sometimes stimulating them by the exaction of tribute in corn. But as their influence declined, and that of their barbarous successors became paramount, no prospect of improvement could be entertained, and the utmost to be hoped for, was the preservation of that which had already been taught. This was, in some measure, insured by the establishment of numerous religious communities throughout uncivilized Europe, who, building churches, founding abbeys, relieving the sick, and providing food for the poor, promoted the civilization of the people among whom they took up their abode. As the lands which these establishments possessed required to be cultivated, not only for their own maintenance, but also for that of their poorer neighbours, some of the body studied the precepts of Agriculture in the works of the Romans, and practised the art with a success to which historians have borne testimony, in their statement of the church lands being always the best cultivated. Gardening moreover was pursued with a skill which was unknown in ancient, and unsurpassed until very modern times.

Agriculture.

Early stages of.

Agriculture being in the present day so extensively practised, and highly patronized throughout Europe, we find a difficulty in representing to ourselves a state of society in which it was not so. But by referring to the records of history, we find that it often required the interference of the sovereign to induce the subject to cultivate that which was not only for his own advantage, but also for the improvement of his country. Thus, Charlemagne, in the eighth century, directed the cultivation in France of no less than seventy-three kinds of fruit-trees and of medicinal plants. The ordonance which he published, is referred to by Montesquieu, as a monument of prudent economy and good administration. He even opened a correspondence with Haroon-al-Rashid, and by that means procured for France the best sorts of pulse, melons, peaches, figs, and other fruits.* From his era, therefore, dates the introduction of many of the best fruits for which France is famous, as well as the establishment of orchards and vineyards.

Agriculture—progress of.

In France.

The revival of learning and the Culture of Arts having taken place in Italy, it was there that agriculture and gardening were first regarded with any thing like the attention they had excited in earlier times. Crescenzio, a senator of Bologna, wrote his work on Rural Affairs and Gardening in the early part of the fourteenth century, though not printed till 1471 at Florence. Irrigation had,

In Italy.

* The Abbé Schinde Mag. Eneye, as quoted by Mr. Loudon, in his Encyclopædia of Gardening.

Agriculture in Italy.

however, been practised previously to 1037, and Silk-worms were imported from Greece into Sicily

First Botanic Garden.

in 1146. The first Botanic Garden was established at Pisa in 1543, and the next at Padua in 1545. The greatest agricultural improvements took place

Improvements in the N. of Italy.

in Tuscany and Lombardy. In the former, the culture of the Vine and of the Olive were brought to great perfection; and the Oil of Lucca, and the Wines of Florence became celebrated. Lombardy excelled also in the management of corn and cattle, and the pastures were the most productive in the world, having the advantages of a climate so temperate in winter, that the grass grows all the year; a soil naturally rich, and an abundant supply of river water for irrigation.

Holland.

Though gardening was first brought into notice in Italy, it attained perfection in Holland and the Netherlands: the climate and soil being singularly favourable for Horticulture and Flower-gardening. The garden of Leyden was began in 1577, when the magistrates, learned men, and citizens, all patronized the introduction of new plants, and the captains of ships were directed to bring them, and seeds from all parts of the world; so that the garden soon contained not less than six thousand species of plants. Before the middle of the seventeenth century, gardens were established in all the provinces; and this century was distinguished by the rage for flowers, which has been denominated Florimania, when particular kinds were sold for such enormous prices. Harte, in his Essays, considers Agriculture to have been brought at an early period from Italy to Basle, the Economical Society of that city being among the oldest in Europe, and the husbandry of its neighbourhood the most perfect on the Continent.

Arts of Culture —Germany.

In France the garden of Montpelier was established in 1597, and that of Paris completed in 1634, after eighteen years of prosecution, and six of culture, according to the description of one of its early superintendents. Since 1786 it has been much improved, and still more so within the last few years, and being connected with a University, forms a school of Horticulture and of Planting, as well as of Agriculture and of Medicine. Other gardens are established in different parts of France, and which pay attention to the Botany and Horticulture of the several districts.

Gardens in France.

In no country, however, of Europe, or indeed of the world, have the Arts of Culture, including in these terms both Horticulture and Agriculture, been carried to higher perfection than in Great Britain. But even here we observe, that they were long in an apparently stationary state, that their advance was slow, and that it is only in comparatively recent times that they have made great progress; the impulse having been given either by the patronage of the sovereign, the works of remarkable individuals, the institution of Societies, or by some extraneous circumstance. The Romans no doubt introduced their Agriculture,

In Great Britain.

Agriculture

In Great Britain. some of their vegetables, and also a few of their fruits, but attention to such subjects declined with their departure. It, however, was revived by the Improved by Normans. Norman Barons, and especially by the Clergy, who both paid great attention to the improvement of the land, and the latter to the introduction also of fruits, and the practice of gardening.

Early authors. It is curious that many to whom improvements in Agriculture are traced were not professional farmers, but men engaged in other pursuits, who, with cultivated minds turned their attention also to this subject. Thus, the first English Treatise on Husbandry was written by Sir A. Fitzherbert. Sir A. Fitzherbert, Judge of the Common Pleas in 1534, and from this, Harte, Canon of Windsor, in his Essays on Agriculture, dates the revival Tusser. of Agriculture in England. Tusser, the author of "Five Hundred Points of Husbandry," published in 1562, was a scholar of Eton, and afterwards of Trinity Hall, Cambridge, before he Sir R. Weston. applied to Farming and Literature. Sir R. Weston, who was Ambassador from England to the Elector Palatine and King of Bohemia in 1619, introduced Clover into England; his Discourse on the Husbandry of Brabant and Flanders was published in 1645, and is said to mark the dawn of the vast improvements which have since been Evelyn. effected in Britain. Evelyn, who is considered one of the greatest encouragers of improvements that had ever appeared, was, as is well known, a gentleman attached to literature and science, and often employed in the public service. He published, in 1664, his "Sylva, or a Discourse on Forest-trees and the Propagation of Timber in his Majesty's dominions," with many other works, which had a great influence in the improvement of the country. Jethro Tull, who introduced the Drill Husbandry, and published his work on Horse-hoeing Husbandry in 1731, was bred a barrister; he first made experiments on his own estate, and then practised farming.

In Great Britain.

Tull.

Scotland, now so remarkable for careful culture and successful farming, was in a most depressed state in these respects, even so late as the end of the seventeenth century. The impulse to improvement was given by such men as Lord Kaimes, the Earl of Stair, and Mr. Cockburn of Ormiston, who instigated a number of landholders to form themselves into a "Society of Improvers in the Knowledge of Agriculture in Scotland." As this association did not continue more than twenty years, another was established in 1784, and well known as the Highland Society, whose beneficial influence in improving the Agriculture and the landed property of the country is so universally acknowledged.

Scotland.

Improvers of Agriculture.

Highland Society.

In England, the Society of Arts, established in 1753, have also displayed very laudable zeal in encouraging, and have therefore greatly promoted planting, in the colonies, as well as in Great Britain. The Board of Agriculture was established in 1793, and though not effecting all that

Society of Arts.

was expected, yet produced the publication of the "County Agricultural Surveys," which have been fruitful of information. Besides these, numerous

Agricultural Societies.

Agricultural societies have been established in several counties of England, and even very recently "The English Agricultural Society" in the metropolis; the mode in which, and the persons by whom, these are supported, are indications of the value entertained for the labours of such institutions.

Improvers of Agriculture.

From the above very cursory examination, it is evident that the improvements have proceeded from the amateurs and patrons of Agriculture, rather than from those who are best acquainted

Non-professional.

with all the practical details of the art. The latter, indeed, have in general been found rather throwing obstructions in the way of, than forwarding any innovations, which interfered with the routine methods which they had been led to consider as essential to success. But in the progress of society, education becoming more diffused,

Practical men.

and practical men, enjoying in their youth the advantages of a liberal education, have the power, as well as the inclination, to profit by the instructions of their predecessors; and thus being enabled to combine principles with practice, they themselves obtain important results, which have an influence on their own, as well as on future times, as has been evinced in the case of Mr.

Modern authors.

Dawson of Trogden. But even within the last half century, the principal writers, whose instructions form the practice of the times, have belonged to the former, rather than to the latter class; as the celebrated Arthur Young, who commenced a series of useful and excellent publications in 1767, and continued them until 1810. Dr. Dickson's Practical Agriculture appeared in 1806, and may be considered as giving a most complete view of the Agriculture of the time; while Sir John Sinclair's Code of Agriculture is an epitome of the Art of Farming. "The Farmer's Magazine," Mr. Loudon, to whose Encyclopædias we are indebted for many of the above details, states "has done more to enlighten both the proprietors and tenantry of Scotland, than any work which has appeared." This was first conducted by R. Brown, a farmer of Markle, and Dr. Somerville, a Physician of Haddington, thus uniting the advantage of a judicious combination of Science with Art. The establishment of a Professorship of Agriculture in the University of Edinburgh in 1790, indicates the necessity which began to be felt of the combination of Principle with the Practice of Agriculture, as is well displayed in the Elements of Agriculture of Professor Low, the successor of Dr. Coventry, who had been appointed the first Professor.

Arthur Young.

Dr. Dickson.

Sir J. Sinclair.

Farmer's Magazine.

Professorship of Agriculture.

If we examine the progress of that department of Culture which is called Gardening or Horticulture, we find that even what is now considered a national taste, namely, that for Florist's Flowers, is supposed by some to have been introduced

Gardening in England.

Flowers—taste for.

into England by the Flemish manufacturers of worsted, and into Scotland by the French weavers. From Norwich the taste for the culture of Flowers spread to other manufacturing towns, and it is still indulged in by the weavers of Spitalfields, and the operatives of Manchester, and until of late, very conspicuously so by those of Birmingham.

culture of;

One of the earliest notices of the culture of Flowers is that at Sion House, the property of the Duke of Somerset, under the care of Dr. Turner, whom Pultency considers the Father of English Botany, and who had studied at Pisa and Bologna.

introduction of from the East.

During the seventeenth century numerous plants were introduced from the East, through Constantinople, as well as from the East and West Indies. The Oxford Botanic

Establishment of Botanic Gardens.

Garden was established in 1632, and that of Edinburgh in 1680; in 1673 Sir Hans Sloane gave the ground of the Chelsea Garden to the Society of Apothecaries, on condition of their presenting fifty new plants annually to the Royal Society. The Cambridge and Kew Gardens were established about the middle of the eighteenth century. The writings of Bradley, Professor of Botany at Cambridge, and of Miller, the celebrated Curator of the Garden at Chelsea, had great influence on the improvement of Horticulture. The Liverpool Botanic Garden owes its origin, in 1803, to the celebrated Roscoe, who, in the relaxation from commercial pursuits, found leisure for Literature, as well as for Botany. The example of Liverpool has been followed in all the great commercial towns, as in Manchester, Birmingham, Bristol, and Hull.

Gardens in England.

It is curious in reading the early accounts of the Culture of this country, to observe the want of skill, apparent in want of success, and how frequently this is ascribed to unfruitfulness in the soil or to unsuitableness in the climate of England, so that then even "Kitchen Garden wares were imported from Holland, and Fruits from France." Dr. Boleyn ascribes the inferiority to want of cultivation; and Oldys, alluding to the depreciation of the English soil and climate, by some adducing the fine garden of Gerrard, says, hence it would appear that "our ground could produce other fruits besides hips and haws, acorns and pignuts." In the present day we are in the habit of hearing similar statements respecting the unsuitableness of the Indian soil, at one time for the production of Cotton, at another for that of Sugar and of Tobacco; while Indian Coffee is hardly thought of, and its Hemp despised. Its Opium is undervalued in comparison with that of Turkey, and even all its Rice is thought, almost necessarily, inferior to that of America, because most of that is so which is imported here. Its Spices and its Indigo are, perhaps, alone acknowledged to be superior to that of other parts of the world. It will not, however, be difficult to prove that in India, as formerly in England, hasty generalizations have ascribed to poverty of soil,

Depreciation of English Soil and Climate in former times.

In the present day of India.

Owing to hasty generalizations.

India—defective culture of—how to be obviated.

that which is owing to deficiency of skill. Therefore we may reasonably hope, as we shall endeavour to show, that by following the course which has been so successfully pursued in civilized Europe, that is, the *application* of Principles to Practice, we may entertain a rational certainty of obtaining equally successful results.

Improvements in culture,

Improvements in the Arts of Culture have taken place, as we have seen, at different periods, but in none so conspicuously as in the present century, when the improvements in Horticulture have been reflected on Agriculture; and those made in the latter have equally advanced the practise of the former. This is in consequence of both having been founded on the principles of Science. It is only of late years that the peculiarities of Climate have been studied, in conjunction with the Physiology of Vegetation; and the assistance of Chemistry has been called in to explain the nature of Soils, and the changes effected in the Atmosphere. From the writings of Brown and of Humboldt, we have learnt the true distribution of Plants on the surface of the globe; and from those of the latter, the influence of Climate on Vegetation, as well as the zones of Temperature best suited to different Cultures. The discovery of Dr. Wells of the production of Cold and of Dew, in consequence of Radiation; and Professor Daniells' observations on Evaporation, on Dryness, and Moisture, and on "Climate with regard to Horticulture," have had

from attention to Science.

Sciences connected with Arts of Culture.

the most important and extended influence on the practice of Gardening. Davy has shown us, in his Lectures on Agriculture, the Chemical nature and uses of soils. The intimate knowledge of Vegetable Physiology possessed by the late Mr. Knight, the first President of the Horticultural Society, which was founded in 1805, his happy combination of Science with Art, and his constant application of the former to practice, have had the most beneficial effect in introducing just views respecting the influence of external agents on Vegetation, and consequently in improving the Arts of Culture.

Sciences connected with the Arts of Culture.

ARTS OF CULTURE IN THE COLONIES AND EXTRA-EUROPEAN COUNTRIES.

Arts of Culture in the Colonies.

Considering how long and how perseveringly the Sister Arts of Horticulture and of Agriculture have been pursued by the people, and patronized by the Governments of Europe, it was but reasonable to expect that they would endeavour to introduce them wherever their influence extended. This was still more to be expected where they were interested in improving the productiveness of the land, as is the case in their different Colonies.

The Spaniards and Portuguese.

The Spaniards and Portuguese, though paying little attention to such subjects in the present day, at one time took considerable pains in introducing into the New World some of the more valued pro-

Spaniards and Portuguese.

ducts of the ancient continents. The former introduced the Pine-apple and Tobacco into Spain. The West-Indies and South America were indebted to both of them for the Orange, Lemon, Plantain, and Tamarind, as well as for the Sugar-cane, Grape-vine, Fig, Melon, and Pomegranate. The Portuguese probably introduced into India some of the richest products of America, as the Maize or Indian Corn, the Capsicum, together with the Guava, Custard,—and Pine-apple.

Introduction of Plants.

The French.

The French have generally shown themselves more sensible than other nations of the importance of such introductions, as is evident by their constant endeavours to transplant valuable plants of other countries into their own Colonies. Thus they established, in 1630, a Botanic Garden at Cayenne, to which the British West-India islands have been indebted for some of the useful plants of the Old World. The Coffee was introduced by them into Martinique, from a plant from the hot-houses of Amsterdam, which was presented by the Dutch to Louis the Fourteenth. They also introduced Ginger, Pepper, and Cloves, which now form articles of export from that part of the world. The Bourbon Cotton is so named from having been early introduced into that island by the French, though identical with the Barbadoes Cotton of the West-Indies.

West-India Islands.

In the British West-India islands, Gardens were also established, as in Jamaica and St. Vincent's. The former consisted of seventy acres, and had for one of its objects the preservation of the productions of different climates, without artificial means. For this purpose a site was chosen on the side of the Liguane mountain, the summit of which is 3,600 feet above the level of the sea, and where at different elevations suitable localities are found for the useful products of various countries; but this garden was sold by the government in 1812, though much remained to be done in introducing plants suited to the island from other parts of the world. The Garden at St. Vincent's was established by General Melville, and we have accounts of the introduction into it of Cloves, Cinnamon, Nutmegs, and a statement that all East-India plants flourished there. Capt. Bligh, when employed in transporting the bread-fruit in 1793 into the West-Indies, also delivered with it a number of fruit-trees of tropical countries, into the gardens of St. Vincent's and of Jamaica, as well as into that of St. Helena. But these islands have obtained many of the most useful plants from the French colonies, as the Coffee, Black Pepper, and Nutmeg. The fortunate capture, by Lord Rodney, of a French East Indiaman, put them in possession, with other plants, of the Ceylon Cinnamon, and of the true Nankeen Cotton, from which some cloth was manufactured at Glasgow in 1785. Guinea Grass, now of so much importance in Jamaica, as forming the chief food in the graz-

Gardens established.

West-Indies.

Plants introduced.

Introduction of Plants.

ing and breeding farms, was accidentally obtained from the coast of Guinea, as food for some birds which were sent to Chief Justice Ellis.

North America.

North America, having been colonized from Europe, it was natural that the inhabitants should, from the suitableness of the climate, introduce the Corn culture, as well as the Fruit-trees of the Old World. Hence it is not surprising to observe, that their most extensive articles of export are of foreign introduction. Thus,

Rice.

Rice, an undoubted native of India, and where it has been extensively cultivated from the remotest antiquity, now affords food to many of the inhabitants, and forms much of the export trade of parts of the New World. Mr. Dalrymple, Editor of the Oriental Repertory, states "that he was informed by the late Mr. Hazard, who assured him he learnt from one of the parties concerned, that Rice, the staple of Carolina, was the result of a small bag of Paddy, given as a present from a Secretary of the East-India Company to a Carolina trader." In a subsequent page he corrects this statement, mentioning that the Rice was given by Mr. C. Dubois, Treasurer of the East-India Company.

Cotton.

Cotton, now so successful a culture, was introduced from other countries; the Nankeen, according to Mr. Spalding, from China, the Sea-island kind from the West-Indies, and the Green Seed, or Georgian Cotton, he supposes from Smyrna, but its origin is doubtful, as it was cultivated before the Revolution. The present excellence of American Tobacco is not due to superiority of the soil, but is the result of the unwearied attention both of the government and of cultivators to the improvement of its produce; for the American planters seemed to think, in former times, as Indian Zumeendars appear to do at the present day, that "*any thing was good enough for the merchants.*"—Tatham on Tobacco, p. 141.—The government, in 1639, anxious to improve the quality of Virginia produce, issued rules for checking over-luxuriance, and appointed officers (sworn to do their duty impartially) to see them enforced, as well as for rooting up inferior plants. Every hogshead of prepared Tobacco was moreover taken to government warehouses, to be inspected by competent officers before it could be exported, and all of an inferior quality condemned to be burnt.*

Introduction of Plants.

Improved Culture of Tobacco in America forced by the Government.

The Dutch, though jealous of the extension of the Spices beyond the limits they prescribed, yet paid considerable attention to the vegetable products of their colonies. They established a garden of large extent at Cape Town, which was divided into four quarters, each of which was planted with the trees, plants, and flowers, that are peculiar to each of the four parts of the world; and hence in this one enclosure were to be found

The Dutch.

* Tatham on Tobacco, p. 69-106; and 138, 207; London, 1800.

the several gardens of Europe, Asia, Africa, and America. Many of the fruits of Europe were also introduced, and the Vine has been the source of their principal article of export.

Arts of Culture in India.

Arts of Culture in India.

Noticing the different kinds, and detailing the early history of Culture, and the stages of its introduction into different countries, has not been for the gratification either of idle or of curious inquiry, but that we might make the experience of the past serve us as lessons for the future. This especially with reference to that country, which we hope to prove is neither so sterile, nor so stubborn in soil, so limited in range of climate, nor deficient in intelligence of population, as to make it improbable that, by following the course which has in other countries been so successfully pursued, we shall attain, at least, an equal degree of success. For the soil of India is rich in many parts, varied in others; and the climate affords us sufficient variation of temperature, as well as of dryness and moisture, to allow of the cultivation of Rice at one season, and at another of that of Wheat and Barley. The inhabitants also are acquainted with many, and have the merit of originating some, of the approved processes of Agriculture, as the rotation of crops and the drill husbandry. They are probably not more bigoted to the practices of their forefathers, than many an English farmer has shown himself,

Soil and Climate varied as is the Culture.

Hindoos well acquainted with Agriculture.

when he has remained unconvinced, even by the successful practice of a neighbour of his own rank and occupation, nor than the Italian, who stops discussion, by saying, " I do as my father of blessed memory did before me, and that is enough."* Hindoo Cultivators.

The Hindoo cultivator must, however, be taught by example rather than by precept, and those who teach must endeavour to fortify their precepts, as well as their practice, by taking care that both are conformable to principle. Thus, the experience of other nations, as well as of other places, may be made suitable to new situations, where, though all the requisites for successful practice are present, yet they may not be in the same relative proportions as elsewhere. A modification of practice is therefore essentially necessary, to compensate for such variations in the richness or poverty of the soil, the dryness, or moisture of the climate, in order to attain the same ends; otherwise our precepts may be as empirical and as unsuited to the new situation, as they are adapted for the places where they are practised. The result, therefore, may be as unsuccessful as those which we are endeavouring to improve. To be improved by example, and by Practice founded on principle.

That we may have correct data for comparison, as well as be able to ascertain the nature and ex- Information respecting India Culture.

---

* " Facio come faceva la buon anima di miopadre, e cio basta."

India—information concerning.

tent of the information to be referred to in our future reasonings, it is desirable to take a cursory view of the means which have hitherto been adopted to develop and improve, and the knowledge which we possess respecting, the physical capabilities of India.

authentic and varied.

By this it will be seen that the information upon which we rely is sufficiently authentic, and drawn from an extensive enough basis to warrant the inferences which are deduced. The results also which have already been obtained are sufficient to justify the most sanguine expectations for the future. It is not, therefore, premature to state, that our knowledge of the Soil, Climate, and Vegetation of the Indian empire, though not sufficiently minute in all particulars, is yet full enough in many, to entitle us to draw legitimate inferences on a number of subjects. The success also in many cases attending the introduction of new Plants and improved cultures has been sufficiently encouraging. We may therefore state, that perseverance in the course which has been commenced, and a steady application of principles to practice, will ensure the utmost success in the culture of as great a variety of useful and valuable products, within the wide-spread dominions of the Indian empire, as is practicable within the limits even of several different countries.

Results of Experiments warrant future success and varied culture.

British Dominions in India.

As the British dominions in India stretch from 8° to 31° of north latitude, we find the northern limits extending to the points which were reached by the Greeks under Alexander, while the southern points are those first touched at by the Portuguese when they reached India by sailing round the Cape of Good Hope. Further, as the products of India reached Europe both by the Red Sea, and by caravans from the north, it is necessary to consult the works of all the nations which have ever been connected with India, if we desire to acquire a complete knowledge of the early history of the natural Products, the Agriculture, Commerce, and Manufactures of India. As the earliest notices of Indian commerce refer chiefly to Vegetable products, we may notice the information respecting these before proceeding to other subjects; and it is fortunate that the majority of those who are considered as having attended to the vegetation of India only in a botanical point of view, have paid considerable attention to the useful plants, and therefore it is of advantage to notice these authors in connection with the economic history of the country.

India—Products of, treated of by authors of several nations.

Both Greek and Latin authors proclaim the high estimation in which the products of the East were held by the nations of antiquity. We may, even in the present day, trace the limits to which Commerce extended in ancient times by the descriptions which we read, in the authors of those days, of products which we know can only grow in the peninsula of India, or in still more southern latitudes, as the far distant islands of the Indian Ocean. Marco Polo is, however, accounted the

Greek and Latin.

India—writers respecting products of. first who described, from actual inspection, some of the useful Plants of India and of the Indian islands. Garcias ab Orto. Christopher a Costa. The Portuguese physicians, Garcias ab Orto* and Christopher a Costa, long resident at Goa, also gave some of the earliest accounts of many of the valued products of the East. The Dutch paid considerable attention to the vegetable products of India, as well from a desire to transport some to the garden of Leyden, as for the purpose of becoming acquainted with the useful products of the country.

Rheede. Rheede,† Governor of Malabar, had the plants of the country collected, described, and figured, as well as their useful properties indicated. So Rumphius. Rumphius,‡ who went out as Physician to Amboyna, and afterwards became Consul there, described and figured numbers of the plants of the Archipelago. He completed his work in 1696, but it remained in manuscript for thirty years in the possession of the Dutch East-India Company. Plukenet. Plukenet, who was appointed in England to suc-

---

* The work of Garcias ab Orto ("De Aromatis") was first published in 1651. This, as well as the work of C. a Costa, on Aromatics, is included in "Clusius Exoticorum libri decem." Kæmpfer, who accompanied the Dutch fleet to India, described and figured many of the plants of that country, but these are all lost. He then proceeded to Japan, of which, as well as of Persia, he has given some account in his "Amœnitates Exoticæ."

† Rheede, "Hortus Malabaricus," twelve volumes folio, 794 plates.

‡ Rumphius, "Herbarium Amboinense," seven volumes folio, 696 plates, 1741 to 1757.

ceed Parkinson as Herbalist, and to the charge of the Royal Gardens at Hampton Court, had collectors despatched both to the East and West-Indies for plants. In his works, therefore, many Indian plants are figured, as well as in those of the two Burmanns.* That of the first appears to have been principally drawn up from specimens collected by Dr. Paul Hermann, who was sent out in 1670 to Ceylon, where he remained till 1677, at the expense of the Dutch East-India Company, for the purpose of describing all the plants and spices growing in that island.

Two Burmanns.

The systematic investigation of Indian vegetation can, however, only date from the arrival in India of Kœnig, a pupil of Linnæus, and who, in 1769, joined the Danish missionaries at Tranquebar, many of whom afterwards prosecuted Botany, and Dr. John founded the garden at that place. Kœnig finding his means too limited to enable him to pursue his investigations, took employment with the Nawab of Arcot; but as his difficulties were still as great, from irregularity of payment, he applied for assistance to the Madras Medical Board. In consequence of their recommendation, the Indian Government granted him a monthly allowance, with which aid he proceeded to the

Kœnig.

* Plukenet, Opera Omnia, London, 1691 to 1705; 534 plates of nearly 3,000 plants.

Burmann, Thesaurus Zeylanicus, Amsterdam, 1737, quarto, 100 plates.

Burmann 2d, Flora Indica, 67 plates, 1768.

Kœnig. Straits of Malacca and to Siam, from whence he returned towards the end of 1779. One of his first acts was to transmit a number of the useful plants of those regions to St. Helena. From this time he continued to be regularly employed in the East-India Company's service until his death in 1785.

Russell. Dr. Patrick Russell was appointed to succeed Dr. Kœnig, and though then engaged in his great works on the Fishes and Snakes of the Peninsula, he projected another, which is interesting as having given origin to one of the most important works on the useful plants of India. But as he did not remain in India long after this, he recommended Dr. Roxburgh to be employed, "on the score of his ability to be of essential service to the Company in the way the Directors wish, that is, in the application of such researches to the more immediate purposes of utility."

Roxburgh. Dr. Roxburgh, stationed at Samulcottah from 1781, had long known and corresponded with Kœnig, and had made large collections of plants in the Carnatic; but he had the misfortune to lose them all, with his books and manuscripts, in an inundation, at Injeram, in 1787. He, however, recommenced making a fresh collection of plants, and the Court of Directors sent him out a present of Botanical books. He described accurately the plants he collected, which were also drawn, and he added such remarks on their uses as he had learned from experience or had collected from the natives. The plan of the work recommended by Dr. Russell having been forwarded by the Madras Government to the Court of Directors, was returned with a paragraph in the General letter, expressive of the "readiness at all times of the Court of Directors to promote the improvement of natural history, and of their approbation of Dr. Russell's proposal for publishing a select collection of useful Indian plants." Roxburgh.

The first packet of drawings and descriptions sent by Dr. Roxburgh were received in 1791, and the last in June 1794, when the number five hundred was completed. Sir Joseph Banks having undertaken the general superintendence of the work, and Dr. Russell, who was then in England, the correction of the press, the first number was published in 1795 of "a progressive work, in which a preference was given to subjects connected with Medicine, the Arts, and Manufactures," illustrated by elegant engravings, and which is now so well known as Roxburgh's Coromandel Plants.* His Coromandel Plants.

The works of Dr. Roxburgh are remarkable

* The Plants of the Coast of Coromandel, selected from drawings and descriptions presented to the Hon. Court of Directors of the East-India Company; by W. Roxburgh, M.D.; published by their order, under the direction of Sir Joseph Banks, Bart., F.R.S. Three volumes elephant folio, with 300 coloured engravings. 1st vol. in 1795, 2d vol. in 1798, and the 3d vol. in 1819.

for combining scrupulous correctness in description and careful discrimination of species, with constant attention to the practical applications of his subject. This is seen in his observations on the productiveness of different kinds of Grain; on the sources whence further supplies of Food might be procured, as in the various esculent Herbs, Roots, and Fruits, and in his substitutes for Sago and Arrow-root. The value and great variety of Timber trees, fitted both for house and ship-building; Gums of various kinds; Resins, or Dammer, as substitutes for pitch; the Piney varnish-tree, and the Illepie oil-tree, are all brought to notice; as well as Astringents for tanning, as the Kino of the Dhak or Pulass, and the Caducay galls and Myrobolans; Dyes, as the Chaya root, with substitutes for Indigo;* notices of Medicines of various kinds, especially substitutes for Ipecacuanha, Sarsaparilla, and Peruvian bark.†

Grain, and other articles of food.

Timber trees.

Gums: Resins; Varnish, and Oil trees.

Tanning materials.

Dyes.

Medicines.

---

* A botanical description and drawing of a new species of Nerium (Rose Bay.), with the process for extracting from its leaves a very beautiful indigo.

Col. Kyd writes from Calcutta, 22d June 1790, respecting this Indigo, that both he and Mr. Harris are of opinion that the Nerium Indigo possesses the qualities of the *best Indigo*, and falls to be ranked (if not equal in value to the first) to the secondary species which has yet been produced in Bengal.

† A Monograph of Swietenia febrifuga, by Dr. W. Roxburgh, printed by order of the East-India Company.

Culture of Pepper in the Circars.

The desire of Dr. Roxburgh to make his scientific discoveries tend to practical purposes is conspicuous in his endeavours to cultivate Pepper in the Circars, and in the number of useful plants which he introduced into the Company's Pepper plantations established at his recommendation in the neighbourhood of Samulcottah. As the origin and progress of this attempt at a new culture are productive of some useful lessons, we may enter a little more into detail than would otherwise be necessary. Pepper—cultivation of,

Dr. Roxburgh himself states in a letter, dated Samulcottah, 25th August 1788,—"Since the end of 1781, I have been stationed here, and as soon as I became a little acquainted with the Seasons, Soil, and Produce of the country hereabouts, I formed an idea that Pepper and Coffee would thrive as well in this Circar as in any part of Asia; my natural turn for Botany, Agriculture, and Meteorological observations, enabled me to form the idea upon pretty certain grounds." But, on the 25th April 1786, he had written, "I have the pleasure to inform you, that since my return I have, for the first time, discovered that Black Pepper is found growing wild in some parts of the hills to the north-west of this; the natives of these hills bring small quantities frequently down to the plains to sell." Mr. Ross, in a letter to Sir A. Campbell, proposed. Pepper discovered in the Hills of the Circars;

Governor of Madras, in reference to some samples of this pepper sent by Dr. Roxburgh, and which the latter described as equal to, if not better, than the best Malabar or Ceylon pepper, says, that "on comparing it with the pepper from the Malabar coast, which is here in the shops for sale, the shopkeepers say that the former is at least ten per cent. better in quality." Mr. Ross further writes (13th Aug. 1786), "The most particular orders were given in time to the Chief and Council of Masulipatam, to furnish Dr. Roxburgh with all the necessary disbursements, to enable him to proceed, and to give orders to the zemindars to assist and encourage the undertaking." The Court of Directors, moreover, in the General letter to Madras, dated 22d April 1789, expressed their approbation of the undertaking,* and ordered that every encouragement and assistance should be afforded to Dr. Roxburgh.

of excellent quality.

Pepper Culture approved of by the Court of Directors.

Pepper plant brought from Rampa.

The Pepper was brought for sale to Cottapilla, at the skirts of the hills; but the Plants were

* "In our letter of the 31st July 1787, we approved of the measures you had taken to assist Dr. Roxburgh in the cultivation of Coffee and of the Pepper plant in the Rajahmundry Circar; but for want of information, &c. we could not decide how far it was a measure meriting our further encouragement. Having since received this information, and likewise the most favourable accounts of the success of the undertaking, we now order and direct that you afford Dr. Roxburgh every encouragement and assistance in your power, in the cultivation of such useful articles of our commerce, particularly that of Pepper."—Oriental Repertory, i. p. 24.

procured from Rampa, about thirty miles within them, and about fifty directly north from Samulcottah. It was afterwards discovered growing wild in almost every valley amongst the mountains, immediately north of that station. The plantations were established about six miles inland from Samulcottah, and about eight or ten miles from the nearest point of the sea, where they were sheltered by innumerable clumps of mangoe-trees. About five hundred slips were first obtained. These, by the end of 1787, had formed four thousand plants, which at the end of the second year had increased to forty thousand in number, the props being formed chiefly with the branches of the Moochy-tree (Erythrina indica).

Plantation established at Samulcottah.

On the 17th July 1790, Dr. R. writes, "I have brought this species of culture to such a pitch of perfection as must convince every person, that the Pepper-vine will thrive as well on this coast as in any part of India." The rate of its productiveness had, however, yet to be ascertained; but before they were old enough for this purpose a difficulty arose, from Dr. Roxburgh discovering that, instead of the real Pepper-plant of Sumatra and the coast of Malabar (Piper nigrum of botanists), he had found a new species, which though yielding an equally good Pepper, was more difficult of cultivation. This was in consequence of the male and female flowers being on different vines, and there being a third kind, with

Success of Culture.

Unforeseen difficulty.

Pepper of Circars—quality of.

hermaphrodite flowers, or hermaphrodite and female flowers mixed, on the same catkins. Hence Dr. R. has called this species Piper trioicum, which he had taken for the true Pepper-plant before he had an opportunity of seeing that famous plant. The natives had increased the difficulty by supplying him in the first instance only with the barren plants. The pepper of the second kind had less pungency than common pepper, but the third sort ripened perfectly, and when dry was exceedingly pungent. Dr. R. was equally unfortunate with the pepper which he sent to this country by a private hand to have its value ascertained, as it was seized by the Custom-house officers.

Useful plants introduced into Pepper plantations.

Into the Pepper plantations Dr. Roxburgh also introduced Coffee, Cinnamon, Nutmeg, Annotto, and Guinea Grass; also the Bread-fruit tree, which had been found growing luxuriantly in Cochin, called by the Dutch, Maldivy Jack; and also mentions having "thousands of young Sappan-wood trees in the Company's Pepper Plantations." He introduced the Teak into the low grounds of the Circars, though it was common in the hills of the Rajahmundry Circars, recommending its being planted in every vacant corner; and mentions that Lord Cornwallis and Col. Kyd had been for some time introducing it into Bengal. He also procured the eggs of the Silk-worm, and proposed its culture in the Circars, as the Mulberry grew there most luxu-

Teak tree.

riantly from cuttings; and obtained copper sugar-boilers from Bengal, in order to try and improve the quality of the Sugars. His paper on the culture and manufacture of sugar in India is among the most interesting which has been published.* Sugar.

Culture of Cochineal in India.

Dr. Roxburgh further mentions having received slips of the Cactus or Opuntia, obtained by Sir Joseph Banks from the Royal Gardens at Kew, and sent out by the Court of Directors, which, he states, grew astonishingly. Attention had been called to this subject by Dr. James Anderson, physician-general of the Madras army, who was distinguished as much for his professional attainments as for his constant attention to whatever would afford employment to the natives, and improve the productive resources of the country. Dr. Anderson had found an insect, which he imagined to be a kind of Cochineal, and with which he had dyed pieces of

Cochineal—cultivation attempted; by Dr. James Anderson.

* An Account of the Hindoo method of cultivating the Sugar-cane, and manufacturing the Sugar and Jagary, in the Rajahmundry Circar, interspersed with such remarks as tend to point out the great benefit that might be expected from increasing this branch of Agriculture, and improving the quality of the sugar; also the process observed by the natives of the Ganjam district in making the sugars of Barrampore. By Dr. William Roxburgh, Samulcottah, 20th June 1792.

Flannel, Shawl, and Satin. Specimens were forwarded to the Court of Directors, and by their order subjected to various experiments, but were found to be entirely useless in dyeing.

Sir Joseph Banks obtained similar results, but having ascertained (22d May 1787), that the specimens sent him were those of a real species of Coccus, he conceived the idea that the true Cochineal might easily be cultivated on the Coromandel Coast, as the "climate was as good as that of the West-Indies (where it had been introduced); the soil suitable to the production of the Cactus with few spines, and labour as cheap, if not still more so, than in Mexico."* The Committee of Warehouses of the Court of Directors were led to entertain the same view, as they state in April 1788 — "The supposed discovery of Dr. Anderson in the environs of Madras, which, although unsuccessful in the issue, has, nevertheless, led your Committee to conceive that the Insect may very successfully be introduced and propagated in the British settlements in India, to the advantage of the natives, the Company, and the British nation, by giving to the former a new article of Culture, to the second an additional article of Commerce, and to the latter a participation in a lucrative article of Trade,

Cochineal culture in India recommended by Sir J Banks.

By Committee of Warehouses.

* Letters to Sir Joseph Banks, Bart., P.R.S., on the subject of Cochineal Insect, discovered at Madras; 1788. By James Anderson, M.D., Physician-General, Madras.

which has hitherto been enjoyed unrivalled by a neighbouring power." At their recommendation sealed orders were given to the captains of some ships proceeding to the Brazils, to procure, if possible, some of the real insect, and carry it to the coast.

Nopalry or Cactus Garden, established by the East-India Company.

Dr. Anderson was in the meantime permitted to establish, with Dr. Berry placed under him as superintendent, a garden to be called the Company's Nopalry, for the cultivation of the several kinds of Cactus, on which alone the true Cochineal feeds.

Cactus Plants obtained; in India; and from Canton, Manilla, Isle of France, and Kew Garden.

Plants of Cactus were obtained with considerable difficulty. One species, extremely common in many parts of India, was undervalued as being thought unsuited to the insect. It is called by the natives *nag-kalli* and *nag-phunee*, and by Dr. Roxburgh *Cactus indicus*, being thought to be indigenous; but it was probably introduced by the Portuguese. Plants were also obtained from Canton, Manilla, and the Isle of France, as well as from the Kew Garden. All these four, Dr. Anderson states, were alike in appearance. In the course of three years, there were not fewer than two thousand Opuntia plants in the Hon. Company's Nopalry—all obtained from the few Kew plants. Specimens were distributed throughout the Presidency, as well as sent to the Botanic Garden at Calcutta.

Attention having thus been turned to the subject, the Cochineal insect was obtained by Capt.

Cochineal Insect brought from Brazil by Capt. Neilson.

Neilson, of H.M. 74th Regt., on his return to India in June 1795. When the fleet in which he sailed repaired for refreshments to the coast of Brazil, Capt. N., in his walks at Rio Janeiro, saw a plantation of Opuntias, and obtained several plants with the insect on them.* Many of them died during the passage to Bengal; and a few only remained alive on the last plant, of which several of the leaves had withered. Capt. N., on his arrival at Calcutta, sent the survivors to the Botanic Garden, where they were placed on the several species of Cactus, or Opuntia. On the China and Manilla species of the Nopal, and even on that from Kew, the survivors began to die fast. It fortunately occurred to make trial of the indigenous Opuntia, on which they were luckily found to thrive amazingly; and so rapidly, that Captain Neilson himself writes, on the 3d August 1795, that he had the day before seen at the Company's Garden near Calcutta about one thousand fine plants covered with the insects: enough to stock all India. He hopes that Dr. Anderson had received the plants and insects sent by Dr. Roxburgh; and expresses his intention of bringing a fresh supply, with the hopes of "seeing in a very few months the plant and insect an object of cultivation over all the

Sent to Calcutta Botanic Garden;

thrive remarkably.

* Miscellaneous Communications, by James Anderson, M.D., Physician-General, Madras, from March 1794, to October 1796.

Carnatic, which I am inclined to think a more favourable climate for it than that of Bengal:" Capt. N. concludes by saying, that great numbers of gentlemen in Bengal have already begun Nopal Plantations; and that Dr. Roxburgh had sent the insect to different parts of the country.

Insect distributed over India.

The insects sent to Dr. Anderson were delivered over to Dr. Berry, Superintendent of the Company's Nopalry at Madras, who, on the 26th August, reported, that the climate seemed most congenial to them in all exposures, as they had gone through all their stages from 28th July to the 24th August. He found the same want of success with the foreign, and, as in Calcutta, was obliged to have recourse to the country Nopal. As this was common everywhere, the culture and collection of the Insect very rapidly spread, particularly as the Collectors of Revenue were each furnished with a small quantity, and directed to exert themselves in the most strenuous manner; also to enclose spots of ground fifty or sixty feet square at some of the villages under each collectorate. On the 8th December, 1795, Dr. Berry further reported, that this Cochineal dyed casimere, cloth, and flannel with a colour equal in brightness to the best scarlet, but that four times the quantity of the Sylvestre Cochineal reared in India was required to produce the same colour as that produced by the Grana Fina Cochineal of Mexico. In March, 1796, the Madras Government having determined to hold out the most solid encouragement to the

Introduced into Madras;

distributed over the Presidency.

Subsidiary Gardens established.

Used as a dye.

Madras Government offer to purchase the Cochineal.

cultivators of Cochineal, offered one pagoda per pound for the Cochineal, to such of the natives as might be disposed to employ their industry in its culture, this being considered by Dr. Berry an allowance liberal enough to encourage the cultivation.

Sent from India to England;

found to be the Sylvestre, or wild species of Cochineal.

Specimens of the insects collected and dried, both on the coast and in Bengal, were sent to the Court of Directors.* These specimens were submitted to examination by the best judges of the commodity in England, who all agreed that it was the Sylvestre, or wild species; and that there was little prospect of its being cultivated to any advantage for the supply of the Europe market, unless it could be offered at about one-third of the price of the Grana Fina, or at from 5s. to 6s. per pound, freight and all charges included.

Quantity collected and purchased by Madras Government.

The Madras Government had collected, in September 1797, 21,744lbs., and fresh supplies were then coming in, at the average price of nearly one pagoda per pound. By a statement, showing the issue of the sales of the Madras Cochineal in England in the years 1797, 1798, and 1799, it appears that 55,196lbs. were sold at an average of 8s. 8¼d. per pound, which was little more than its prime cost in India. In 1807, the management of the purchase of Cochineal at Madras was transferred to the Board of Trade, who re-

---

* Memoir on the Bengal Cochineal, by Dr. N. Fontana.—Asiatic Annual Register, vol. i., 1801.

ported that since the date of the Court's letter of September, 1800, with the above statement, 73,366⅛lbs. of Cochineal, amounting to pagodas 40,883:14:29, had been sent to England; and that from the London Price Current, it did not appear to be an article of profit to the Company; and they, therefore, suggested the propriety of discontinuing the purchase, or reducing the price to two and one rupee per pound. The Government, in reply to this date, directed purchases to continue; and in this determination the Court of Directors expressed their concurrence in the following terms:—"As the prices which we have obtained for the Cochineal on sales have not been such as to reimburse the prime cost and charges, our sole reason for continuing to suffer a considerable annual loss upon this article, has been with a view to encourage the breeding of the insect, until it should become perfectly understood among the natives."

Board of Trade recommend the purchases being discontinued, as not profitable.

Ordered to be continued by Court of Directors.

In 1807, Mr. William Webbe, of the Madras Civil Establishment, suggested through Dr. Anderson to the Governor in Council, the expediency of advertising a reward for the introduction of the Grana Fina, or real Mexican Cochineal, into India. The Court of Directors concurred in the reward offered by the Indian Government of two thousand pounds for this purpose.*

Reward offered for the introduction of the Grana Fina Insect into India.

* Measures which have been pursued by the Court of Directors and the Governments in India with a view to the

Observations on the causes of failure in both the Pepper and Cochineal cultures.

The details which have been given with respect to the Pepper and Cochineal cultivations are important, as shewing that, even with the greatest energy in individuals, and the utmost necessary patronage in the Government, success is unattainable, unless equal precaution be taken with every part of an experiment. Here the utmost degree of success was obtained that was possible with the materials. The plants succeeded perfectly, but it is doubtful whether any of them was the true Cochineal-Cactus of Mexico; and, in fact, the Insects (certainly the inferior kinds) preferred the Cactus already in India to that which had been procured expressly for them, though this was found an excellent remedy for scurvy, and a vegetable for voyages at sea. The Grana Sylvestre Insect—unfortunately the only kind procured—being one-third only of the value of the Grana Fina, while the expenses of its cultivation, collection, and drying, were necessarily the same; the price also paid for the Insect being high, because intended as an encouragement in the first instance, made this culture, like all experimental ones, more expensive than would be necessary when success was established. The results also appear more unfavourable than they actually are. The Cactus, instead of requiring the best grounds

The same expenses incurred in the Sylvestre as would be necessary for the Grana Fina.

Introduction of the True Cochineal Insect into the British Territories in India.—Trans. Asiat. Soc. of Calcutta, vol. vi.; Appendix, p. 85.

and garden culture, will flourish in the most sterile parts of the country, needing but little subsequent attention; and as women and children may be employed in the care and collection of the insect, the expenses should, therefore, not be great. The experiment was so successful with the Grana Sylvestre, that no doubt can be entertained respecting equal success with the Grana Fina Cochineal, whenever it can be introduced; and this, with the same care and no greater expense, would be so much more valuable as a dye, and as an article of commerce.*

Observations on the result of the experiments on Cochineal culture.

With regard to the Pepper Cultivation, we have seen that complete success was not attained; in fact, as far as a profitable culture was concerned, the Pepper Plantation at Samulcottah was a failure. Every thing, however, appeared favourable, for the Pepper of the Hills was pronounced by dealers to be of excellent quality: the Garden was established close to where the plant was indigenous; and Dr. Roxburgh was a most careful, and at the same time skilful Superintendent; but at that time, never having seen the true Pepper

On the Pepper cultivation.

---

* It is not easy to estimate the expenses of the experiment, as so many small gardens were established in different parts of the country: but those of the principal one at Marmalong, near Madras, were restricted to 200 pagodas a month: £500 was paid to the brother of Capt. Neilson; and 13,397 pagodas, 17 fanams, and 20 cash, to Dr. Anderson in 1795, for disbursements, on account of the introduction of the Cochineal and Silk-worm upon the coast.

Causes of failure in Pepper cultivation; by Dr. Roxburgh, a wrong plant.

plant, he mistook for it a nearly allied species, yielding excellent Pepper, but which for the reasons stated (p. 65) was more difficult of culture. Dr. Heyne, however, (v. infra), has given a different reason for the want of success in the culture.

by Dr. Heyne, imperfect culture;

He succeeded Dr. Roxburgh in the charge of the Pepper Plantations, and, having afterwards an opportunity of visiting Bencoolen, he made particular inquiries respecting the culture of Pepper in Sumatra.

Culture in Sumatra.

He learnt that the Malays plant the Pepper vine at distances of five cubits in every direction, and support it on pieces of the Mootchy tree (Erythrinæ, sp.); that the Pepper grew luxuriantly where it had much moisture, and hence the vallies were the most favourable situations for Pepper gardens. After the first planting in September the vine required but little attention, being left to its fate for twelve or eighteen months, when it received a peculiar treatment, which Dr. Heyne thinks, is the cause of its great fertility. The whole plant, with all its branches, being then *buried* in such a way "that only a small arch of the stem remains above ground."

Plant buried in the ground when twelve or eighteen months old.

From this arch new shoots soon sprout out, three or four of which are allowed to climb up the prop tree, and are expected to produce flowers and fruit in a year after this operation. Dr. Heyne supposes, that by this practice the strength and vigour of the plant,—by the multiplication of its organs of nourishment, the roots—being so much increased, it cannot only produce large crops of flowers, but bring the fruit also to its greatest perfection. The omission of this practice, Dr. Heyne supposes, was the cause of failure at Samulcottah, as he says, "the plants that were raised from cuttings seemed indeed to thrive well, and soon produced blossoms; but such as had male flowers only. To account for this circumstance, we supposed that the hermaphrodite plant had been withheld by the people who sent us cuttings from their hills, where pepper is cultivated to a small extent, when, in fact, we had *starved our plants into celibacy*. (Tracts, p. 402.) It would be an interesting and very useful experiment, as well as one easily put into execution, in any of the Botanic or Horticultural Gardens favourably situated in India, to ascertain whether the Malayan treatment applied to the Pepper Vine of the Northern Circars would make it more fruitful.

Causes of failure in Pepper cultivation.

Experiment suggested.

At the same time that so much pains was bestowed on the cultivation of the Pepper, Cactus, and Cochineal, considerable attention was also directed to the culture of the Mulberry and the Silkworm, as well as to that of Sugar, and to the introduction of Indigo. But as these were attempted in consequence of their success in Bengal, their notice may be deferred.

Other cultures attempted.

Mulberry; Silk: Sugar; Indigo.

It is interesting to observe, that even at this early period the indefatigable Dr. Anderson was employed in sending "Mauritius Cotton Seeds," as well as "Brown Cotton Seeds," to different parts

Cotton.

Useful plants introduced into India. of the Peninsula. The latter had been brought from Malta to India by Major Macdonald, Governor of Penang, in 1796, who, in writing for some useful plants to be sent him, says, "I forward two boxes of plants from Mr. Smith, the Company's Botanist here, addressed to Dr. Heyne, Botanist at Samulcottah; No. 1, containing 360 plants of the India Rubber, and No. 2, 353 of the Dammar."

Dr. Heyne, Dr. Heyne, so favourably known by his "Tracts on India," succeeded Dr. Roxburgh at Samulcottah, and afterwards acted as assistant to Col. Mackenzie, Superintendent of the Mysore Survey. his attention to Botany and He paid considerable attention to Botany, made a large collection of Plants, some of which are contained in the East-Indian and Banksian Herbaria, and some were described by Roth;* but he Mineralogy. chiefly studied Mineralogy, and his Tracts† are full of original information concerning the Rock formations, the Minerals, and Soils of the Peninsula. With respect to practical subjects, it is in- Introduction of Potatoes. teresting to find him observing, that Potatoes were first introduced into the neighbourhood of Bangalore and of Nundydroog by Col. Cuppage, and since 1800 by himself among the natives, whom,

* A. G. Roth, Novæ plantarum species præsertim Indiæ Orientalis ex collectione Doct. Benj. Heynii. Halberstadii, 1821.

† Tracts, Historical and Statistical, on India; with Journals of several Tours through various Parts of the Peninsula, &c. By Benjamin Heyne, M.D. F.L.S., Surgeon and Naturalist on the Establishment of Fort St. George. London, 1814.

he says, " I was enabled by Government to supply with Seed Potatoes of the best kind from the St. Helena stock, and to offer them a sale for their produce, which, however, they soon found for themselves, in all parts of the country where Europeans reside. Since that time they have even supplied Madras, where their potatoes are preferred to those of Bengal."* Introduction of Potatoes.

Botanic Garden established at Calcutta.

The Botanic Garden of Calcutta was first established in 1786, part of it having been previously cultivated as a private garden by Col Kyd, to whom the genus *Kydia*† was dedicated by Dr. Roxburgh. Dr. Carey, in his Introduction to the *Hortus Bengalensis*,‡ justly says, "The un- Calcutta Botanic Garden established. Col. Kyd. Dr. Roxburgh.

---

* Dr. Heyne not having had leisure to publish the results of all his observations, says, " I have in the mean time not been sparing in communicating my specimens to such as will be able to make them useful; and this, on the whole, was and is the primary object. It matters but little whether it be known by whom a thing is collected, provided it only be used for the good of the community. Many of my friends seem to be of the same opinion!" Tracts, Preface, p. vii.

† "In memory of the late Col. Robert Kyd, whose love for the science induced him, at the desire of the Honourable the English East-India Company, to begin the Botanical Garden and Public Nursery at Calcutta, in Bengal, which he conducted with much success during his life." Roxb. Corom. Plants, iii. p. 11; published in 1819.

‡ *Hortus Bengalensis*, or a Catalogue of the Plants growing in the Honourable East-India Company's Botanic Garden at Calcutta. Serampore, 1814. Introduction by Dr. Carey.

Results of Dr. Roxburgh's labours.

remitted attention paid by Dr. Roxburgh to the improvement of the Garden, and his eminent abilities as a Botanist, are far more fully exhibited in the following Catalogues than they could possibly be by any eulogium from a friend." The number of described species now in the garden amounts to about 3500, for the knowledge of no fewer than 1510 of which, as named and described in this Catalogue, we are indebted to his indefatigable and discriminating researches. Among these are a great number of new genera, some of which have already a considerable number of species ascertained. To these should be added those plants contained in the second Catalogue, which, though not yet in the Botanic Garden, have been described, and many of them accurately drawn by him—these amount to 453. This, indeed, forms as important a part of his valuable labours, as the description of those already in that rich repository of Indian Plants. The total number of Plants drawn and described by him is 1963. (Introduction, p. 2. 3).

Catalogue of the plants contained in the Calcutta Botanic Garden.

Dr. Carey.

Dr. Carey, celebrated for his missionary labours, and knowledge of Asiatic language, whence he was appointed Professor in the College at Calcutta, as well as for his attention to Botany, justly remarks in his Introduction, that by the formation of Botanic Gardens the labours of scientific men have been called forth and greatly aided, as these afford facilities for the improvement of Botanical Science, which might have been sought for in vain without the aid of such institutions. "But the

Uses of Botanic Gardens

Botanical Gardens, and other noble collections of Plants in Europe, could never have been brought to the perfection in which they now appear, had not public or private repositories of plants been formed in the different settlements in Asia, Africa, and America." This, however, as he further observes, is not the only use of such institutions, as they are intended chiefly for the benefit of the country in which they are established. Useful plants, such as Grains and Timber-trees, are first introduced, and then spread into the culture of the country; others also employed in the domestic economy of the inhabitants, or which by their beauty contribute to the enjoyment and pleasure of mankind. Thus are introduced Flowers, Shrubs, and Timber-trees, Grains supplying food for man and beast, Esculent and Medicinal Plants, and those which yield Colouring matter, or are employed as Mordants.

Botanic Gardens— Uses of. Introduction of useful plants.

" It is readily granted," continues the venerable Carey, " that Agricultural Societies would more effectually accomplish the object of improving the culture of Grain, and that the premiums bestowed by them upon successful candidates in the various branches of husbandry, would operate with greater success, where these operations must necessarily be carried forward on a large scale, and a comparative view made of the advantage attending different modes of culture, and of the produce of different kinds of soil. This is, however, impracticable in many of our

Agricultural Societies— benefit of.

Experimental Farm attached to Botanic Garden.

foreign possessions, and must necessarily be attended with many defects in them all, which it is not necessary here to mention: the best substitute for such a society seems to be, the attaching of an Experimental Farm to a Botanical Garden, a measure which the liberal views of the Government of British India have induced them to adopt, and which has been well repaid by the experiments made there on the cultivation and produce of different kinds of grain, on the strength and durability of the fibres of the bark of various plants, and upon various other subjects, highly important to the Agricultural interests of the country."—Introduction, p. 4 and 5.

Dr. Roxburgh.

Though Dr. Roxburgh had very indifferent health, having been obliged during his Superintendence to make three distinct voyages, between the time of his first coming to the Garden, in 1793, and that of his death, which happened in 1813, once to the Cape of Good Hope, and twice to Europe, few men have laboured with greater zeal, assiduity, and success; and even during his absence, some of the men who acted for him were well qualified to do justice to the institution. Dr. John Fleming, President of the Medical Board, and who is well known by his Essay on Indian Medicinal Plants and Drugs, acted as Superintendent when Dr. Roxburgh went to the Cape of Good Hope; and on another occasion, Mr. Colebrooke, distinguished as a Sanscrit scholar, and for his Philosophical Essays

Dr. John Fleming.

upon the Literature and Philosophy of the Hindoos, as well as for the attention he paid to the useful Plants of India, as displayed in his Papers on Olibanum, Camphor, &c. in the Asiatic Researches; as likewise by his "Remarks on the Husbandry and Internal Commerce of Bengal." Dr. Carey also seems to have been in constant communication with the Calcutta Botanic Garden, of which he published the Catalogue in 1814, and a complete edition of Dr. Roxburgh's Flora Indica in 1831 and 1832.

Mr. Colebroke.

Dr. Carey.

The Botanic Garden of Calcutta has been useful in introducing many important plants into India. So long ago as 1814 Dr. Carey states, "The Mahogany tree, for instance, which but a few years ago was brought from Jamaica to this country, thrives so luxuriantly in Bengal, that many thousand trees of it are growing here, and even small pieces of furniture have been already made of the wood. The Pimento and Coffee prosper now as well in Bengal as in their native soil, and the Nutmeg, notwithstanding the climate is somewhat too cold for it, already produces fruit every year." The Nutmeg was but imperfectly known until it was correctly described by Dr. Roxburgh from specimens growing in the Calcutta Botanic Garden, which were obtained from the Molucca Islands, while they were in the possession of the English from 1796 to 1802.

Useful plants introduced into India.

Mahogany.

Pimento.

Nutmeg.

A Spice plantation was established by the E. I.

Spice plantation established by the E.-I. Company in Sumatra.

Company, under the charge of Dr. C. Campbell, on Mount Carmel, about sixteen miles south of Marlborough. Mr. Cole, a Civil servant of the

Mr. Cole's plantation at Bencoolen;

Bencoolen establishment, was the first who took measures to cultivate the Nutmeg and Clove Plants on a scale that merited attention. "His plantation, however," Dr. Heyne says, "was the only one of its kind until 1803, when it began to produce, and convinced the sneerers that the Spice did not only grow well, but produced in the greatest perfection." (Tracts p. 412.) From that period, plantations sprang up on every side, and the settlement thereby wonderfully improved. The number of plantations amounted in 1812 to about thirty-three, most of which had trees bearing fruit, and their produce in the market, particularly the Mace and Cloves, was found equal to that from the Eastern Islands: the Nutmegs were not quite so large as those from Banda. Dr.

also in Penang.

Roxburgh states that at Prince of Wales' Island, where by far the most extensive plantations were formed, the plants were in a middle state, between those at Bencoolen and in Bengal, but did not thrive by any means so well as in Sumatra, where they are perfectly at home in every respect, and fruit earlier than in the Molucca Islands. (Fl. Ind. iii. p. 845.)

Cinnamon.

In addition to the Spice trees, the Cinnamon was introduced into the Calcutta Botanic Garden

Camphor tree.

from Ceylon; and the Camphor tree from the

Cape of Good Hope, where it had been conveyed by the Dutch; also the Benzoin tree from Sumatra, and the Culitlawan from Amboyna. Camphor and Benzoin trees.

Among other subjects of great national importance, which at that time attracted Dr. Roxburgh's attention, were Barilla, Cotton, Sugar, Indigo, Hemp, and Caoutchouc. Experiments were made on these in the Botanic Garden, but of which, though very important in nature, it was long before their results and value were appreciated, or before imitators were found among those most interested in the improvement of the soil. Useful Indian products;

Potash and Barilla, which are imported in such large quantities, the former chiefly from America and Russia, and the latter from Spain and Sicily, he proposed to supply from India. The two species of Salicornia, and one of Salsola, which he described, and which are extremely abundant on the Coromandel Coast, he says might be made to yield *barilla* sufficient to make *soap* and *glass* for the whole world; as labour is cheap, population abundant, and, except in years of remarkable drought, there is always more grain produced than can be sold on the spot. But as the natives can scarcely procure a sufficiency of food during the dry season of the year, when there is little or no employment for them, it appears the more necessary to institute such branches of manufacture as will employ them during that season, — such as gathering these plants, and burning them for the Alkali. "Our Barilla in India. abundant; would afford the natives useful employment.

extensive, and I may also say impenetrable forests which cover such large tracts of the best lands in India, might by degrees be cleared and turned into Potash, for the same reasons, and by the same means. Certainly labour is as cheap here as in Russia. In this hot country we have many advantages, *viz.*, immense tracts of wood of the most solid texture, which requires little labour to prepare it for the fire, on account of the great drought and heat which prevail at the season this manufacture could best be carried on. The same heat and drought is fully sufficient to evaporate the ley without the least assistance of fire. All that could be necessary would be some broad shallow vessels exposed to the sun and wind." Dr. Helenus Scott, however, received a gold medal from the Society of Arts for sending from Bombay, as a substitute for Barilla, considerable quantities of Mineral Alkali, which he describes as being dug out of the ground, and which, though intermixed with a little common salt, yielded as large a proportion of Barilla as the Spanish.—v. Trans. Society of Arts, vol. vi.

Potash from India.

Mineral alkali sent from India.

Caoutchouc from Assam.

Caoutchouc, or India Rubber, long appeared a substance of trifling importance, but we see it every day becoming a more extensive article of commerce. From a source of this substance, discovered in Assam by Dr. Roxburgh above thirty years ago, it has only now entered the market, in consequence of letters written by the Author in 1836. It is now rapidly increasing in quantity, and is of so excellent a quality as already to have reduced the price, nearly thirty per cent. of that which had been so long and almost exclusively imported from Para. Though an agency house in Calcutta, to whom it was sent in 1828 by desire of the late Mr. D. Scott, informed him that "the article being unknown in this (the Calcutta) market, we are sorry we can give you no idea of its value;" and this, in March 1828, when it was selling in London for two shillings a pound; in the year 1837, 514, and in 1838, 925 Bazar maunds were exported from Calcutta; the former of the value of 4,112, and the latter 7,400 Rupees.

Caoutchouc from Assam;

Wood Oil, which is also a remarkable substance, and contains a large proportion of Balsam of Copaiba, is yielded by several trees described by him.* This has never become an article of commerce, but no less than five hundred gallons of it have been sent by a single individual, in consequence of a letter, also written by the Author, stating that it might become an article of commerce if made known here. The Custom-house officers, however, refuse to pass it except at the highest rate of duty, namely that, for a manufactured article, though it is actually obtained merely by tapping

Wood Oil.

imported;

high duty required.

* Species of the genus *Dipterocarpus*, as *D. turbinatus*, *D. costatus*, *D. incanus*, *D. alatus*, belonging to a family rich in valuable trees, as that yielding the Camphor and Camphor Oil of Sumatra; the Piney tree, which yields a liquid varnish, Indian Copal, and a Vegetable Tallow; the Saul tree, yielding a valuable timber, and Dammer, an excellent resin.

Wood Oil. the tree. The selling price is hence increased before it is even known, and it may thus perhaps be prevented from becoming an article of commerce.

Culture of Cotton in India.

Cotton; Among the various products of the soil, there are few, if any, which are at the present day of greater importance than the wool-like covering of the seeds of a tropical genus of plants, which is so well known under the name of Cotton. This is one of those products of the Vegetable Kingdom, which is common to both the New and the Old World. It is mentioned by the Greeks, as Herodotus states, that the Indians possess a plant which produces wool of a finer and better quality than that of sheep, of which the natives make their clothes, and Nearchus describes it as flax made from trees. That it was also indigenous in America, we know from its having been found in some of the ancient Peruvian tombs, together with specimens of Cotton cloths; some of the woven patterns of which, it is curious to observe, very closely resemble some modern patterns. From India, Cotton seems to have been first introduced into and cultivated in the islands of the Persian Gulf, and subsequently into Egypt, where, though known as an article of commerce, it does not seem to have been cultivated until later times, nor could it have been very common

known to Greeks as a native of India.

Indigenous also in America.

From India introduced into Persia and Egypt.

as an article of clothing, for the Mummy Cloths are found to consist of linen. Linen.

Though the Flax plant and Linseed are well known, and extensively cultivated in India, it is remarkable, considering the early and constant communication between the two countries, that the Hindoos should not have learnt from the Egyptians the art of separating the Flax, and of weaving linen out of a plant, which they extensively cultivate on account of its seeds. This is most easily accounted for, by their possessing a substance like the Cotton, which is obvious to the senses, and easily spun into thread, and which, when made into cloth, is so well suited to the climate. Its inferior conducting powers making, it like flannel, more efficacious than linen in preventing chills, in a climate where perspiration is so copious and evaporation very rapid, which is necessarily accompanied with a certain degree of cooling.

not known to Indians.

Advantages of Cotton clothing in hot climates.

Seeing that Cotton is one of the indigenous products of India, and one which has been so long cultivated in the country for the uses of its inhabitants, it strikes one as extraordinary to hear India frequently adduced as a country incapable of producing the finer kinds of Cotton. In the history of the nation, it is only in comparatively recent times that it has been of such great importance to provide what is so much valued by the English manufacturer, that is, Cotton of a good length and quality of staple, as well as of

India erroneously supposed unfavourable to growth of Cotton.

Indian Cotton carelessly collected;

a certain degree of cleanness. From the earliest times, the Hindoo, with his patient habits and prodigal labour, because this was so cheap, though he collected his Cotton carelessly, yet cleaned it with care before weaving it into the matchless fabrics, emphatically denominated "woven air," for which India is still unrivalled. Cotton Piece Goods long formed an extensive commerce from India to England, but the improvement in English machinery has caused a revulsion in commerce, from which, as it is not easy to change the habits of a nation, the weavers of India continue to suffer. Their country is inundated with the proceeds of the incessant working of English machinery; and the English manufacturer requires to be constantly supplied with the raw material of a certain quality, instead of the English merchant importing, as heretofore, the manufactured products of Indian looms.

but cleaned before weaving.

India not yet recovered from the revulsion in the commerce of Cotton.

Cotton; improvement of dependent on careful culture, and clean picking.

To improve the length or the quality of the staple of Cotton, and to collect it in as clean a state as possible, are two very different, though nearly equally important processes—one entirely mechanical in nature, the other depending on the application of the principles of Science to the culture of the plant. These, we shall endeavour to show, depend not only upon a proper selection of kinds of Cotton,—that is, of species suited to particular situations, — in reference to peculiarities of soil and of climate, embracing in the latter term not only temperature, but also dryness and moisture, and everything which is now included under the comprehensive term of Climate. Few of those who have written on the subject seem to have been aware of the paramount necessity of attending to the influence of the different Physical agents on the growth and secretions, and therefore on the Products of Plants, though the importance of so doing may any day be proved, even in the growing of a Cabbage, or the blanching of a Lettuce, or of Celery.

Culture of Cotton.

The Court of Directors called the attention of the Government in India, as early as the year 1788, to the cultivation of Cotton in India, "with a view to affording every encouragement to its growth and improvement in general, but particularly to the species manufactured into the finer sorts of thread in use for the superior goods of the Dacca fabric." Reports were called for, from the Collectors of districts. Mr. Bebb's and Mr. Duncan's are among the most valuable of those received. In the year 1794, a machine was sent out for cleaning Cotton from seeds or other impurities. A few years afterwards a bounty was offered for its cultivation on the coast; a plantation was then established at Rhaudaterra on the Bombay side, under the superintendence of a Mr. Brown. Instructions for the proper cultivation of Cotton were also sent out: and it was intimated that seeds of the West-India and American Cottons would be procured, and sent out to India.

Culture of Cotton encouraged by E.I. Company; Reports required; Machine sent out; Bounty offered Cotton Farm; Instructions sent out, &c. Seeds.

Means adopted by E.I. Company for encouraging the culture of Cotton in India.

In consequence of the position of public relations with the United States of America, the Court of Directors, at the commencement of 1809, sent out instructions to India. The result of which was, that about thirty millions of pounds weight of Cotton-wool were sent by the month of August in 1810; of this quantity, somewhat less than five millions only were sold, the intercourse with America having then been renewed. In the year 1810, one point especially noticed, is "the foulness, dirt, and seeds which are suffered to remain mixed with the Cotton, and for the continuance of which no excuse would hereafter be admitted." It was further stated "it is our positive order that the commission be not paid to any commercial resident, whose provision of cotton shall be faulty in this particular." But even this failed to improve the culture of Cotton.

Cotton sent from India; a small portion only sold; its dirty state particularly reprehended.

In the year 1811, the Court of Directors expressed their intention of consigning to the different Presidencies, a sufficient quantity of the seed of the Cotton produced in the Isle of Bourbon, with a statement of its mode of cultivation, and the nature of the soil best suited to it. This was done to enable the Governments in India to make a decided experiment, and ascertain whether a considerable quantity of Cotton-wool of good staple, which might in all respects be equal to American Cotton, could not be successfully grown in India. The Court, however, were not unmindful that the experiments previously made with Bour-

Bourbon seed.

bon Cotton in India had not been very successful. We have seen (p. 66) that seed had been introduced from the Mauritius into the Peninsula of India by Dr. Anderson, but it did not succeed, evidently from want of attention to the soil it requires. Dr. Roxburgh early ascertained that "it succeeds better in the more elevated, dryer, and less fertile soil of Coromandel, than in Bengal, where the plant grows to a great size, yields less Cotton, and the cultivation is very generally relinquished, though there must be many situations near the mountains of our northern frontier where it would thrive." (Flora Indica iii., p. 187.)

Cotton—culture of; soil suited to Bourbon Cotton;

Dr. Roxburgh also describes with the above, the green-seeded Cotton as a native of America, and five other species, with their varieties, as natives of Asia, stating that, "after a search of thirty years, he had been unable to find more well-defined species of the genus." Among the varieties described, is the famous Dacca Cotton, which is figured in his Coromandel Plants. This Cotton was described by Mr. Bebb, Resident at Dacca, as the finest in the world, and as producing cloth of astonishing beauty and fineness; the best quality of this was cultivated only in a tract to the eastward of Dacca. But whether its superiority was owing to the soil, the quality of the air, or to any particular art of cultivation, was uncertain, and probably could not be ascertained. Dr. Roxburgh states, that the most intelligent people of that country (Dacca) think the great difference

Species of Cotton; American; Asiatic; Dacca Cotton.

Dacca Cotton. lies in the spinning, and allow little for the influence of soil.

Want of attention to principles in culture of Cotton.

In the experiments hitherto made, we do not observe, however, that any attention was paid by the Experimentors and Cultivators to what is now thought so essential to success in a new culture, or in, what is the same thing, the improvement of an old culture by the introduction of new species, and the adoption of the practices of other places. Such as, ascertaining whether the soil and the climate of the new situation are similar to that of the place of which we wish to adopt both the plant and the practice; or, supposing differences of soil or of climate in the country into which a plant is introduced, whether such modifications may not be introduced into the culture, as to be more suitable to the new situation, and thus enable us to obtain the same products as elsewhere. This we know may be done by duly apportioning the influence of the several physical agents, as light, air, heat, and moisture, on the delicate and easily altered vegetable structure, according to the richness or poverty of the soil, the dryness or moisture of the atmosphere. Though we cannot alter the quantities of the above agents, we may modify their effects, either by open or close planting, by a richer or more sterile soil, pruning or irrigation. We shall afterwards see that those who succeeded best in their experiments, were those who paid attention to the influence of physical agents on vegetation.

Culture of Sugar in India.

Sugar-cane a native of India.

Sugar is one of the ancient productions of India, which was early known to the nations of the West, and to the Greeks, four or five hundred years before the Christian æra. It was at first called "honey of canes," and afterwards *sakkhar*, which is its Indian, and evidently the origin of its European names, as *sukkhar kund* is of Sugar Candy, thus indicating very clearly their Eastern origin. The Saracens introduced the Sugar-cane into Sicily and the South of Europe, and the Portuguese into the Canaries; from thence it was taken to Hispaniola in the year 1506.*

Introduced into the South of Europe, the Canaries, the West-Indies.

The remarkable effects produced by the introduction of a vegetable are in no cases more conspicuous than in the transportation of the Coffee and of the Sugar-cane into the West-Indies. There, before the middle of the eighteenth century, no less than three hundred sail of ships went annually from Great Britain, besides those from other places. The navigation of France also

Sugar trade of West-Indies.

* "The first Sugar-canes found in the West-Indies were at Hispaniola in 1506, an inhabitant of La Vega, named Acquillor, having brought them from the Canaries. Bachilla Vellosa and Pedro Atiença were the first who planted them, and extracted Sugar from them. They yielded so well, that in a short time there were on the island forty Water and Horse Mills. The first was made by Christoval and Francisco de Tapia, at Laguate."—Tablas Chronologicas por Claudio Clemente. Valencia 1689; 4to. p. 168, as quoted by Dalrymple in the Oriental Repertory, i., p. 2.

Sugar-cane introduced from India into America.

was described even in 1701, in a memorial by a French Chamber of Commerce, as "owing all its increase and splendour to the commerce of its sugar islands;" and this owing to the introduction of a plant which came originally from India. Yet that country has long been supposed, and still is so by many, incapable of manufacturing the product of the Cane, so as to compete with those countries to which it has so freely given this, as well as many other of its natural riches,—as Rice, Ginger, Indigo, Tamarinds, the Mangoe, the Orange and Lemon tribe. Coffee, Cloves, Nutmeg, Cinnamon, and many others, have also been derived from parts of Asia.

India supposed incapable of producing good Sugar.

East-India Company called upon to import Sugar from East-Indies.

In the year 1792, Sugar rose by degrees to an enormous price, in consequence, it was supposed, of the annual importation being very unequal to the increased consumption of Great Britain, combined with the demand for exportation. The East-India Company were called upon at a General Meeting of the Public to lend their assistance towards effecting a reduction of the price of Sugar, by encouraging importations of it from the East-Indies. A General Court of Proprietors was held, on the 15th March 1792, for the purpose of considering an application intended to be made to His Majesty's Ministers or to Parliament, for lowering the duties then payable on East-India Sugar. Upon this occasion a Report by the Committee of Warehouses, dated the 29th February 1792, relative to the culture and produce of Sugar in British India, was read. As further authentic information appeared still indispensable, the Court of Directors ordered, agreeably to a suggestion in this report, that the Collectors of the Indian revenues should be called upon "to ascertain various particulars relative to the existing state of the Sugar cultivation, its increase or decrease; whether it laboured under any peculiar disadvantages which could be removed by proper encouragement."

Sugar culture in India; Information called for.

It had, however, been directed in the year 1789, that a quantity of Sugar and some other articles should be sent for trial. In the year 1790 a quantity of Benares Sugar, with samples of other Sugars and of Tobacco in the leaf, the produce of Bengal and Behar, were transmitted to England. In February 1791, Lieut. J. Paterson, of the Bengal Establishment, addressed a memorial to the Court of Directors, stating that Sugar could be cultivated in Bengal with many superior advantages, and at less expense than in the West-Indies; though after making his contracts, and returning to India, he does not seem to have found the facilities so great as he expected.

Sugar sent from India. also Tobacco. Lieut. Paterson contracts to manufacture Sugar on the West-Indian method.

The result of the above orders was a series of valuable reports by the Collectors of Revenue upon the culture of Sugar in India. Among these, that of the political resident at Benares is the most full and comprehensive in its views, and it may be profitably referred to, even now, for the improvement of the culture of Sugar

Reports on Sugar culture in India.

Reports on Sugar culture in India; in India. With these were obtained a few essays on the subject by scientific persons in India,—as those drawn up by order of the Supreme Government by Drs. Roxburgh and Buchanan Hamilton. Large quantities of Sugar were also imported, as is fully related in the "Papers respecting the Culture and Manufacture of Sugar in British India." The result may be briefly summed up, as is done in the above report of the Committee of Buying and Warehouses 11th December 1822: "In the course of the thirty years which have elapsed since the former proceedings of the General Court of Proprietors relative to East-India Sugar took place, this article has risen, by a regular gradation, to be an important branch of the national commerce; the quantity of East-India Sugar imported in the year ending the 5th of January 1821 having amounted to about fourteen thousand tons, and in the year ending the 5th of January 1822, to thirteen thousand five hundred tons."

Reports published.

Quantities of Sugar imported from India.

Effects of the introduction of East-India Sugar.

The great extent of the Indian territories in which Sugar may be grown, the quantities which were imported, and the cheapness with which it can be manufactured, had, no doubt, considerable influence in reducing the price of Sugar, and would perhaps have injured the commerce of the West-Indies, had not this been prevented by the great distance, high freights, and the very unreasonable duties, amounting to £37. 16s. 3d. per cent. charged on this country on East-India Sugar.

At this time English metals were admitted free of duty, and English manufactured Goods, Cottons even, entered India on paying only two and a-half per cent. The continued demand for Sugar, of which the consumption seemed to increase in proportion to the extent of its production, had also its influence in preventing any very great reduction of price taking place.

Increased demand for Sugar.

But at the very time that these efforts were making in India, the West-Indians were assisted by the introduction of a new kind of Sugar-cane, which far surpassed that originally introduced from the Canaries, in size and in productiveness of juice. This was the Otaheite cane, of which Capt. Bligh says, "some very fine Sugar-cane was brought to me, each of the pieces was six inches round." The French, about the year 1794, introduced three new kinds of Sugar-cane into Martinique, and into their other West-India colonies. One from the island of Bourbon, another from Otaheite, and a third from Batavia. The Bourbon and Otaheite Canes were found to be nearly of the same nature, both, being much larger than the old West-India Cane; many of their joints measuring nine inches in length, and six in circumference. When trimmed and fit for grinding, some of the canes weighed seven pounds, being about two pounds heavier than the largest picked canes of the old kind. They ripened quicker, and were fit for cutting in ten months; their juice also granulated sooner, and threw up less scum

Otaheite Sugar-cane introduced into the West-Indies by the French, of great size, rich in juice.

Otaheite Sugar-cane.

Sugar estates greatly increased in value.

in the boiling than that of the old canes. They also resisted the injuries of excessive dry weather, and the ravages of that destructive insect, called the *borer* in the Sugar islands. So that in one season, in a year, wherein the dry weather and the borer were particularly fatal to the other canes, a proprietor estimated the produce at 3,500 pounds of sugar from an acre. In a subsequent season, however, 5,700 pounds an acre are recorded as having been produced. Macpherson, in his Annals of Commerce, says, "After such proofs of their superiority, the new canes, generally under the name of the Bourbon canes, were soon spread over all the British West-Indies, where they very quickly superseded the old canes, and with such advantage to the proprietors of sugar plantations, whom they have inspired with the most splendid hopes, that the introduction of them will undoubtedly constitute an important æra in the history of the West-Indies."*

Bourbon Canes.

It is a curious coincidence that the Otaheite

* A proprietor of the greatest respectability in the Island of Tobago, writes on the 20th September 1797, "my properties here, since we were restored to the British Government, have become very valuable. I have for three years averaged five hundred hogsheads of sugar, and a large proportion of rum, and the Bourbon canes are so wonderful, that I expect from six to seven hundred hogsheads next year, if I can make them. This cane passes wonder, and renders the appearance of the old canes unpleasant. I would not, as a planter, have credited a report of what I have witnessed of it."

Cane should have been introduced into the West-Indies at the very time that vigorous efforts were making for establishing the Sugar trade of the East-Indies. It is remarkable also, that among the numbers who at that time paid attention to the subject, so few should have thought of improvements in the Culture of the Cane in India, or even in the Manufacture of the Sugar, and still fewer of the introduction of new kinds of Sugar-cane from other countries. Some, however, acquainted with the West-India method, forcibly called attention to the unthrifty manufacture in India, where, from delays in the processes, much of the saccharine principle was destroyed, before the juice was boiled down into Sugar. The Bourbon, or Otaheite Sugar-Cane, was at that time probably little known, but Dr. Roxburgh was well aware of the importance of this subject, as at the beginning of the year 1796, he applied to Government to write to the Supercargoes at Canton for the seeds of all vegetables that yield *flax* and *hemp*, or that produce substances employed in their stead, as well as for the various sorts of *Sugar-cane*.

Little attention paid in India to improved culture or manufacture of Sugar.

Among the plants received from China, towards the close of 1796, in consequence of this requisition, was a kind of Sugar-cane, which Dr. Roxburgh considered a new species, and has called Saccharum Sinense, or Chinese Sugar-cane. Of this, he writes at the close of 1799, that it "has been cultivated with the utmost pos-

China Sugar-cane imported in 1796 into Calcutta Botanic Garden,

China Sugar-cane extensively distributed.

sible success. Many *hundred thousands* have been distributed over the country amongst the cultivators of that article." It possessed the advantage of being so hard and solid as to resist the forceps of the white ants and the teeth of the jackal, two great enemies to the East-India Sugar Plantations. It was found, however, too difficult to express the juice with the common Bengal Sugar-mill; but Dr. Roxburgh was of opinion that this might be obviated by introducing the simple, and at the same time powerful mill of the Coast of Coromandel. The cane he further describes as bearing drought much better than the sorts in general cultivation, producing moreover a profitable crop even to the third year; while the common cane of India must be annually renewed. According to the report of Mr. Touchet, the commercial resident at Radnagore, and of Mr. R. Carden, Superintendent of the Honourable Company's Sugar Plantation Farm at Mirzapore Culna, it not only resists the ravages of the white ant and jackal, but yields about double the produce of the common Bengal Cane. (v. "Report on the Sugar Trade," p. 258, and Roxburgh's "Flora Indica," 1 p. 239).*

Its advantages.

Report from E.I. Company's Sugar Farm.

* Though anticipating events, it may be mentioned, that the Otaheite Cane was only introduced lately into the Botanic Garden at Calcutta by Captain Sleeman of the East-India Company's service, and thence into India. It has since spread rapidly, seems highly esteemed, and the climate appears suitable to it all over India. A European house, however, em-

In examining the accounts of the Sugar-cane Culture in India, several subjects of inquiry present themselves as worthy of investigation, and respecting which, accurate experiments seem still to be required. It is evident that every part of the extensive plains of India is well suited to the cultivation of Sugar; but we do not know what peculiarities of soil and climate are best suited to produce the richest secretion of juice; nor which cane is best suited to the different degrees of dryness and moisture, heat or cold of the different parts of India. The differences in these respects it would be extremely desirable to have accurately ascertained. In the culture also of the cane, many peculiarities must have considerable influence in the nature of the secretions, and consequently on the quantity of Sugar that is produced, besides what is dependent on difference of species. Such as the more or less deep ploughing and planting, as well as whether the latter be close or open, (so as to exclude or admit air and light,) the copious or scanty weeding, or the frequent irrigation. In addition to this, any improvement in the unthrifty mode of manufacturing it will ensure the production of Sugar of as superior quality in every,

Principles to be attended to in the culture and manufacture of Sugar.

Culture;

Manufacture;

---

ployed in the culture and manufacture of Sugar, and in the distilling of Rum, in the north-west of India, writes, that they found the China Cane to be superior to that introduced from the Isle of Bourbon, and now spread over India under the name of the Otaheite Cane.

Culture and Manufacture of Sugar in India. as we now know to be produced in some, parts of the Indian empire. Samples of East-India Sugar sent to this country have been pronounced equal to any from the West-Indies. But to ensure success, as well as to make it profitable, it is necessary to pay as much attention to the culture of the cane, as to the manufacture of the Sugar.

Culture of Indigo in India.

Indigo, Product of India, Indigo, which like Rice, Pepper, Cotton, and Sugar, is a natural product of India, and has like them, been successfully introduced into other countries, is still better calculated to prove, that the success of the manufacture of a vegetable product, and therefore the extent of its Commerce, depends as much upon skill, combined with energy in the cultivators and manufacturers, as upon suitableness of climate to its culture. That Indigo is an original product of Hindostan, known to ancients, is proved by its name *Indicum* among ancient authors, and hence it was, until very recent times even, called *Indico* in European commerce. That this was the substance which we now call Indigo, is evident by the directions given by Pliny for detecting spurious kinds, as he states, that "the proof hereof is by fire, for cast the right indico upon live coles, it yieldeth a flame of most excellent purple." It might be adduced as an objection, that the substance alluded to is sometimes called the *stone indicon*, but so even in the present day is Catechu, also an Indian and equally a vegetable product, called *Terra Japonica.* Indigo.

With regard to the commerce of Indigo, it is mentioned in the Periplus of Arrian, as exported from Barbarike on the Indus, to Egypt. In the seventeenth century, the consumption of Indigo in Europe was so considerable, that the sale of Woad was much diminished, and the use of Indigo was prohibited in an imperial edict, published in 1654, when it was denominated the *devil's dye.* The Nuremburgers, moreover, compelled the dyers annually to swear that they would never use Indigo.* In the "Report of the Proceedings of the East-India Company, in regard to the Culture and Manufacture of Indigo," we learn that it formed a prominent article of importation during the first century of their commerce; and we find in the earliest notices respecting it, that like so many other Indian products, though intrinsically good, its value was diminished by carelessness in preparation as well as in packing. It was then recommended that the sand and dirt which adhere to the outside should be avoided, as frequent complaints had been made, that the sand injured the mills in grinding it.

Commerce of.

Use of prohibited.

Imported by East-India Company.

Carelessly prepared and packed.

In the markets of Europe, however, the East

* Bancroft; Phil. of Permanent Colours, 1, p. 166.

Indigo, in Mexico, were again to be supplanted by the West-Indies. On the discovery of Mexico, a dye like Indigo was known to the Aztees, and, according to Humboldt, a species of Indigo plant is seen among the most ancient hieroglyphical paintings of that country. But it was not from improvements in the ancient culture there, that the East-India Company were obliged to discontinue their imports from India, but in consequence of the British colonists in the West-Indies and the southern parts of North America, giving their attention to the culture and manufacture of Indigo, in such large quantities and so successfully.

in West-Indies.

Cultivated by French, Portuguese, Spaniards,

The culture and manufacture of Indigo had also been introduced into St. Domingo by the French, who greatly improved the process, while by the Portuguese it was carried into Brazil, and by the Spaniards into Mexico. About the year 1747, most of the planters in the British West-India possessions relinquished the cultivation, and Great Britain, with the rest of Europe, was supplied by the Spaniards and French, who manufactured the finest kinds of Indigo.

By whom Great Britain and Europe supplied.

Efforts of East-India Company.

But, about 1779-80, the Court of Directors of the East-India Company made extraordinary efforts to increase the production of Indigo, and to improve its quality, foreseeing that if they succeeded, the result would at once be highly advantageous to India, and beneficial to this country. A contract, at prices which were intended to encourage the growth, was therefore entered into with Mr. Prinsep,* who at this time conceived that India might supply Europe with Sugar and Cotton, as well as Indigo: and for a supply of the latter, they continued to make other engagements of a similar kind until 1788. But, on reviewing the issue of all the sales prior to the year 1786, it was ascertained that the several parcels yielded a remittance of only 1s. 7d. 67 dec. for the current rupee, which was a loss in the first instance of upwards of seventeen per cent., independent of freight and charges, which may be reckoned at full ten per cent. more. In 1786, several contractors delivered in Indigo, which was sold in London,— of this, that supplied by Mr. J .P. Scott was the only parcel which yielded a profit, and this to the extent of 11d. 01 dec. per pound. Notwithstanding this, the losses upon the aggregate of the above consignments were very considerable; as that which stood the Company in

Indigo in India; imported into England.

Losses sustained.

Cost and charges	£30,207
Produced only	21,596

so that there was a loss of £8,611, or equal to twenty-eight per cent.

* Having been kindly allowed access to papers left by Mr. Prinsep, I find that as early as 25th Jan. 1780, in a letter to Lord North, he writes of his "objects of introducing Indigo, Sugar, and Tobacco into Great Britain from the East Indies;" and in another letter it is stated that he had, "with the utmost trouble and expense, collected round him Europeans bred to different arts and sciences, as well as the most intelligent mechanics and planters of the East."

Means adopted for improving Indigo in quality.

Though these losses had been sustained, important results were the consequence. Europeans acquainted with West-India methods having proceeded to Bengal, considerable improvements took place in the manufacture of Indigo. Some transmitted by Mr. Boyce, even so early as 1787, was pronounced by a competent judge in London "equal to Spanish, 9s. 6d to 10s. 6d. the pound the second sort." From the proved practicability, therefore, of making superior kinds of Indigo, and contrasting this with the inferior qualities of that sent from Bengal, as well as the high prices at which it was tendered, the Court came to the determination that the Company should cease to purchase for at least three years. This, it was supposed, would have the effect of creating competition among individuals, and would not "fail to operate in bringing the article to its greatest possible state of perfection;" at the same time, the lowest rate at which it was possible to be manufactured would be ascertained.

Company discontinue purchases for three years.

To insure due attention being paid to all parts of the process, and to afford the requisite facilities for attaining success, instructions were sent out concerning the mode of manufacture, as well as directions respecting the square forms in which it was desirable that the Indigo should be sent home. Specimens also of the good kinds which it was desirable to rival, were sent to India, and also the reports of the Dyers and Brokers on the several samples which had been successively

Instructions, Specimens, and Reports, sent out to India.

transmitted from India. Besides this, some of the duties were remitted for the seasons of 1789 and 1790, and relief also afforded both as to tonnage and freight. Advances were likewise made by the Government to some manufacturers, and "as a further aid, the Company made large advances of money secured on the Indigo, on a plan of remittance to London, and this course was followed for many years."*

Relief in duties.

Advances of Money.

It is extremely interesting and instructive to find these measures followed by rapid improvement in the quality of the Indigo. It is stated in a letter of the Court of Directors of the 30th of May 1792: "It affords us much pleasure to remark that the article, as to quality, is still increasing in reputation. It has already surpassed the American and French, and there is no doubt but, by perseverance and attention on the part of the planters, it will effectually rival the Spanish." In fact, a parcel of five chests, belonging to Messrs. Gilchrist and Charters, was declared to be superior to Spanish, and was sold at a higher rate; while the buyers deemed it to be possessed of every requisite that could be wished. By the accounts of the quantities of Indigo imported into Great Britain, during ten years, ending in 1791, it appeared, that in proportion as the imports

Improved quality of Indigo.

Surpasses the American, French, and Spanish.

* Vide "Report of the Proceedings of the East-India Company in regard to the Culture and Manufacture of Indigo," p. v.

from Bengal increased, there was a diminution from other parts. The consumption of French Indigo in this country was even then nearly supplanted by that from Bengal, and it was a still more favourable circumstance, that the cultivation in St. Domingo diminished nearly one-half in the course of the seven years which preceded 1789, in consequence chiefly of the increased cultivation of Coffee.

French Indigo supplanted by Bengal.

Large quantities imported from India.

From the success of the culture, it was prosecuted with undue vigour, as this in the year 1795 caused an importation of 4,368,027 lbs., of which the consignments from Bengal alone amounted to 2,956,862lbs. From this immense quantity being thrown into the market, and from four-fifths of it being of a very inferior quality, a considerable reduction in price ensued. These fluctuations continued to characterize the commerce in Indigo, and this not only for the above reasons, but also because the consumption of Indigo depends upon the condition and progress of other manufactures. The reduction in price was at no time more remarkable than between 1824-25 and 1829-30, having been 11s. 5¾d. a pound in the former, and 4s. 3¾d. in the latter. But the trade increased gradually to a great extent, as no less than 9,913,010 lbs. were imported in 1828, though not more than 6,545,873 lbs. in the year 1837: of these importations ninety-four per cent. was supplied by India.

Reduction and Fluctuation in prices.

Great extent of commerce in Indigo.

Few histories of commercial products are more

instructive than that of Indigo, which we see an article of export in the earliest times, from the country where the plant is indigenous. It formed one of the principal articles imported by the East-India Company in the first century of their commerce, but was soon supplanted when European skill was applied to the culture of the plant, and the manufacture of Indigo, in the West-Indies and southern parts of North America. It was restored again to the country of its birth, by the very means by which it had been wrested thence, that is, by the application of European skill and energy, as well to the culture of the plant as to the chemistry of the manufacture. Accurate information was also supplied, and specimens of the quality of drug it was desirable to rival.

Observations on the previous history.

But all these would hardly have sufficed, had it not been for the extensive purchases made by the East-India Company, the losses which they sustained, and the advances which they still continued to make. The manufacturers eventually attained a degree of skill, which in a climate favourable to the plant, and backed by the cheapness of labour in Bengal, enabled them to bid defiance even to the more practised manufacturers of the West. The culture and manufacture being established, Indigo has continued one of the staple products of Bengal. Its goodness is permanently secured by the planters in Bengal and the south-east provinces attending to the culture of the plant and the manufacture of the Indigo,

Indigo manufactory established by purchases of East India Company.

Observations on history of Indigo Culture:

while those in the north-western parts of India supply them with seed. The moisture and richness of the Bengal soil and climate are favourable to the luxuriant growth of the parts of vegetation, in which the colouring matter is secreted; while the comparative dryness of the northern provinces enables them more easily to perfect the parts of fructification. The whole history, culture, and manufacture afford most useful lessons for the means to be adopted for ensuring success in other cultures, which at first appear equally unprofitable, but are not more hopeless, inasmuch as they are substantive products, which do not depend upon the state of other manufactures for their sale and consumption.

Culture of the Poppy in India.

Poppy, an exotic introduced into India.

Opium, so well known, and so extensively produced, need hardly be adduced as an instance of the physical capabilities of India for producing valuable commodities; were it not that the cultivation of the Poppy gives us an instructive lesson, not afforded by the other cultures successfully practised in India. Cotton, the Sugar-Cane, Indigo, and Pepper, are all indigenous products of the country, while the Poppy is a striking instance of the successful introduction of a valuable plant of more northern latitudes, into a hot country.

The history of the Poppy, and of Opium, its inspissated juice, are imperfectly known. Though extensively cultivated in India, the Poppy is also common in the gardens of England. Very good Opium has sometimes been prepared even in this uncertain climate, and in France and Germany it has been so very frequently. The Opium, so called Turkish, is chiefly collected in Asia Minor, and is exported to the extent of about 400,000lbs. from Smyrna. It is produced at several places, at from ten to thirty days' distance in the interior; but that grown at Caisar, about six hundred miles from Smyrna, is the most esteemed for its cleanness and good quality. Besides this, other kinds of Opium are known in commerce, as that of Constantinople, and of Trebisond, as well as the Egyptian.

Poppy and Opium—history of.

Opium—varieties of;

The oldest notices of the Poppy are found in the works of the early Greek Physicians, where not only the plant, but also its juice, is mentioned. Opium, however, does not appear to have been so generally employed as in modern times, or the notices respecting it would have been more numerous and definite. It seems also probable that it first came into extensive use in Egypt. But, from having been so long and so generally cultivated in Europe, and the northern parts of Asia, the Poppy has spread, and become so completely naturalized in different countries, that it is now difficult to ascertain where it was originally indigenous. But, extensively as it is cultivated in India, it is remarkable that nowhere are even a few stray plants to be seen in a wild state; a

Poppy; earliest notices of.

where indigenous;

cultivated in India, but not found wild;

sufficient indication that it is not a native of the country. This supposition is still further confirmed, by no other species of Poppy being found in the plains, though the Author discovered one in the mountains, and Mr. Griffith has sent the seeds of a species of wild Poppy from Caubul. The names of the Drug seem also to assist us in tracing

Opium—origin of name.

its origin to countries beyond India. *Opium* is, no doubt, derived from the Greek *opos*, (juice;) which may also be the origin of the Arabic *afioon;* and this latter, of the Hindee *aphim.* According to Professor Wilson, the only Sanscrit term for Opium, is *ahiphena*; this occurs in the Medical Dictionary, called the "Raja Nighanta," and has every appearance of being borrowed and adopted from the Arabic term. By the Chinese, as we learn from the Memorial of Heu-Naetse, Vice-President of the Sacrificial Court, it is called *Afooyung* in the Materia Medica of Le Shechin, of the Ming dynasty.—(Correspondence relating to China, 1840, p. 156.)

The Poppy, not being a native of tropical countries, is not cultivated in India during the seasons which are characteristic of those climates, that is, during the hot weather or rains; but in what are

Poppy cultivated during the cold season.

the winter months of European climates, namely from October and November to March. The great heat is then sufficiently reduced to allow of the successful cultivation, not only of this, but also of other valuable plants requiring only the summer heat of northern latitudes; such as Wheat,

Barley, and European Kitchen-garden Vegetables. As low temperatures enough occur throughout the plains of India, the Poppy may be successfully cultivated from Behar, even to the banks of the Sutlej, or in the several independent states of the partially elevated table land of Central India, which are usually comprehended under the name of Malwa. The Behar, or Patna Opium, has long been esteemed of the finest quality for the China market; but that of Malwa, containing a large proportion of the narcotic principle, has rapidly attained almost equal value. For this it is probably indebted to the climate of Central India; but the north-western provinces could no doubt produce it of as fine a quality; since a specimen prepared at Bareilly was found to contain the largest proportion of the narcotic principle. Some Opium prepared by the Author at Saharunpore, was pronounced equal to the best Turkey, for medical purposes, and this was very similar to some procured in the Himalayas. The latter is grown there much later in the season, and collected nearly in the same months as in Europe and Asia Minor, that is in May and June. It can, no doubt, be prepared of the best quality for the European market, both in the hills and plains, whenever it is thought desirable to do so.

Culture of the Poppy.

Behar, or Patna Opium;

Malwa Opium;

Opium in N. W. provinces,

and in Himalayas.

Though in the preparation of many of the valued articles of commerce, the Hindoos preceded most nations, yet they have usually been surpassed, whenever European skill and energy have been

Collection of Opium requiring only care;

Preparation of Opium; applied to the improvement of these very discoveries. It is remarkable, therefore, to find that with Opium they should have attained complete success, and this too, without the aid of European science. But, in the preparation of Opium, nature does everything, and man has only to wait patiently and carefully to collect the secretions of her laboratory.

dependent upon state of atmosphere; The cultivation of the plant, however, requires some degree of attention, such as good soil, manure, and also careful management of the irrigation. The strength of the juice depends upon the quantity of moisture, and also, as Dr. Butter has shown, upon that of the dew which falls upon the surface of the capsule. A deficiency of dew prevents the proper flow of the milk, while an excess, besides washing off the milk, causes additional mischief, by separating the soluble from the insoluble parts of the Opium. This deteriorates its quality, as well as increases the quantity of moisture, which must afterwards be got rid of. This, together with the adulterations practised by the Ryots, causes the chief difficulties experienced by the Opium agents.

easier to make good Opium in Northern than in Southern India. This dependence upon the state of the atmosphere will in many cases explain the greater or less facility experienced in the preparation of Opium of the best quality in different parts of India. Also, why though the soil be less fertile, it is easier to prepare Opium of fine quality in Malwa and the north-western provinces of India, than in Bengal. But the history of the Opium culture is as instructive as that of Indigo, though in a different way. The latter being an indigenous plant, has continued to be cultivated by the natives according to their own methods, while the manufacture of its dye has been improved by the application of European energy and science. The Poppy, on the contrary, is a foreign plant, successfully introduced by the natives themselves, of which the produce requires care, but not science on their parts. It is well calculated though, to show the important results which may follow the introduction of a plant, suited to the soil and climate of a country. When the Poppy was first culivated in India, is not known, but it had attained considerable importance in 1786, as there is a memorial of the Marquis Cornwallis of that date, respecting the best mode of deriving a revenue from Opium. In 1826, the Finance Committee estimated that the government might derive from it about £1,000,000 yearly of revenue.

History of Opium; instructive as that of Indigo;

Indigo indigenous;

Poppy foreign.

Poppy, and its juice, a source of Revenue.

The Poppy has been adduced as a remarkable instance of a foreign plant successfully cultivated in India, but chiefly on account of the lessons which may be drawn for the culture of other plants from similar climates. For we are led to enquire whether it be so peculiar in nature, as to be the only useful plant from similar climates cultivable in India, or whether it may not rather be an instance which may be successfully imitated. Therefore that other plants, as important as arti-

Inferences from successful culture of Opium.

Inferences from successful culture of Opium.

cles of commerce, which like it succeed in the summer of European climates, may with equal success be introduced into the cold weather culture of the plains, or into the summer culture of the mountains of India.

Culture of Flax and Hemp in India.

India looked to for substitutes for Hemp;

We have seen, that on the occasion of the high price of Sugar, India was looked to, for a supply of what in some countries is considered a luxury, but in Great Britain almost a necessary of life. When a deficiency began to be felt in the best materials for Canvas, Cables, and Cordage, so essential for the safety of our navy and mercantile shipping, India was again looked to, and expected to send an adequate supply of Hemp, or of some efficient substitute.

growth of Hemp in India recommended.

The Lords of the Privy Council for Trade and Foreign Plantations, in a letter, dated the 4th of February 1803, recommended to the Court of Directors of the East-India Company to encourage as much as possible the growth of strong Hemp in such parts of their dependencies in India, as might be best suited to the production of that article. On the 23d of the same month, the Court replied that they would take the needful measures for accomplishing the object of their Lordships' wishes. But attention must have been directed to this subject long previous to this, as in the Treatise on Hemp,* &c., by Mr. Wisset, he quotes from the Board of Trade consultations in Bengal, of the date of 1792, referring to the Reports of the Collectors of Revenue, which impart much valuable information respecting the culture of Sunn, in India. We learn also from a letter of Dr. Roxburgh's, dated 24th December 1799, that the Court of Directors had sent out Mr. Sinclair to establish the cultivation of Hemp; but he, having died shortly afterwards, the experiment was continued by Mr. T. Douglas, and, according to Dr. Roxburgh, in a most expensive manner.

Culture of Hemp in India;

Mr. Sinclair sent out to establish it.

India being an anciently civilized country, and its inhabitants practising various arts and manufactures, must necessarily have possessed some plants, of which the fibre could be employed for the purposes of Cordage. This we know is required for many purposes, besides being essential for the rigging of the vessels of their extensive river navigation. In fact, in investigating the subject, we find that the natives of India possess no less than between forty

Many cordage plants in India.

* A Treatise on Hemp, including a comprehensive account of the best Modes of Cultivation and Preparation as practised in Europe, Asia, and America, with Observations on the Sunn Plant of India, which may be introduced as a substitute for many of the purposes to which Hemp is now exclusively employed. By Robert Wisset, Esq., F.R. and A.S. London, 1808, Clerk to the Committee of Warehouses of the East-India Company.

India—cordage plants of; and fifty different plants which yield them materials fit for cordage. The fibres of some of these plants are remarkable for their great strength; those of others more easily cultivated, are deficient either in softness or strength: but as these are produced in the greatest abundance, their characteristics have come to be considered as those of all Indian plants of this nature.

described and cultivated by Dr. Roxburgh. Dr. Roxburgh,* described many of these and cultivated them in the Botanic Garden. He also prepared their fibres, in general by maceration, &c., as is done with Hemp and Flax in Europe; and had them made into cords, for the purpose of comparing their respective strength (plain, tanned, and tarred). The details it would be out of place to enter into at present, as we shall recur again to the subject, and be able to show, that besides those usually cultivated in India, there are some others which are in request in the English market, and which are well suited to the soil and climate of different parts of that country. On the present occasion, we need only

* Observations of the late Dr. William Roxburgh, Botanical Superintendent of the Honourable East-India Company's Garden at Calcutta, on the various Specimens of Fibrous Vegetables, the produce of India, which may prove valuable substitutes for Hemp and Flax, on some future day, in Europe. Edited by a Friend, and published at the expense of the East-India Company, for the information of the Residents, and the benefit that may arise therefrom throughout the Settlements in India. London, 1815.

mention the Flax and the Hemp plants; the former is extensively cultivated on account of the oil contained in its seeds, but the plant itself is thrown away. Of this, Dr. R. says, "Samples of the Flax have frequently been procured by the Board of Trade, and sent to England to the Honourable Court of Directors, so that it is from home we may expect to learn its properties. If the Flax has been found good, large quantities may be reared at a small expense, as the seed alone which the crop yields must be more than equal to the charges to render it profitable to the farmer."—Observations, p. 17, and Trans. Soc. of Arts, 1804, xxii. p. 389.

Flax cultivated in India;

sent to England.

The Hemp, like Flax, seems to have been cultivated from very early times, being mentioned in old Sanscrit works, and in some European works it is referred to as a native of India. It is the *ganja* of the Hindoos, and is valued by them only for a resinous secretion, which is elaborated by the leaves and green part of the flowers. This is of a stimulant nature, and taken by some of the natives for the purposes of intoxication; they call it by various names, though that of *Bang* or *Bhang* is that most commonly known. The plant is therefore cultivated everywhere, and grows apparently wild in the north-western parts of India, at the foot of the Himalayas, and very abundantly, and of large size, in the mountains themselves. It is well known to the Persians and Arabs, and

Hemp,

native of India;

cultivated in India;

Hemp plant, where indigenous.

it is probable that its name, *kinnub*, gave origin to the Greek Cannabis, as it did to the European *hemp;* as another name, *husheesh*, is thought to have done to the word assassin. Though an Asiatic plant, it is also extensively cultivated in many parts of Europe, especially Poland, Russia, and Italy, and it is matter of doubt whether it may not have been originally indigenous in some of the southern provinces of Russia.

Indian Flax and Hemp; planted so as to secrete oil and resin, &c., and not to produce softness and length of fibre; causes of defects;

The Flax, or Linseed plant, being valued by the natives of India on account of the oil of its seed, and the Hemp on account of the resinous secretion of its leaves, are both cultivated so as to favour the production of the largest proportion of these secretions, that is, the Flax usually on the borders of fields, and the Hemp nine feet apart. In Europe, it is well known, that if it be wished to prevent a plant secreting the principles, bitter, acrid, or otherwise, which are natural to it, the practice is to exclude it from the influence of light and air, as in tying up Lettuces, and covering up Celery. So, to ensure a full secretion of the principles natural to a plant, an opposite treatment is necessary, and is practised with the Hemp in India by openness of planting, and consequent exposure to the full influence of Light, Heat, and Air. But this very exposure will produce hardness of fibre, as is well known in the best timber being produced in exposed situations. Therefore, as in the case of the Indian Hemp, a diminution is produced, of the softness and flexibility, which are as essential as strength to good Flax and Hemp.

Indian Flax and Hemp;

This hardness, and consequent inflexibility, of fibre, produced by open planting, and which may have caused a prejudice against the fitness of the plants of Indian growth for the production of Flax and Hemp, is a defect, probably, most easily remedied. Mere sowing thick, necessarily causes the plants to grow close to each other, and as they extend themselves most in the direction of the light and air, they will shoot upwards, and produce but few lateral branches. The rapidity and extent of growth produces not only length, but also softness of fibre, with some diminution of strength, but probably with not more than is necessary to ensure the requisite degree of softness and flexibility. Thus, even in Europe, when Flax is required for Cambric, it is sown much thicker than when it is to be made into Linen.

hardness and inflexibility of;

how to be remedied.

Flax was prepared by Dr. Roxburgh in India, and he was of opinion that it could be produced profitably, and in any quantities. So he also obtained Hemp, from the true Hemp Plant (Cannabis sativa) both on the Coromandel Coast and in Bengal. He was led to think that it might be cultivated to greater advantage over the interior parts of Bengal and Behar; and especially in Rohilcund, also in the adjoining mountainous tracts to the northward of that district, (Observations,

Flax prepared by Dr. Roxburgh;

also true Hemp;

might be cultivated in India.

Hemp in India; p. 2). In a subsequent page (31), however, he fears that it can never be cultivated to advantage in India, as numerous expensive experiments had been made by Government without any prospect of real advantage. But this opinion is of less weight, as he calculates the freight at £16 per ton, and because his experiments were made in Bengal, which, he states, is unsuited to the culture. He was also unacquainted with the fact of

abundant in north-western provinces; the great abundance of this plant in the north-western provinces, and also until a late period,

and in Himalayas. that the Himalayan mountaineers value it for its bark, of which they make a coarse sackcloth, (much used for grain bags by the merchants in the plains), as well as the strongest ropes, for crossing their broad and rapid rivers.

In this part of the country, therefore, the practicability of preparing Hemp for the European market ought first to be ascertained, and if successful there, as will probably be the case, it may then be spread to other parts of India.* The capabilities of the country for growing cordage plants, and the habits of the people in preparing

Quantities of Hemp and Flax exported. them, are evident from the large quantities of the substitutes for Hemp and Flax which have been exported;—as of Indian Hemp (probably Sunn) 18,955 maunds, and of Jute 14,565 maunds

---

* *Vide* a letter by the Author, on the Cultivation of Hemp in India, published in the Proceedings of the Agricultural and Horticultural Society of India, 12th February 1840, Calcutta.

were exported from Calcutta in 1828-29, besides 1,013,277 pieces, Gunnies and Gunny bags, made of these very materials, while in the following year no less than 9,006,415 were exported. Export of Indian substitutes for Hemp.

Silk Culture in India.

Having noticed the progress of the culture in India, of several vegetable substances which enter most largely into the commerce of the world, and endeavoured to explain the causes of success or of failure in the experiments which were instituted for their improvement, we might now proceed to investigate the principles which require to be attended to in the culture of plants, whether for amusement, or for increasing our comforts, or the resources of a country. But there are some animal products which depend so entirely upon the proper culture and suitableness of their vegetable food, that we cannot well omit them even in the present cursory enumeration. Animal Products dependent on Vegetable culture.

Silk is one of those rich productions of the East, which even from ancient times has been highly valued by the nations of the West. There can be no doubt that the Silk-worm was originally a native of China, and that Silk has been produced there from the most remote antiquity. Chinese annals assign to its discovery a date equivalent to two thousand seven hundred years before the Christian æra. It has also been known in India from very ancient times, as it appears that Silk is Silk. Silk-worm, a native of China; long known in India.

Silk mentioned in oldest Sanscrit Works.

mentioned in the *Amera Kosha*; though it may be doubtful whether the worms most common there be indigenous or introduced. In some of the older Sanscrit works, Silk is called *Cheenam-Sokam*, or cloth of China; and in the Mahabharat, which is supposed to have been written before the Christian æra, Patta-keetas, or Silk-worms, are described as having been brought by Chinese as a present to Yoodhestera during his reign at Endraprastom.* Several distinct species of Silk-worm are, nevertheless, indigenous in India, as we shall immediately see, and yield silks which are very distinct from those of China, and which

Silk-worm, some species of, indigenous in India.

* In the 2d part of the Mahabharata, entitled *Sabha Parvam*, chap. 86, we have the substance of the following verses:—

"Cheenas, Hoonas, Kashas, and Cauchas,
Who lived on mountain summits,
And who were famous,
With obedience brought (to Yoodhestera)
Ten thousand Caps and Haircloths,
And also Silk and Silk-worms."

Translation by Teroovercaudoo Mootiah in Anderson's Communications. Madras 1795.

The Author having submitted the above quotation to the first authority, Professor Wilson, he was good enough to look through the above book of the Mahabharat, and has favoured him with the following note:—

"The reading of other copies of the Mahabharata does not exactly agree with that consulted by Mutiah. As it stands in the printed edition, with which in all essential respects a good copy in the East-India Company's library agrees, the passage occurs thus: 'Chinas, Sakas, Barbaras, Hunas, &c. brought fine cloths, made from the wool of the sheep and goat, produced from worms—from Patta, and made from or with valued for their useful qualities in India, are now beginning to be esteemed and desired for some of the manufactures of this country. At what period the Silk of India was first introduced into Europe, it is probably impossible to ascertain, for it must often have been confounded with that from China; as the sources of both were so little known, that the accounts of Silk are frequently confounded with those of Cotton.

Import of Indian Silk into Europe.

The Ancients describe Silk under the names of Sericum and Bombykia, the latter derived from *Bombyx*, the insect, and the former from *Serica* and *Sereinda*, the remote country beyond the Ganges, where Silk was produced, or from *Seres*, the people who inhabited it. This country probably was China, from the frontiers of which the Persians conveyed merchandize across central Asia to the coast of Syria. A portion of this was, no doubt, diverged from some part of the route, towards India, and in works now in use there,

Silk, ancient names of;

probably obtained from China.

---

kuti (?), soft sheep skin, sharp swords, &c.' There can be no doubt that by *kíta jam* we must understand Silk; *pattajam* is more questionable, *patta* meaning a plant, from the fibres of which a coarse cloth or canvas is made: what is meant by *kute kritam* I do not know. The most important difference in the reading is that regarding Silk-worms, which is the sense Mutiah attaches to *patta kítán*. No such compound occurs in my copies, the version being there, '*pattajam kìtajam tathá.*' It is, therefore, very questionable if the Mahabharat is authority for the introduction of the worms from China into India. Silk, both raw and manufactured, was no doubt an article of import from China into India at a very early date."

the country whence it came is noticed, under the name of Kathai, (China) the old Cathay of our own Authors.

Silk from China esteemed by the Romans;

The Romans esteemed Silk so much that Marcus Antoninus sent an embassy to China, to open a direct communication with that country; but the Ambassadors, who proceeded by way of Egypt and India, do not seem to have been more successful than those of modern times. Silk-worms, as is well known, were subsequently introduced into Europe by two Persian monks, in the year 552, conveying the eggs in a hollow cane to Constantinople. The worms were fed upon the leaves of the Mulberry tree, which was, fortunately, indigenous in Europe.

Silk-worms introduced into Europe;

Culture of, long confined to territories of Greek empire;

The culture of the Silk-worm was for six hundred years confined to the territories of the Greek empire. Yet it might have been supposed that the eggs of an insect so highly valued, and which had been brought from China to Constantinople, would in this long period have been introduced into other parts of Europe. This, however, did not take place till Roger I. of Sicily carried into captivity a considerable number of Silk-weavers, whom he compelled to settle at Palermo, and to impart the knowledge of their art to his subjects. Twenty years afterwards the silks of Sicily are described as having attained a decided excellence. By degrees, a knowledge of the several processes spread over the greater part of Italy, and was carried into Spain. It is said, that Silk

introduced into Sicily;

Spain;

was first introduced into France by Louis XI., who obtained workmen from Genoa, Venice, and Florence, and established them at Tours in the year 1480, under very extensive privileges; but it was not until the reign of Francis I. that much progress was made in the Silk Manufacture in France.*

Culture of Silk introduced into France;

In those days so little encouragement was afforded in England even to machinery, that the Rev. W. Lee, of St. John's College, Cambridge, who invented an engine for knitting or weaving stockings, was induced to comply with the invitation of Henry IV. of France, and, accompanied by several journeymen, established his looms at Rouen, in Normandy. Colbert, minister of Louis XIV., was so anxious to increase the production of Silk, that he not only gave trees from the Royal Nurseries, but also caused them to be removed and planted at the Government expense. But, as the trees thus easily acquired, were found to be but little valued, a reward was afterwards offered to cultivators for every Mulberry tree that should be found in a thriving condition, three years after it had been planted.

and much encouraged.

The Silk-worms having, though with difficulty, been introduced into Europe, have now been spread over a great extent. Being indigenous in China, Silk is extensively produced there, chiefly to the south of the Yellow River, and especially

Silk, cultivation of, in China.

* The Author has referred for these historical facts, which are sufficient for the present purpose, to the volume of the Cabinet Cyclopædia on the Silk Manufacture.

Silk, cultivation of, in India. about the neighbourhood of Nankin, in 32° N. lat. but it is said not to flourish in the most southern provinces. In India, on the contrary, the Silk culture flourishes only in the southern parts, that is, in Bengal; and all the East-India Company's filatures were confined to that province, and did not extend beyond 26° N. lat. Silk has long formed commerce of, from India; an article of commerce from India, but in inconsiderable quantities before the middle of the eighteenth century. It was, moreover, very inferior in quality, "being wound from the cocoons, and reeled into skeins after the rude manner immemorially practised by the natives of India," and which is now distinguished by the name of "*country wound.*" It fell into so much disrepute, that the Court of Directors informed the Bengal Government, that unless the defects could be rectified, the Company must abandon the exportation of it to England."*

The Court were induced, in the year 1757, to send Mr. Wilder, "a gentleman who had the Bengal Silk improved by East India Company. Mr. Wilder sent out. reputation of being perfectly acquainted with the culture and preparation of Silk in every stage," out to Bengal. He remained in India till the time of his death, in 1761, and laid the foundation of great improvements in the winding of the Silk. "Subsequently to the acquisition of the Dewannee, the cultivation of the Mulberry was recom-

* Report of the Proceedings of the East-India Company in regard to the Trade, Culture, and Manufacture of Raw Silk. London, 1836.

mended in the strongest manner to the Zemindars and landholders, and all possible encouragement afforded for the clearing of such lands as would best answer for the purpose." "The Government also was directed to make such deductions from the rents of the lands planted with it, as should have the effect of a bounty in its favour, and render it more profitable than any other kind of culture." By these means a very great increase took place in the importations of Silk from India.

Culture of the Mulberry encouraged.

Increase in importation of Silk.

But hitherto the better modes of preparing the Silk had been but partially successful, and as "considerable dealers and manufacturers had given it as their opinion that the staple of the Bengal raw Silk was equal to that of the Italian or Spanish, and capable of being used for all the purposes—if reeled in the same manner,"—it was determined, in 1769, "to introduce into Bengal the exact mode of winding practised in the filatures of Italy, and other parts of the Continent." For this purpose several Englishmen and foreigners, as Messrs. Wiss, Robinson, and Aubert, and others—as drawers, winders, reelers, and mechanics,—were retained, for the purposes of proceeding to India. It was also determined that the method of spinning and drawing the Silk as practised at Novi,* in Italy, was to be adopted throughout all the filatures. The first Silks pre-

Italian mode of winding introduced;

Europeans sent out to Bengal.

* "Various tools, implements, and models, manufactured in London, and at Novi, were forwarded to Bengal for the use of the Establishments."—Report, p. xii.

Silk wound by Italian method; pared by the Italian method were sent to the Court of Directors in 1771, and reached England in 1772. The report, which was made here received and reported on. on their arrival was, that "Mr. Wiss had succeeded to admiration in drawing a tolerable Silk from the most ungrateful cocoons that the sickliest worms under the most unfavourable season could produce; that the coarse Silks could not be much improved; that it was the finer sizes that required reformation, which, if accomplished, the Company would view the advanced price, and eager demand for it, with astonishment."

Silk-worm introduced from China. About this period the Bengal Government applied for, and received from China, a quantity of the China Silk-worms, as well as Mulberry plants, which were planted in the Governor-general's garden. It is unnecessary to follow the history more minutely, as "It has been shown that the introduction of the Italian method of winding Silk in Bengal may be dated from about Italian method of winding fully established; the year 1770; but it was not until 1775 that the new mode could be considered as in full operation. In the intermediate period much time was unavoidably taken up in erecting buildings, fitting up furnaces, reels, &c.; and in instructing the natives, whose long established prejudices it was difficult to remove, so scrupulously averse are they to innovations of any kind."

the results of this improvement. The result of the successful efforts for improving Bengal Silks was quickly seen, by the decline of importations from Aleppo, Valencia, Naples,

Calabria, and other places in the Mediterranean, so that, in a very short period, the whole of the Silks used in this country were furnished only from the northern provinces of Italy, from Bengal, and China.

Success of Bengal culture.

In the deficiency of the supply of Hemp from Russia, and in that of Sugar from the West Indies, we have seen that India was looked to, to relieve the wants of the British public. So in 1808, when the decrees of Napoleon occasioned an entire cessation of the customary importations of Italian raw silk into this country, the Silk trade held a meeting at Weavers' Hall. It was then resolved unanimously, "That Bengal Silk was become highly necessary in many branches of manufacture, and that from experiments lately made, it is found fit for purposes to which it had not before been thought suitable." That it was highly desirable that its quality should be further improved, and that a greatly increased quantity should be brought over. A Committee was also appointed to confer on the subject with the Chairman and Deputy-Chairman of the East-India Company.

Deficient supply of Silk from Italy in 1808.

Bengal looked to for a supply;

In consequence of this, orders were sent to the Bengal Government to adopt all possible means for increasing the supply of Silk, and to arrange, as soon as circumstances would admit, that the whole of it should consist of the filature-wound class. Instructions for reeling Silk were

Increased quantities ordered;

instructions for reeling Silk sent out; translated into native languages; furnished by Mr. Wiss,* and these were sent out to Bengal, and directed "to be supplied to the Residents at the several Silk aurungs, and to be translated into the native languages for the information and direction of the native servants, who are entrusted with the care of the minor establishments. The Indian Government was also recommended to consider whether it might not be practicable to a certain extent to establish Mulberry Plantations on its own account.

specimens of silk sent out; To remove uncertainty respecting the exact sizes of Filature Silk required, the Court transmitted to Bengal sets of regulating specimens, with directions that the Silk should in future be manufactured strictly in conformity with them

specimens of cocoons, and reports required. Specimens of the cocoons reared in the vicinity of the several factories were also required, with reports on the varieties of the Bengal Silk-worms by the different Commercial Residents. The Commercial Resident at Santipore having suggested that a certain quantity of Mulberry land should be cultivated, and that the Silk-worms should be

---

* Mr. Wiss having returned to England, was presented by the Court of Directors with £1,000, for the assiduity and skill with which he had established the Italian mode of winding at one operation from the pod. He was also appointed Silk Superintendent, and "continued in the Company's home service for many years, and was eminently useful in furnishing the Residents in India with suggestions for improving their Silks."—Report, p. xvii.

reared, and the cocoons formed under his immediate superintendence, his recommendation was sanctioned both by the Indian and Home Government. The experiment was continued until 1830, but the Silk was not found improved in proportion to the expense incurred.

Experimental Silk Farm established.

From the foregoing cursory view of the means adopted for improving the Silk culture of India, we observe that there, as in Europe, improvements have generally, if not always, been urged upon cultivators by the influence and expenditure of the Government. In later periods of the history of nations, individuals are sufficiently well informed to adopt suggestions for a prospective advantage; though this is never found to be the case, nor indeed can it be expected, in nations less advanced in civilization. The results of the measures which had been adopted were, as we have seen, firstly, great improvements in the Silk of Bengal, and secondly, the quantity imported into England was increased from 401,445lbs. in the year 1792, to 1,387,754lbs. in 1829, though in subsequent years it was somewhat less.

Results of the measures of the East India Company.

Great improvement in the Silk.

The culture of Silk, though susceptible of further improvement, having succeeded to so great a degree in Bengal, ought to afford the best encouragement for the ultimate success of other cultures. Many of these are not more hopeless than that of Silk appeared when the East-India Company determined upon attempting its improvement. In fact, any difficulties must be fewer

Inferences from success in Silk culture;

Requisites for Silk culture. in number, and less in degree. For in that we had not only to procure the animal which was to prepare the Silk, but also the leaf upon which it was to feed; and, thirdly, a climate was required suitable, both for the growth of the vegetable, and for the healthy existence of the animal.

Species of Silk-worm in India, The species of Silk-worm indigenous in India are sufficiently numerous, besides those which have been introduced from China, and latterly from Italy. An account of the indigenous Silk-worms has been given by Drs. Roxburgh and Buchanan Hamilton, Col. Sykes, Dr. Geddes, Mr. Hugon, and Dr. Helfer, as well as by the Residents at the East-India Company's Silk Filatures.

as described by Residents; Annual Worms; The Residents describe the Silk-worms which yielded the investments of Silk, as—1st. The large Annual Worm reared only once in the year, and yielding its produce from the middle of March till May. Dessee; 2d. The Dessee, or Indigenous Silk-worm of Bengal, of which the cocoons are obtained throughout the year; that is, there are four or five collections annually; of these, the worm of the cold weather, or November breeds, and that of the dry weather, or March and April breeds, are superior to the others, from the more nourishing nature of the leaves at those seasons. 3d. The China; China Silk-worms introduced into Bengal, which are next in estimation to the annual and country breeds; of these, both the yellow and white cocoons are abundant in the Radnagore district.

The Residents also describe, firstly, the Nistry tribe of Worms, which is said to include three distinct kinds, the *madrassie*, *soonamooky*, and *cramee*, and these yield a portion of what was formerly the Company's investment of Silk; secondly, the Tusseh Silk-worms, of which the *mooga*, *teerah*, and *bonbunda* are described as different kinds; the cocoons of these are collected in September, and are called the Rain weather sorts; but there are others of the dry weather months, which are denominated *dabba* and *buggoy*. *Tarroy* is an inferior sort collected in December.

Nistry Worms; Tusseh.

The Tusseh, or Tussar Silk, is very extensively diffused, the Residents describing the Worm as being reared in all the western forests from Ramghur to Midnapore. Dr. Roxburgh mentions it as a native of Bengal, Behar, and Assam, and that it is the same as the Bughy insect of other districts. The Jaroo is also described as a variety, by Dr. Buchanan Hamilton, and as occurring in the districts of Bhagulpore and Dinajepore; by Col. Sykes it was found in the Bombay, and by Dr. Geddes in the Madras Presidency.

Tusseh Silk-worms extensively distributed.

Mr. Hugon, Sub-Assistant to Captain Jenkins, Political Agent in Assam, describes six species of Silk-worm as being found in the central part of that province. Of these, the Mulberry Silk-worm, (Bombyx Mori); the Tusseh Silk-worm (Saturnia (Phalæna), Paphia) and the Eria, or Arindy

Silk-worms of Assam, described by Mr. Hugon;

Silk-worms in Assam; Silk-worm, (Phalæna Cynthia,) were previously well known; but the others have been described by himself and by Dr. Helfer. The Mooga Silk-worm (Saturnia Assamensis, Helfer), was also evidently known to the Residents, (v. Report, p. 52). The Joree Silk-worm (Bombyx religiosæ, Helfer), is a new species discovered by Captain Jenkins on the Peepul tree (Ficus religiosa). This is said to yield a Silk certainly equal to that of the Mulberry Silk-worm. Saturnia Silhetica, Helfer, is a native of the Kassia mountains, and of Silhet and Dacca. It also yields Silk, as do two other species, the wild Silk-worm of the central provinces, and another, which produces its cocoon upon the Mangoe tree. This the people of Malda gather, and mix with Arindy Silk cocoons in spinning. There are probably other species in different parts of India, which may be found to yield useful products.

(Margin: and by Dr. Helfer.)

(Margin: The wild Silk-worms: important as affording employment, and clothing.)

These wild Silk-worms may be thought by many unworthy of notice, as they do not yield the kind of Silk most valued in commerce; but they are more important than they at first appear to be. We must remember that the culture of some in the forests, and the collection of all, affords employment to considerable numbers of the natives in the parts of districts least productive of useful occupation. They afford also clothing for many of the inhabitants, as Mr. Hugon informs us that Silk from the Eria, or Arindy worm, is the daily wear of the poor in Assam, and is used by every class in winter. It is remarkable for its very great durability. Arindy Silk;

The Tusseh Silk is still better known, having also afforded the natives in Bengal, &c. a coarse durable Silk, which is much esteemed in India, both for ladies' and childrens' dresses; for the latter especially, on account of its cheapness and durability. This Silk will probably become an extensive article of commerce, as some of it, having been sent on speculation to Paris in its unbleached state—was there employed as a covering for parasols, and was found to answer so well, that an instantaneous demand for it sprung up. The price advanced, and the quantity imported has greatly increased; in 1835, only 158 pieces, in 1836, 830, in 1837, 2,647, and in 1838 no less than 4,249 pieces were imported. Other uses will probably be found for it when it is better known, and from the extensive tracts over which the Tusseh Silk-worm is distributed, we know that this commerce is susceptible of great extension. As an instance of the quantities in which the Tusseh Silk is produced in India, we may adduce the evidence of Mr. R. Montgomery of the Bengal Civil Service, for one district only. In an abstract statement in 1837, of the results of the survey and settlement of the district of Azimghur, giving accurate returns of the total area of cultivated, culturable, and of waste land, with the revenue of the district, Mr. M. has also given an

Tusseh Silk; becoming an article of commerce; quantity imported into England; quantity manufactured in Azimghur.

Tusseh Silk; quantity manufactured in Azimghur.

estimate of the quantity of Cloth, Silk, and Tusseh, manufactured, which Mr. Tucker and himself obtained from looms at work. In this statement 318,772 pieces of Tusseh Silk are given as the quantity produced annually.

Food of the various Silk-worms.

The food best adapted to these Silk-worms requires attention to as great a variety of points as the animals themselves. As the leaf of the Mulberry is required for their food, it is evident, that if a species of Mulberry had not been indigenous in Europe, the Silk-worm could not have been introduced from China into Constantinople. The Black Mulberry (Morus nigra) being the only European species, must originally have been employed as the sole food for the Silk-worm; as it is in the present day in the small experiments in this country. It is also occasionally cultivated in France. The White Mulberry (Morus alba), however, is infinitely to be preferred—and this has been introduced from China into Europe, as well as into India, —but so many varieties have been produced from cultivation, that it is difficult to ascertain whether they all belong to one species. Thus Morus Indica, the species most common in Bengal, is thought by Dr. Wallich to be only one of its varieties. Morus atropurpurea is a species introduced into India from China, where it is employed as food for the Silk-worm, though Dr. Roxburgh states, that it had not been found to answer for that purpose in Bengal. Two varieties (one, the Doppa Foglia), of the Italian White Mulberry,

Species of Mulberry; varieties produced by cultivation.

received from St. Helena, were established in the East-India Company's Botanic Garden at Dapooree, in the Bombay Presidency. The then Superintendent, Dr. Lush, forwarded to Calcutta young plants, which, in September 1833, were reported by Dr. Wallich to be in a flourishing condition. Two other species are common in the plains of North-western India, and others have been introduced there from Caubul and Cashmere; one distinct species occurs, moreover, in the Himalayas.

Species of Mulberry in India.

Morus multicaulis proposed to be introduced into India by Col. Sykes.

Col. Sykes has drawn attention to the great importance of introducing into India the Mulberry called Morus multicaulis, a distinct species or variety introduced by M. Perrottet into France, in 1821, from the Phillipine Islands, where it had been brought from China. It is now thought by many, both in Italy and France, to be the most valuable sort for cultivation, and has become a favourite variety in America. It is said, besides growing easily, and affording abundance of leaves of the most nourishing kind, to be able to withstand a considerable degree of cold.

Other plants fed on by wild Silk-worms.

We see, therefore, that the various species of Mulberry are nearly as numerous as those of Silk-worms; but all the wild Silk-worms feed upon different trees, such as the Jujube, Ficus religiosa or Peepul, the Castor Oil Plant, some of the Laurel tribe, and others, which are found in almost all the forests of India.

Mode of culture of Mulberry; Great importance is necessarily attached to the kind of Mulberry to be selected, but it is of hardly less consequence to determine upon the best method of cultivation. Respecting this, there are considerable differences of opinion, some conceiving (bush;) that the *bush* system usually adopted in Bengal is the only eligible method; while others recommend that the Mulberry be allowed to grow (standard.) into a *standard* tree. It will probably be found that both methods are suitable to different situations, according to the respective soils and climates of the places.

Properties desirable in leaf. The object being to obtain such food for the Silk-worm as will enable it to spin the strongest and finest Silk, we must first ascertain what properties in the leaf indicate its being best calculated for this purpose; and we must then inquire, what effects the different modes of planting are most likely to produce on the leaf. From the testimony of various observers, it is evident that too herbaceous or watery a leaf, though eaten voraciously by the worm, produces sickness in it, and (Effects of physical agents on different modes of planting.) weakness in the Silk. This state of leaf will be produced whenever, from too moist a soil and atmosphere, combined with heat, there is rapidity of growth. This is experienced in many parts of Bengal, though the climate there is on the whole so well suited to the growth of the Mulberry and the culture of Silk.

Bush culture. The Bengal mode of cultivating the Mulberry

Bengal or bush culture of Mulberry.

by cuttings planted rather close to each other, produces rapidity of growth, and, consequently, succulence both of branches and of leaf. The abundance of foliage prevents evaporation from the surface of the soil, at the same time that much watery vapour escapes from the surfaces of the leaves by their transpiration. Everything, therefore, contributes to increase the moisture, which, according to circumstances, may be an advantage or a disadvantage. That the latter is sometimes the case is evident, from Dr. Roxburgh having given it as his opinion, that the only improvement in the native culture which he could suggest, was, that a little more space should be allowed to the plants; as he conceived that more light and air would render the leaves better food. Dr. Wallich also has more recently stated it as his opinion, that it would be extremely desirable to cultivate the arborescent kinds of Mulberry.

Standard cultivation of the Mulberry.

In the standard cultivation, the trees being planted apart from each other, will be freely exposed to light and air; rapid growth will thus be checked, but a more healthy state of the secretions will be induced; though such exposure may sometimes produce too much dryness, and even harshness of leaf. But in many moist situations the standard will undoubtedly be preferable to the shrub cultivation, as it will partially obviate the tendency in such situations to run too much into leaf. It may also be preferable in some dry soils, where the difficulties of irrigation are great,

Standard cultivation of Mulberry, known to natives of Bengal.

as when the plant is once established it would send its roots into the earth in search of moisture. This practice is not entirely foreign to the natives, as the resident at Bauleah states that the annual worm prefers the leaf of the shrub which is well matured, to that which is young and tender; and therefore he infers that it would thrive better with the tree leaf than the shrub leaf. He also says that the tree is cultivated in parts of the Rungpore and Radnagore districts for the production of cocoons. The resident at Hurripal states, that there, the method of cultivation differs from that in use about Bauleah and Malda, the leaves being gathered only from *standard trees*, which are preferred on account of the dryness of the soil in that district. (Reports, p. 137 and p. 142.)

Soil suited to Mulberry in Europe.

In Europe it is found that when the Mulberry is required to feed the Silk-worm, rich soils are not suited to it, but that such as are sandy or gravelly, or even hilly situations, are better. In such places, less copious nourishment, combined with exposure to light and air, produce effects analagous to the Standard cultivation.

Signor Mutti introduces standard cultivation into Bombay Presidency.

Signor Mutti, in 1830, offered to the Bombay Government to produce Silk at Poona. A grant of land was given him, and he first tried the bush system; but not finding it suited to Bombay, he introduced the Italian method of growing the Mulberry as a standard tree. His success in the latter has been so considerable, that both the

Agricultural Society of Bengal and that of Bombay awarded him premiums for the benefit which had been derived from his great merit and indefatigable exertions, in introducing the method of producing superior silk into the Bombay Presidency.

Standard cultivation introduced into Western India.

Dr. Roxburgh, in reply to a query of the Bengal Board of Trade, respecting the influence of Climate on the Silk-worm, observes, but hardly with his usual sagacity, "that meteorological knowledge would operate but slowly in the improvements the Board (of Trade) have at heart." There is no doubt, however, but what considerable advantage may be derived from attention to peculiarities of climate.

Effects of climate on Silk culture.

It is remarkable to see both the Mulberry and the Silk-worm diffused over so wide a space, that is, flourishing in the hot and moist climate of Bengal, in the mild and dry climate of the South of Europe, and in the cold and changeable one of England. The same species of plant, however, is not found in these different situations; the black Mulberry, or old European species, being alone common in the north, and the others in southern latitudes. The worm which is exposed to all the influence of the climate in Bengal, is in Europe reared in houses, and is therefore subjected to a much more equable temperature.

Great diffusion of Mulberry and of Silk-worm.

It is interesting to contrast the East-India Company's filatures all confined between 22° and 26° of north latitude, with the absence of the Silk-

In India confined to Bengal.

worm from the more northern provinces of India. This must be ascribed to the greater temperature and dryness of these plains in the months from March to the middle of June; for excess of heat in Bengal, and even in the south of Europe, is often fatal to myriads of the worms. Heat alone, however, does not seem adequate to explain the whole of the phenomena, as the worms are often in the most healthy state previous to their being suddenly destroyed. But as the weather is described, then as being very hot, the air very dry, and evaporation very considerable, at the same time that the atmosphere is highly charged with electricity, it is possible that the latter state may be fatal to the worms, at the time when they are ready to spin a non-conducting material like silk. This may, perhaps, also explain why thunder-storms are sometimes so fatal to myriads of Silk-worms. If such should be proved to have any influence, as the author hopes to be able to ascertain by experiment, the obvious remedy would be to diminish the heat and dryness by exposing surfaces of water, or by having it thrown on *tattees* (thatched coverings), to be attached to the doors of well-secured buildings. This would diminish the heat, dryness, and also the electricity. At all events, well-built houses, with glazed doors or windows, which would give light and allow a modification of temperature, with the requisite circulation of air, as recommended by Mr. Marjoribanks, would enable the

Heat of Northern India hurtful to Silk-worms; probably also electricity of atmosphere; how both may be obviated.

silk culture of the annual worm at least, to be carried into drier parts of India, which now appear unsuited to the culture of silk;. and also along the vallies of the Himalayas and into Assam. That the expense in establishing experimental Silk farms if attached to Indigo, or other Factories, would not be excessive, has been proved by Mr. Speed, in the Transactions of the Agricultural Society of Calcutta.

Silk culture might be carried into other parts of India.

In the preceding review, comparatively little notice has been taken of the recent endeavours to introduce the Silk Culture into Bombay (owing chiefly to the exertions of Signor Mutti), as the recital would, as far as principle is concerned be only a repetition of what took place in Bengal, or, perhaps, more correctly in Madras about 1791. The earliest attempt to introduce the Culture of Silk into Bombay, was probably that of Dr. H. Scott, about 1795, mentioned in Dr. Anderson's Correspondence. Dr. Lush states, that there was nothing like a Silk filature in Bombay, and that the worm was first introduced by Mr. Baber, about 1823, into the jail at Dharwar, and that a few maunds of Silk were subsequently made for home consumption. But the determined perseverance of Signor Mutti was required to contend against the difficulties which attend all new undertakings. It has been mentioned in the text that he first tried the *bush* system, and then had recourse to the *standard* cultivation, and removed from Bombay to the neighbourhood of Poona. A house was given him, and land free of rent for several years; but time was required before the superiority of the standard cultivation could be proved. He was appointed to survey and report on the Deccan, and afterwards made Superintendent of Silk Culture. The Transactions of the Agricultural Society of Calcutta, vol. vi., contains Mr. Mutti's remarks on the superiority of standard Mulberry trees for the culture of Silk in Bengal and the Deccan, as well as his Guide to Silk Culture in the

Experiments on Silk culture in Bombay and in Madras.

Deccan. The Report of the Bombay Chamber of Commerce, for the first quarter of 1839-40, contains his reports on the Progress of the Silk Culture in the Deccan, and the Proceedings of the Agricultural and Horticultural Society of Bombay, Dr. Burns' Report of his progress in the same culture; forwarded by the Revenue Commissioner, Mr. T. Williamson.

The Silk Culture was commenced in the year 1791 by the Madras Government; ground, generally, to the extent of ten acres with twenty labourers, was allotted by the Collectors of Districts in the neighbourhood of different stations, where various gentlemen were appointed Superintendents of Mulberry Plantations. Silk-worms were obtained from Bengal; but so little information was possessed respecting the culture even there, that Dr. Anderson supposed that Silk was not produced in Bengal in the cold weather; so that Mr. Glas, of Boglepore, writes him, 11th June 1791: "Believe me, it is quite the reverse of what you have been told; the Mulberries are in high order all the cold season, and the three principal Beens (or hatchings) of the year are in November, January, and March." The Bengal workmen, afterwards sent from Cossimbazar, found fault with the mode of feeding the worms with the leaves gathered at noon, when they are flaccid, instead of in the morning, when they are fresh. The Mulberry was found in gardens all over the Presidency, in the state of trees and in hedges, but the Bengal, or Bush system, was adopted, though objectionable as requiring much irrigation in a dry climate. Various means were adopted for encouraging the natives to undertake the culture. Some of the native princes also attempted the culture of Silk, as Tippoo Sahib, in Mysore, and the Court of Hydrabad in Berar, as well as some of the smaller princes; and the Court of Directors encouraged the attempt in the Madras Presidency, as we learn by the Extract of a General Letter from England, dated 21st May 1794, published by Dr. Anderson.

"Par. 53. The directions contained in the 4th paragraph of our Revenue dispatch of the 3d July last, sufficiently evince our earnest desire to afford every reasonable degree of encouragement to Dr. Anderson's endeavours for establishing the Manufacture of Silk on the coast of Coromandel, and we shall cheerfully consent to your rendering such pecuniary assistance to the undertaking, as shall give it a fair chance of success. With respect to what is stated in the 5th and 6th paragraphs of your letter, in the Public Department, of the 28th February 1793, concerning the charges already incurred by Dr. Anderson, in his laudable endeavours for furthering an object of so much utility, we can only say, that we are not only willing to discharge the amount thereof, but shall have great satisfaction in giving Dr. Anderson a more substantial proof of the sense we entertain of his zeal and ability."

Experiments on Silk culture at Madras.

"54. Of the samples of Silk received by the contractor, the following report has been made to us, that it is of good quality, was admirably well wound, and if it is procurable at a rate of cost equal to what the article is afforded for at Bengal, it would answer for sale in this country."

PRODUCTION OF WOOL IN INDIA.

Wool, a produce of the East.

Considering the tropical nature of many of the substances of which we have treated, and that Wool of a good quality is usually thought to be a produce only of cold countries, it may startle many but partially acquainted with India, to hear of Wool as a product of that country. Yet from the oldest records which we possess, we find the tending of sheep, and the preparation of clothing from their wool, one of the earliest occupations of mankind in the warm and dry regions of the East. The open plains of these countries, from their great absorption of heat at one season, in

India climate, peculiarities of.

summer become scorched up, but from its free radiation at another, are cooled to an almost equal degree in winter. The northern plains of India are in a great measure similarly situated with respect to climate, though under the influence of the tropical rains at one season of the year. But in the winter, the cold is sufficient to require their inhabitants to be clothed in the fleeces of their sheep, or in coats padded with cotton.

As in the culture of Silk, so in considering the probability of the production of Wool, we have to consider the best breeds of the animal suited to the climate in which they are to be placed, as well as the pastures upon which they are to feed.

India, parts of unsuited to sheep;

The wide-spread territories and diversified climates of the British territories in India, can in no case be made more evident than in the different districts suited to, or unfit for the production of Wool. The coasts of the Peninsula, and the plains of Bengal, may be unsuited to the support of such sheep as will be valued for their fleece alone, but no where is the mutton finer than that of the grain-fed sheep of the plains of India.

suited to wool-bearing sheep.

The table-land of the Peninsula, however, commencing with the Neelgheries, and proceeding along Mysore to the Deccan, Candeish, and Guzerat, presents large tracts of country affording a favourable climate, and abundant pastures for numerous flocks of sheep. If from thence we proceed in a north-east direction, passing Marwar, Malwa, Rajpootana, to the district of Hurriana, and the province of Delhi, we shall see supported on the natural pastures of the country, immense herds of cattle, and numerous flocks of sheep. The latter affording Wool employed by the natives for making blankets *(Kumlees)*, of different degrees of fineness, which form a considerable article of the commerce of these provinces.

India, natural pastures of.

Again, the Himalayan mountains, on their Southern face, present a European-like climate, remarkable however for being influenced by the periodical rains. The temperature varies according to the elevation; but they afford everywhere rich pastures, and support a fine breed of sheep, of which the Wool is employed by the Mountaineers to form their clothing. The Northern face of these mountains is as remarkable for its dryness, as the Southern is for its moisture; the cold is excessive, and the animals which are pastured there are covered with shaggy hair, or with long Wool, and a fine down. It is here that the Shawl Wool Goat finds its most congenial climate.

Himalayas; southern face of; northern face of.

Attention was early turned to the possibility of deriving some benefit from the Shawl Goat, but, in the first instance, England was alone thought of. We learn from Dr. Anderson's publications, that in consequence of the establishment of a Society for the Improvement of British Wool, which was instituted at Edinburgh, on the 31st January 1791, Sir John Sinclair made ap-

Shawl Wool Goats imported into England;

Attempts to introduce Shawl Goats into England.

plication to the Court of Directors, and wrote on the 10th of March of the same year to Dr. Anderson, requiring "in the first place, as much information as possible respecting the sheep and other animals in the East, carrying any species of fur;" secondly, "to have specimens sent over of such breeds as are likely to answer in this country." In a letter to Sir John, dated 11th June 1794, from Dr. A., written in consequence of one to the latter from Dr. Roxburgh, we learn of the arrival at the Botanic Garden at Calcutta, of eighteen Shawl Goats, which had been procured by order of the Court of Directors, for the purpose of being sent to Sir John Sinclair. Attempts were also made to obtain "Carmenian Goats from Persia;" and we learn that Dr. Anderson had procured a ram with six horns from Mount Ararat, which on arrival in England, with the exception of having six instead of four horns, was found to be nearly identical in appearance with another which had been procured from Sweden.

Sheep's Wool of Tibet:

In the country of the Shawl Goats, some Sheep's Wool of very good quality is also produced. This might, no doubt, be easily improved, but the country is little under the influence of European advice or example, even if it were proffered. Attempts were made to divert a portion of this Wool trade towards India; but the difficulties were found to be considerable. Mr. Moorcroft, who was deputed in 1814, to that part of Little Tibet, in Chinese Tartary, where the Shawl Goat is pastured, for the purpose of opening to Great Britain the means of obtaining the materials of the finest woollen fabric, found that the Hooneas were obliged to send all their best Wool to Cashmere.* In the year 1819, considerable advantage was anticipated from importing this Wool into England; as a gentleman who was consulted, and who professed to have a practical knowledge of the English Wool Market, valued it at eight shillings per pound. The Bhyragee Wool, however, when imported was found to be unsaleable; as of 189 bales of Shawl and Bhyragee Wool, imported in the years 1821, 1822, and 1823, costing exclusive of freight and charges, £5,444, the gross sale proceeds amounted only to £809. This Wool was bought from the Hooneas, who keep sheep with the Shawl Wool Goats, by the people of Kunawur, and brought by them to Rampore, the capital of Bissehur, on the Sutlej. Specimens of the same kind of Wool, procured by Mr. Hodgson from the Booteas, who visit Nepal, were forwarded to the Court of Directors of the East-India Company, in 1835, by

Mr. Moorcroft on Sheep's Wool of Tibet.

imported into England;

losses on investment.

Specimens forwarded, by Mr. Hodgson to Court of Directors.

* "This is caused by strict injunctions to all the owners of flocks, not to sell any shawl-wool except to the Cashmerians or their agents, in consequence of a representation having been made to the Government, that the Jouaree merchants had bought some last year, and that the Cashmerians would suffer if any of this kind of wool were to pass into other hands." Moorcroft's Journey to Lake Manosarovara.—Asiatic Res., vol. xii.

Bhyragee Wool, value of.

Dr. Wallich. Of this the sorted Wool was valued here, at from 10*d.* to 11*d.* per pound; some in the unsorted state at 5*d.* to 7*d.*; and some was sold in the London market in 1834, at from 2½*d.* to 7*d.* per pound; the low price was chiefly owing to its dirty and mixed state.

Wool imported from Bombay;

Attention was turned in England to the subject of Indian Wool, by Mr. Southey, of Coleman Street, addressing a letter, 24th November 1836, to the Committee of Agriculture of the Royal Asiatic Society, respecting some Wool imported here from Bombay. He suggested more attention being paid to the assortment of the Wool, and improvement in the breed of the sheep; and stated that last year there were imported into London 773 bags, and into Liverpool 624 bags of Indian Wool, which were sold by Public Auction at 4¼*d.* to 1*s.* 2½*d.* per pound. The Wool was chiefly white, but with black hairs occasionally interspersed; and he understood that it was produced in the province of Guzerat. In the following year, Mr. Southey again called attention to the subject, stating that the quantity exported from Bombay had enormously increased; but that what came here was entirely of middling and secondary quality, and had, consequently, realized no higher prices than from 4½*d.* to 10½*d.* per pound.

prices obtained;

great increase in quantities exported;

The great and rapid increase of the exports of Wool from Bombay, is evident from an inspection of the following extract from the official Report of the Commerce of Bombay, for 1836-37.

It is there stated, that "the article Wool is particularly deserving of attention, from having so lately become an export (the first shipment having been made in 1833), and from the rapidity with which it has risen into an extensive and valuable staple; as will appear from the following statement, taken from the Records of the Custom House: *Exports of Wool from Bombay;*

"In the official year ending 30th April

1834	69,944 lbs.
1835	486,528
1836	1,196,664
1837	2,444,019."

The Report of 1837-38, goes on to say, "The quantity of Wool exported has increased from 2,444,019 lbs. to 2,700,086 lbs., valued at 98,564 rupees."

It was rather hastily concluded that the whole of this was the result of the opening of the Trade of the Indus; for Col. Jervis, of the Bombay service, has stated, "that the first exports of Wool from Bombay were the produce exclusively of the Deccan sheep. But the merchants of Affghanistan, and other northern countries, who are in the habit of resorting to Bombay for trade, perceiving Wool (an abundant produce of their own country) a marketable article at that Presidency, turned their attention to it for the first time." *supposed to be from opening of Indus; but from Deccan, and Affghanistan.*

A great part of this supply is derived from Cutch and Sinde, and from Marwar, *via* Gujerat, *Sources of supply;*

Sources of Bombay Wool.

and small quantities are also received from the Persian Gulf and Red Sea. Capt., now Sir A. Burnes has lately given an account of the quantity and quality of the supply of Wool likely to be derived from the great pastoral countries of Cabool and Bokhara. These are—

Sir A. Burnes on Wools of Cabool and Bokhara;

1. The Wool of Toorkistan, obtained chiefly in the neighbourhood of Bokhara and Samarcand, is more celebrated than that of Cabool. This is sent to Umritser in the Punjab, where it is used to mix with the Shawl Wool of Tibet, in making what are called Cashmere shawls. It is the produce of the Goat, and not of the Sheep, of Toorkistan, and is called *put*, in contradistinction to *pushm*, which is used to express the fleece of the Sheep. 2. The Wool or Put of Cabool, not at present exported, being entirely consumed in the Native Manufactures. It is procured from Goats, and chiefly from the Hill Country of the Huzaras to the West of Cabool, and between that city and Herat, which has an elevation of about 6,000 or 8,000 feet above the level of the sea. 3. The countless flocks of flat-tailed Sheep in Cabool, which produce an abundance of Wool. The fleece is of a glossy white colour, and is in Cabool called *pushmi burra*, and the fabrics prepared from it *burrak*, in contradistinction to *puttoo*. It sells at from two and a half to two Cabool rupees the seer, or sixteen pounds. It is brought in from all directions for sale in Cabool, and Sir A. Burnes states, that he "can scarcely put a limit to the

of Goat of Bokhara.

of Goat of Cabool;

of Sheep of Cabool.

supply, since the extent of pasture land in these countries is not over-rated at four-fifths of the whole surface of the country, and a very large portion of the population, such as the Lohanees and Ghilgees, are shepherds, who remove from pasture to pasture, and rear their flocks with great care and attention. Nature, however, does as much as the people; for aromatic plants in which sheep delight, are exceedingly abundant, and it is universally believed that they have considerable effect on the quality of the Wool."—*Notice on the Wool of Cabool and Bokhara, by Sir A. Burnes.*

Sir A. Burnes on Wool of Cabool.

The relative value of Wools, however, like that of all other commercial products, can only be ascertained when submitted to the examination of competent persons, or to the test of sale in an open market where there is a demand for the article. Thus, twenty-four bales of so-called Cashmere Wool, shipped from Bombay on account of Maharajah Runjeet Singh, arrived in London, valued at more than two rupees a pound. But it was of such a description that the brokers here could give no satisfactory report on it; two bales therefore were sold in order to ascertain its value. One of Black Wool sold for 2*s.* 6½*d.*, and one of white at 5½*d.* per pound.

Market value of the above wools.

The foregoing have been notices of the importation of the indigenous Wool of Asia for the use of the Manufacturers of Europe. The first attempt at the introduction of Sheep for the

First introduction of Sheep into India.

Foreign sheep introduced into India.

benefit of India, appears to have been previous to the year 1796. Mr. Lionel Place, collector of the Jaghire lands, now the collectorate of Chingleput, in a letter to Dr. Anderson,* acknowledges his obliging offer of two Abyssinian sheep, for which he states he would lose no time in sending, adding, that "the three sheep you before sent are doing well, the one of which I despaired, having recovered,—I have attached them to a small flock of Coimbatore sheep."

A flock of Merinos imported by the Bengal Government,

This very humble commencement was followed by an experiment on a sufficiently large scale, on the part of Government. This was not attended with any useful result, even in point of information. It does not appear to have been any person's special business to attend to the sheep, and the public officers to whose care they were entrusted, having their time fully occupied, had neither the leisure to give attention, nor probably the information to direct the measures, which a subject of this kind requires on its first introduction.

proposed by Mr. H. Wood.

Mr. H. Wood, a Member of the Board of Superintendence for the Improvement of the Breed of Cattle in Bengal, when at the Cape of Good Hope for the benefit of his health, conceived the idea that "the introduction into India of the Spanish Ram would probably produce Wool

---

* Letters on the subject of Cochineal, by Dr. James Anderson, Physician-general. Madras, 1788—1791.

Miscellaneous Communications, by the same. 1794, p. 9.

worthy of mercantile notice, and thereby add an important article to the exports of the country." The Bengal Government, in accordance with the proposition of the Board of Superintendence, and to give the experiment a fair trial, authorized at an expense of 9,450 rupees, the provision, either from the Cape or New South Wales, of twenty Merino rams, and twenty Merino ewes; with 1,000 country ewes, to form the flock.

Flock of Merinos imported into Bengal.

After a trial of two years, the soil and climate of the north-western provinces not having proved so congenial as the Board had anticipated, the flock was divided, and removed to the stations of Deyra Doon, and of Sabathoo. These being within the Himalayas, sanguine anticipations were entertained of the result, from the abundant and excellent pasturage, and the facility of changing the climate according to the season of the year. But these were never realized, as the Board of Superintendence were informed on the 3d of August, 1829, that the whole of the original stock of Merino sheep had died of old age, and that difficulty was experienced in rearing the produce, from the delicate nature of the animals and the exceeding moisture of the climate. To avoid this, it was suggested that the sheep of Sabathoo should be annually sent to the dry country beyond the snowy range, where little or no rain falls, or where, at least, there is no regular rainy season. In September, 1832, the Government finally reported, that in conse-

Climate of north-western India not suited to them;

sent to Himalayas;

experiment still unsuccessful.

Merino flocks in Himalayas; quence of the large sums expended upon the Sheep without any apparent corresponding benefit, the Governor General (Lord William Bentinck) directed that the flock of Sabathoo should be gratuitously distributed among such of the Hill Chiefs as might be disposed to receive them. Also, that the flock in the Deyra Doon should be transferred to Mr. Vet.-Surgeon Hodgson, of the Hauper Stud, free of charge, on condition of his furnishing periodical reports and specimens of the Wool.

ordered to be distributed;

Mr. Moorcroft's flock of small Tibetan sheep.

Mr. Moorcroft, in his journies to Tibet, had also in view the improvement of the breed of sheep in India, as in his letter respecting the Prangos Hay Plant, from near Droz, he writes: "I have purchased and made arrangements for the keep of upwards of a hundred head of a race of sheep, the smallest perhaps known, but which in fineness of fleece may vie with the Merino, under the advantages of a much hardier constitution and of a better carcase."

Improved breeds of sheep in the Madras Presidency.

Some little attention, we have seen, was early paid to the improvement of the breed of sheep in the Madras Presidency. In the beginning of 1838, the Government there sanctioned the purchase of Merino rams which had been recently imported from Australia by Col. Hazlewood, of the Madras army. These were of the Saxon breed, though imported from Sydney. Colonel Hazlewood, in a letter to Captain Jacob, of the Bombay Artillery, mentions that experiments had been made in the Neilgherries by Mr. Sullivan with Merinos, and by Sir William Rumbold with South-downs, and that his own flock consisted of 700 white-wooled country ewes with Saxon rams. The ewes appear to have been obtained in Coimbatore and Baramahal; but Jalna and Beder are mentioned as the best places whence to obtain the white-wooled breed. The results obtained both at Bangalore and on the Neilgherry Hills, from crossing the white-wooled sheep of the country, with Saxon, Merino, and South-down rams, are stated to be most satisfactory, both as to quantity and quality of Wool, and size of carcase.

Improved breeds of sheep in the Madras Presidency; in Mysore and on the Neilgherries.

The most decisive results have been produced by Major (now Colonel) Jervis, of the Bombay military service, who was first most active in urging the adoption of measures for the improvement of the breed of sheep in that Presidency, and has since submitted his improved fleeces to the judgment of competent persons in London. Colonel Jervis originally represented, in 1835, that many parts of the Deccan and of Gujerat are well adapted to sheep pastures, and stated that, "if the Wool which is at present produced, and which, though of an inferior sort, finds a ready market, were improved by means of a superior breed of sheep, there can be little doubt of the benefit which would ultimately result to this country." The Bombay Government, accordingly, ordered rams and ewes of the Saxon breed

In the Bombay Presidency. Proposed by Col. Jervis.

Sheep imported from Cape of Good Hope, Affghanistan, and Cabool;

from the Cape of Good Hope; and as the best Wool imported into Bombay was understood to be produced in Affghanistan and Cabool, Colonel Pottinger, as well as Lieutenant, now Sir A. Burnes, were each requested to obtain three hundred ewes and eight rams of a pure white colour from the pastoral districts in the vicinity of the Indus. A few were also ordered from Bussora, as the sheep there yield a very fine and lengthy fleece. The Court of Directors of the East-India Company, likewise, on being applied to, sent out 120 rams and ewes of different breeds, including the South-down, Leicester—Cotswold, and Merino (Lord Western's) under the charge of the son of a respectable farmer, who delivered them, with but few losses, in good order in Bombay.

a flock sent out from England by East-India Company.

Sheep Farms established in Bombay Presidency.

The Bombay Government subsequently reported that "the Sheep obtained from England, the Cape, and Cabool, have been distributed throughout the country; many of them having been entrusted to the care of gentlemen who understand the management of these animals, and take an interest in the undertaking. A sheep farm has been established at Ahmednugger, and another at the fort of Jooner, where the climate is good and pasturage plentiful; and these farms have been entrusted to the charge of Mr. J. Webb, of the Civil Service, who has a good practical acquaintance with the management of Sheep.*

* In the Proceedings of the Agricultural and Horticultural

The natives in the interior who breed sheep are supplied from these farms with half-bred lambs, and are allowed to send their ewes to the Government farms to be kept with the rams. Many of the rams have been given to wealthy natives and Patells of villages (by whom they appear to be much prized), who have flocks of their own, and who breed sheep for the sake of the wool and not for the market." Sheep Farms; benefits of, participated in by natives.

The result of the experiments have led to the conclusion that the Cape-bred Merino sheep are far better adapted to the country than those imported from England; so much so, that the Bombay Government have determined to import for the future only from the Cape of Good Hope. The Report of the Commerce of Bombay for 1836-37 states, "from the active measures taken by Government to improve the fleeces of the Sheep in the extensive pastoral country of the Deccan, so well adapted for the carrying of such an improvement into effect, the export trade in Wool promises, in a few years, to be one of the most important and valuable from Bombay." Result of experiments.

Society of Bombay 1838, p. 4, it is stated that at Faria Bagh, near Ahmednuggur, Major Byne is trying the cross betwixt the Saxon ram and Cutch ewe. "The Wool of Cutch sheep is particularly long in the staple, though not fine; it is principally exported to Persia for the making of carpets. A gentleman conversant with the Wool trade in London has stated that Wool of that sort is much wanted in this country; it will make Blankets, Carpets, and other coarse articles."—Committee of House of Commons. Commerce and Finance, p. 467.

Col. Jervis's Sheep Farm.

Colonel Jervis, at whose recommendation the above experiments had been instituted, in the mean time established a Sheep farm on his own account in the Deccan; and imported for the native ewes of his flock a large number of the finest Merino rams from the celebrated breed

Lord Western's breed.

of Lord Western. The results which he has obtained have been most satisfactory, as is evident from the following opinion of Messrs. Southey of Coleman-street, eminent Wool-brokers. 1. The wool or rather hair of the native ewe of the Deccan may be set down as being of the value in London of 3d. per pound. 2. The fleece of a yearling shorn near Poonah, in February 1839, the produce of the Deccan ewe crossed

Greatly improved fleeces.

by the Merino rams imported from Europe, was pronounced "a remarkable clean well prepared fleece of Wool, being fine in the hair, longer in staple, and of a better quality, than we have hitherto seen produced in the Indian Peninsula, and worth 15d. per pound. 3. A white fleece, inferior to the above, from having some dead hairs interspersed through the fleece, 12d. to 12½d. 4. A black fleece, with longer staple than the ordinary breed of Indian wool, 7d. to 7½d., having become more valuable from the increased length of the staple.

Pasture Grasses of India.

The production of Wool in India having so recently attracted attention, and the information respecting it being scattered in publications not easily accessible, has been treated of more in detail, than other products of at least equal importance. From the numerous flocks of Goats and Sheep which we see spread over the Northern parts of India: Camels traversing its deserts, with Buffaloes and Bullocks employed in its agriculture, and for draught carriage, as well as for carrying burdens; besides the Rhinoceros and the Elephant, abounding in the jungles of the Southern parts, as well as along the foot of the Himalayas, and everywhere Deer and Antelopes, it is evident that there must be abundance of food for these various herbivorous quadrupeds in every part of that widely-spread empire. **Pasturage in India.**

The Camel, it is well known, can feed upon the prickly shrubs of the desert, and the Cattle in the districts which border upon it are fed upon the leaves and cut branches of the various plants which thrive in such arid situations. In the provinces, besides grain, Camels and Elephants are fed upon the leaves of various trees. The Goats, Sheep, and Cattle are pastured upon what are called the waste land or the jungles of the villages; the last are fed also upon chopped straw, and the stalks of the joar (Sorghum vulgare), cut into small pieces; while Horses, besides grain, are fed **Food of different herbivorous animals.**

Pasturage in India.

upon grass brought in by men called grass-cutters, but who rather scrape off the ground the creeping stems and young leaves of the grass called Doob.

Doob-grass;

This Doob-grass (Cynodon Dactylon of Botanists), which grows throughout the year, is fortunately the most common species throughout India, and succeeds particularly well in the Northern parts where lawns and pastures of moderate extent are made by planting pieces of the creeping stems of this grass. It is also much used for forming a covering for the banks of rivers, ramparts, and esplanades. The high lands of the

Spikenard grass;

Ballaghaut also possess a grass of which cattle are amazingly fond, and which has so strong an aromatic and pungent taste, that the flesh of the animals, as well as their milk and butter, become scented with it. This species is allied to the Lemon grass, and is very abundantly diffused towards the North-west of India. There are, however,

other Indian grasses.

numerous other grasses common in India which cattle delight in; but the greater number of these flourish most in the rainy season. Their rapid growth, and the great height they attain, as well as their withered and dry nature towards the close of the year, soon however unfit them for pasture grasses. The inhabitants of many parts of India remedy this, by burning down the old and dried up grass, when the young blade shoots up and affords excellent pasturage.

India being at one season deluged with rain,

and at another parched up with heat, with only a few months of temperate climate, cannot be expected to possess any pasture grasses similar to those of European countries. But as grasses are among the most universally diffused of plants, we find some suited to every season, indigenous in all parts of India, and affording food for its various herbivorous animals.

Climate in reference to pasture grasses.

For the purposes of pasturing improved breeds of Sheep, the hills and table-land, from Coimbatore to Kandeish, and the frontier provinces from Gujerat to Hurriana and Saharunpore, seem alone suited. But the Himalayas, enjoying a temperate climate, and a European-like vegetation, have also abundant and excellent pasturage. During the rainy season, when the temperature is moist but equable, we have many grasses resembling those in the plains. These are associated with others belonging to European genera, which are able to withstand the winter's cold: so that throughout the year nearly, there is abundant pasturage in the neighbourhood of Himalayan villages. Of this the inhabitants avail themselves, by driving their herds of cattle, and flocks of goats and of sheep, to different ranges and elevations, according to the season of the year. The sward upon these mountains is short and thick, and very closely resembles that which we meet with on the mountains of Scotland and Wales; while the Sheep are as much esteemed for their mutton as those fed in the plains upon grain.

Parts of India suited to improved breeds of sheep.

Himalayan pastures.

Pasture grasses of the Himalayas.

These grasses, the author has already elsewhere stated,* belong to such genera as Agrostis, Fox-tail grass, Cat's-tail, Meadow-grass, Fescue, Cock's-foot, Bent-grass, Oat-grass, and others. Also, that many of the same species which are accounted the best pasture grasses in England are among those found in the Himalayas, as Cock's-foot grass; Annual, Narrow-leaved, and Smooth-stalked Meadow-grass; Cat's-tail or Timothy-grass, Purple Fescue-grass, which from its greater produce is considered preferable to that specially called Sheep's Fescue-grass. In the climate where these grow naturally, nothing would be easier than the introduction of any other of the superior pasture grasses of England; but this is hardly necessary where the natural pasturage is so good.

Pasture grasses required for plains and table land of India.

But it would be of considerable importance to find some pasture-grasses suited to the plains of India, or to the Table-land of the Peninsula and of the Deccan, and such a series as would afford pasturage, in the season of the year when deficiency is most experienced, whether this be in the cold, the hot, or the rainy weather. In England, attention is paid to hay-grasses, both of temporary and of permanent duration; also to those adapted for pasturage, and to these, as yielding early or late pasturage, as well as to those suited to diffe-

* Illustrations of the Botany and other branches of the Natural History of the Himalayan Mountains.

rent kinds of soil.—Illustrations, &c. of Himalayan Botany, p. 423.

Though the Himalayas may thus be naturally provided with the best pasture grasses, and it may be unnecessary to introduce others, yet, as dried leaves are stored up for winter fodder, and green food may be deficient at some particular seasons of the year; it might be advisable to introduce in some situations an earlier or a later variety of grass to fill up the gap between the seasons. Also some hay grasses, in case, which is far from improbable, any Sheep Farms are established by Europeans on these mountains. **Improvement of Himalayan pastures;**

The table land of the Peninsula we have already seen also possesses some excellent pasture grasses. These were so much valued by the Native Governments, that some of the pasture of the Sandstone-hills, south of the Kistnah river, where the lemon grass is found, were reserved for their own cavalry, or the right to cut and sell it was rented to the highest bidders. As we possess no account of the natural pasture of the tracts where experiments are going on for improving the breed of Sheep, we are unable to say whether it be desirable or possible to introduce other pasture grasses. But it is probable that in some parts of the year, as the hot weather, any grass would be a valuable introduction which was only later in the season. The warm parts of Spain, or the pasture lands of Italy, per- **of those of the Peninsula and Deccan.**

Improvement of the pasture; haps also those of the neighbourhood of the Indus, or of North America, of the Cape of Good Hope, or of New Holland, might yield some species which would be suited to the soil, or to the season when the natural grasses of the country were most deficient, and thus come in as a seasonable relief.

of the plains of India. To improve the pastures or increase the quantity of fodder in the warm and moist parts of the plains of India, it will be necessary to have recourse to the grasses of other climates, as to those of the West-Indies and of South America. The Guinea grass and the Scott's grass of Jamaica are both highly esteemed in that island, while some of the pasture grasses of Brazil and of the banks of the Amazon, are described as being of a gigantic size, and at the same time perfectly tender and delicate.

Green food for Camels and Elephants. Closely connected with the subject of the pasture grasses is that of providing green food for horses, camels, and elephants, and one to which little attention has been paid, though the supply has much diminished in the neighbourhood of towns and large stations. To this Dr. Wallich called attention in his evidence before the Committee of the House of Commons in 1832, stating, that for any number of animals, either for conveyance or for consumption, any quantity of food might be produced in the utmost possible abundance in India, but suggested that a more ready and plentiful supply of food for elephants and camels should be provided by planting those trees (such as particular Indian fig-trees) which form the staff of life for them, and which are extremely easily cultivated. On the Madras Presidency, considerable exertions were made about the year 1796, in everywhere planting what was called the Bastard Cedar (Guazuma ulmifolia) as green food for cattle.

Green food for camels, &c. in India.

Improvement of the Breed of Sheep in India.

The nature and abundance of the Pasturage being ascertained, the next, and also the most important points of consideration, are, whether it is advisable to introduce new, and what varieties, of foreign sheep into India, or whether it be preferable to attempt improving those already so abundant in the country; and, in the latter case, what are the best modes of effecting the object.

Improvement of Indian, and the introduction of foreign Sheep.

It is necessary, in the first place, to consider, not only the intrinsic merits of the breed of sheep which it is proposed to introduce, but also their suitableness to the pasture and climate into which they are to be introduced. This, first in the case of the pure breed being preserved, and also for the produce of any cross breed which it may be proposed to form. Sheep, we know, are now spread over a great part of the world: we may, therefore, infer their capability of sup-

Considerations to be attended to.

Considerations on improving the breed of Sheep.

porting a great variety of climate. This is probably owing to their being able to adapt themselves by degrees to the circumstances in which they are placed, rather than to any positive indifference to the great diversities of climate in which they are now found. The varieties of sheep have, no doubt, arisen, in the first instance, from peculiarities induced by differences of soil, food, and climate. These having become propagated by descent, now form our several permanent varieties. Others have been created by the arrangements of the different breeders who have attended to this subject.

Influence of food on the flavour of the mutton.

Every one acquainted with India knows the great difference in flavour, of the ordinary grass-fed and of the private grain-fed mutton of that country; but it has been mentioned that the grass-fed sheep of the Himalayas are equally well-flavoured with those fed on grain in the plains. Here the striking effects of different kinds of food are very evident in the change produced on a part which is less easily altered than the external covering, whether this be of hair or wool.

Influence of climate on wool.

The effects of climate in altering the wool may be seen in the differences of this covering in the sheep of the plains, and in those of the Himalayas, also between these and the sheep of Tibet. The sheep of Southern India must evidently have been introduced originally from the Mountains, or from the countries to the north-west of Hindoostan; and yet the differences are as great as any where, between some of the hairy sheep of Mysore, and the wool-bearing sheep of the plains of north-western India. This can only be ascribed to differences of pasture and of climate.

Influence of Climate on wool.

It is generally supposed that cold climates are best suited to the production of fine wool; but in fact we find that fine wool countries, such as Spain and Tibet, Australia, Van Diemen's Land, and the Cape of Good Hope, rather have dry climates, with a warm summer and a cold winter. The culture in Germany is so peculiar, consisting in great care and confinement of the sheep, that it cannot be adduced as militating against, or as favouring this view. Mr. Blacklock, in his admirable little "Treatise on Sheep" has said, that sheep, though capable of thriving in a great variety of climates, seem to prefer such as are temperate, and that "regular warmth is absolutely necessary for the production of a good animal and a fine fleece, and is only to be obtained by attending to the drainage and clearing of land, so as to dissipate moisture, and allow currents of air to play freely across the country. Hence one of the reasons why sheep thrive best in a rather elevated situation." The Yolk, or thin film which covers the other tunics of the skin, is most plentiful on fine-woolled sheep, those of the south possessing more than the sheep of the north of Great Britain, while Merinos possess most of all. So that there is apparently some

Dry climate with warm summer and cold winter, preferable for production of fine wool.

Warmth necessary.

The Yolk on fine-woolled and on Sheep of the South.

Influence of Climate on production of wool.

connection between a fine fleece and a good supply of this Yolk. The Australians are said to produce it by penning their sheep in roofed buildings, and thus producing heat, make them sweat before they are shorn. These considerations respecting temperature, and the fact of the existence already, of wool-bearing sheep in India, prove the country to be well adapted for the introduction into it of some improved breeds of sheep, or for attempting to improve those already diffused throughout the country.

Principles to be attended to in improving the breed of Sheep.

In reference to the improvement of the breeds; the experiment, we have seen, is already being carried on. The principles to be adhered to, require to be settled, both for the prosecution of the present experiments and the institution of the new ones, which will, no doubt, be attempted. The different methods for improving the breed of animals have their advocates in India as well as in England. "The one most in vogue is that of choosing individuals of the same family, and breeding *in* and *in*," but the objections to this system are very great; and though "no evil has ever so clearly shown itself as such, yet it is only recently that people have opened the intellectual eye to the dangers of a practice against which the ablest pens were long and vainly blunted." (Blacklock, p. 106.) Mr. Dickson also says, "The evil of breeding *in* and *in*, or, in other words, producing too great refinement of tone, is manifested, in the first instance, by a tenderness of

Breeding in and in.

constitution; the animals not being able to withstand the extremes of heat and cold, rain and drought." These defects must necessarily attend any attempt to keep pure whatever race is introduced into India, with the additional disadvantage of our not knowing whether the climate, soil, and pasture are likely to be suitable either to the new race or to their progeny.

Breeding in and in.

The next mode of breeding, that from different families of the same race, is that which Mr. Blacklock says, "is of all methods deservedly the best, as the males, which are interchanged, have always had shades of difference impressed upon them, by various soils and treatment, so that the defects of each family have a good chance to be counteracted by the perfections of the other, the bad points are gradually exhausted, and their valuable properties as gradually heightened." But this in India is more impracticable than the first, inasmuch as it pre-supposes the establishment of several varieties of the same race in different parts of the country. This has yet to be done; but when it has been effected, advantage will, no doubt, be taken of it, by the different breeders, in continuing to keep up, as well as to add to, the improvement of their flocks.

Breeding from different families of the same race.

Some amelioration might, no doubt, be effected in the wool-bearing flocks of North-Western India by judicious treatment, nutritious diet, and careful selection of the healthiest and most perfect specimens procurable in the country. Yet, as

Improvement of some Indian breeds without aid of foreign blood.

Improvement of some Indian Breeds without the aid of foreign Sheep.

the progress in this, though certain, would be slow, and perhaps not sufficiently great in degree, few are likely to attempt or to persevere in such an undertaking. It may, however, be suggested as an interesting subject for experiment to the many intelligent gentlemen who are favourably situated for the purpose on the north-western frontier and in the Himalayas. It will be requisite, in the first instance, to consult some of the treatises on the subject, that experimentalists may be aware of the points requiring attention, and thus benefit by the experience of those who surmounted great difficulties, and obtained the most signal success in this country. Mr. Ellman, of Glynde, it is well known, obtained his well-earned fame from the zealous manner in which he so materially improved the South-down sheep, without any admixture of foreign blood.

Crossing the Indian with some foreign Sheep.

The only method, therefore, which remains for improving the breed of the wool-bearing sheep of India is, that of "crossing two distinct races, one of which possesses the properties it is desirable to acquire and wants the defects we wish to remove." But here the difficulties are as great, and require as many points of consideration, as any of the other modes of breeding which we have noticed. Mr. Blacklock's observations on the subject are marked with the good sense which pervades his Treatise, where he says, "that if you wish to have a particular kind of sheep, you must first of all be in possession of a pasture suitable for the new comers. You must consider the influence of the individual parents on the progeny, the size of the animals, their habits and dispositions, and their peculiarities in regard to the time of their maturity and fattening properties. Having anticipated these apparently trifling affairs, you must see that the surface of your farm, its degree of exposure, and the quantity and quality of its productions, are calculated for the profitable maintenance of the animal in view," as "no animal can be made to forego a long-used food, an ancient locality, peculiarity of clime and season, and the instinctive habits that have been long nurtured by these, without both it and its progeny suffering from the change." Having considered these preparatory measures, it is necessary to select well formed parents, not much disproportionate in size, and such, that their progeny will be rather under than above what the pasture is capable of supporting. It is better, when some increase has been attained, to bring the breed to the required size or fineness by one or two crossings, than attempt at first what we may ultimately wish for, as Nature abhors sudden extremes, and does every thing in the most gradual manner. (Blacklock, on Sheep.)

Considerations requiring attention in crossing one race with another.

Aspect and produce of form.

Selection of parents.

Gradual improvement.

In crossing, the full effect can only be produced by several years of constant exertion. It is thought on the Continent, according to Mr. Blacklock, that any race of ewes, however coarse

Several crossings necessary.

Number of crossings necessary to attain full effect.

and long in the fleece, will, on the fourth cross of the Merino ram, give progeny with short wool equal to the Spanish. Dr. Parry, of Bath, however, considers that one cross more is necessary to produce the desired purpose. "If we suppose," he says, "the result of the admixture of the blood of the Merino ram to be always in an exact arithmetical proportion, and state the native blood in the ewe as 64, then the first cross would give $\frac{32}{64}$ of the Merinos, the second $\frac{48}{64}$ the third $\frac{56}{64}$, the fourth $\frac{60}{64}$, the fifth $\frac{62}{64}$, and so on. In other words, the first cross would leave thirty-two parts in sixty-four, or half of the English quality; the second, sixteen parts, or one-fourth; the third, eight parts, or one-eighth; the fourth, four parts, or one-sixteenth; the fifth, two parts, or one-thirty-second; the sixth, one, or one-sixty-fourth, and so on." Communication to the Board of Agriculture.

Changes produced on Bengal Sheep in Australia.

Great changes may, no doubt, be produced in the wool of the Indian Sheep, by crossing with appropriate breeds. This is evident from what has been effected in Australia* with Bengal sheep,

* New Holland had no sheep of its own, but a number were procured from Bengal to provide the colonists with mutton and wool, and to establish a permanent flock. They are described as having "an accumulation of bad qualities." Yet such were the primitive New Holland sheep, more, according to Mr. Atkinson, resembling goats than sheep, and from such animals emanated all the improved flocks now in the colony.—*Vide* Youatt's work on Sheep, their Breeds, Management, and Diseases. London, 1837.

which were first crossed with South-down and Leicester rams, and, subsequently, with Merinos from England and Germany. It is probable that the sheep of Southern India were alone taken to New Holland, and these, we know, are far inferior to those in the Hurriana, Shekawatty, and Jeypore districts; where the country is naturally favourable to flocks of sheep, and is therefore well suited to breeding experiments.

Changes effected on Bengal Sheep in Australia.

The experiments already made in India seem to have decided, for the present at least, that the Merino breed is the best fitted for introduction into that country, though the South-down, and some other English breeds, may eventually be found eligible. The next subject for consideration is the country from which they should be imported into India; whether direct from Spain, from England, or from Saxony, or whether from the Cape of Good Hope or New Holland. Judging from the energetic zeal at present displayed, it is probable that some will be introduced from all these countries. But it is desirable, in the first instance, to import a breed from the climates most similar to that into which it is to be introduced. The sheep of the Cape and of New Holland being already much improved, and the climate of both being more like that of Northern India than is either that of England or of Germany, it would appear preferable to import chiefly from these two colonies, for introduction into the Table-land or northern plains of India. But, as

Merino breed best suited to India.

Whence to be introduced.

Cape of Good Hope and New Holland, in the first instance.

English breeds of Sheep probably suited to the Himalayas.

the pasturage of the Himalayas, as well as the temperature and moisture, more nearly resemble those of England, it would appear, for the same reason, that some of the English breeds would be better suited to the mountains than the Merinos, which require both a warmer and a drier climate.

Improvement in Sheep as probable as that which has already been effected in Horses and Cattle at the Government establishments.

That great improvement in the breed of sheep may be effected in India, will be readily believed by those who have seen the highly improved breed of Horses now produced at the Government Studs, for mounting both her Majesty's and the Company's regiments of cavalry, as well as the horse artillery in India. So also the Breed of Cattle produced in the Government Establishment at Hissar,* in the Hurrianah district, for

---

* The Cattle employed at the Hurrianah Establishment consist of the Nagore, Guzerat, Angole, Hurrianah, Sinde, and Mysore breeds. The qualities of the Nagore breed are height, substance, and speed; of the Guzerat, height, greater substance, but of a duller disposition than the Nagore. The Angole has height, and very great substance; can endure great fatigue upon coarse food, and lives to a great age. The Hurrianah can endure great fatigue upon coarse food, but has not the height or substance of the former breeds. The Sinde has great substance, but is low and lazy. The Mysore is strong, and active for its size, but is too low for ordnance purposes.

The most successful crosses are from the Nagore, Guzerat, and Angole tribes. The best draught cattle are from the Nagore; Angole, Guzerat, Hurrianah; and the Guzerat, Nagore, Angole; the latter promises to be the best cross we have made. —Memoir by Capt. Parsons, Superintendent of the Hissar Establishment. Proceedings Agricultural Society of India, 1838.

the ordnance and carriage department of the foot artillery, are vastly superior to the ordinary cattle of the country, in consequence of the great pains taken to improve them. The cattle known as the Mysore breed, and noted for their great activity and spirit, are also the produce of a breeding establishment kept up by Government, and called the Amrit Mahal, of which the object is to supply bullocks for the gun-carriage department and commissariat. It is, therefore, far from problematical that sheep may be improved in the very districts where these fine cattle are produced, and be as superior to the ordinary sheep of India as the Government bullocks are to the ordinary bullocks of the country.

Improved breeds of cattle in the Government establishments.

That a trade in wool may be established even in the Bengal Presidency by the produce of the N. Western provinces being brought down the Jumna and Ganges rivers, is quite as probable as that in Hides and Horns, which is now fully established. These were pointed out, in 1806, by Mr. Colebroke only as articles which *might* be exported from Bengal. From the circular of Messrs. Whyte, Holmes, and Co., of the latest date, we learn, that of Hides there were exported to Great Britain in the year ending 29th February 1840, 904,755; to France, 132,430; to North America, 492,383 pieces: and of Buffalo horns, to the same date, to Great Britain 317,082; and to France, 269,788 pieces; and of Deer horns to the former 3,076 maunds, and of Horn tips 4,518

Trade in wool might be established from N.W. India.

Wool might be exported from Calcutta.

maunds. That wool might in the same way become an export from Calcutta, even without the improvement of the breed of sheep, is evident, from a portion of the Bombay exports being from Marwar. The wool of the similar country more to the north-west, and which would reach the Jumna with less land carriage than does the Cotton of Central India, would be found of at least equal quality, and would probably yield a profit, as the fine sheep of the Shekawatty district sell for ten rupees a corge, or for about a shilling a piece. The exporters from Bombay expected to realize 5d. to 6d. a pound for their wool, which, it is stated, would give an ample return. Sheep wool is already much employed for making the *kumlees* or native blankets. Some of these are even employed in making rough coats by the officers in Northern India, while the finest from Jyepore sell for a high price among the natives. Blankets also form a considerable article of trade between the northern and southern provinces of India; and we find blankets and rugs exported from Calcutta to the extent of 27,517 pieces in the years 1829-30, and in 1837-38, 39,929 pieces, chiefly to the Mauritius.*

Procured from N.W. Provinces.

Sheep abundant and cheap.

Wool now manufactured into blankets, &c. by Natives.

---

* To show the importance of the Wool Trade, and the large quantities which are annually imported, the Author extracts the following, as containing the most recent information:—" A return to an order of the House of Commons gives, as the total quantity of sheep and lambs' wool imported in 1839 into the United Kingdom, 57,395,944lbs.; of which, 57,379,923lbs. are

Labours of Dr. Roxburgh's Successors.

From the connection of the several cultures with one another, we have been led to trace their history further than is consistent with a due attention to priority of date. But having commenced with stating that Dr. Roxburgh had paid attention to the culture of all the great staple products of India, we have shown that his experiments, whether on Pepper, Sugar, Indigo, Cotton, Flax, Hemp, or Mulberry, or his obser-

---

foreign, and the remaining 16,021lbs. the produce of the Isle of Man. The total quantity of foreign wool retained for Home Consumption was 52,959,221 lbs., and the quantity re-exported 695,049lbs. The quantity of foreign sheep and lambs' wool remaining warehoused under bond on the 5th of January 1840 was 7,451,016lbs. Of the foreign countries, by far the greatest quantity of wool was imported from Germany, being 23,837,805lbs. The second and third, as to quantity, were Russia and New South Wales, from the former of which, 7,966,954lbs., and from the latter, 6,621,291lbs. were imported. The quantity of British sheep and lambs' wool exported during the same year was 4,603,799 lbs., and the quantity of yarn (including that of wool mixed with other materials) was 3,320,441 lbs. Of the wool, the largest quantity, being 3,625,896lbs., was sent to Belgium. Of the yarn, the largest quantity, being 1,770,536lbs., was sent to Germany. The total value of British woollen manufactures exported in 1839, was £6,271,645. The value of the manufactures sent to the United States was considerably the highest, being £2,142,352. The value of those sent to Germany, the East-Indies and China, and the North-American Colonies, was also high, being respectively £816,604, £530,687, and £511,190." —*Times, May* 14, 1840.

Dr. Roxburgh's Experiments.

vations on the production in India of Potash, Barilla, Caoutchouc, or of Wood Oil, were conducted on the soundest principles, and anticipated much of what has been subsequently done.

Dr. Buchanan Hamilton succeeds Dr. Roxburgh.

Dr. Roxburgh, having proceeded to England for the benefit of his health, died there in the year 1814.* He was succeeded in his office of Superintendent of the Botanic Garden at Calcutta by Dr. Francis Buchanan, of the Bengal Medical Establishment, who afterwards assumed the name of Hamilton. He was as distinguished for laborious research as for the variety of his attainments, and the zeal with which he endeavoured to develop the resources of the various parts of India which he visited, as displayed in his Journey to Nepal; his Surveys of Mysore, and of the South-eastern Provinces of the Bengal Presidency, in his account of the Fishes of the

---

* Dr. Roxburgh's 'Coromandel Plants,' and his 'Hortus Bengalensis', have been already mentioned, pp. 51 and 69. Besides these he published several papers in the Transactions of the Asiatic Society in Calcutta; and in those of the Linnean Society and of the Society of Arts in London. The work, 'Flora Indica,' which would probably have had the most extensive influence, unfortunately remained unpublished for a great many years. An edition of this work was commenced by Dr. Carey, with Descriptions of the more recently discovered Plants, by Dr. N. Wallich, and published at Serampore, the first volume in 1820, and the second in 1824. Dr. Wallich having had, subsequently to this, to visit the North-western provinces, and then Ava, Pegu, and Tenasserim; after which he returned to Europe, in

Ganges, and in his Commentaries on the Works of Rheede and of Rumphius.* Dr. Buchanan Hamilton's Works.

---

consequence of continued attacks of fever ; delay took place in the completion of the work. The sons of Dr. Roxburgh, therefore, published an edition of the Flora Indica, as left by their father, which was printed at Serampore, in 3 vols. 8vo. 1832.

I am informed by Mr. Brown, that it was intended to have published an edition of the Flora Indica in this country, in consequence of Mr. Colebrooke and himself, with two other gentlemen, having been requested by Dr. Roxburgh, in his will, to look over his manuscripts, and determine what was fit for publication. Dr. Fleming, who was then in England, having offered to provide what money was necessary, it was determined to publish the Flora Indica ; but the appearance of the first volume by Drs. Carey and Wallich from Serampore, caused the idea to be abandoned.

* *Works of Dr. Buchanan Hamilton* :—

1. A Journey from Madras through the countries of Mysore, Canara, and Malabar, performed under the Orders of the Most Noble the Marquis Wellesley, Governor-General of India. London, 1807.

2. A Journey in Nepal, 1 vol. 4to.

3. A Statistical Survey of the Districts of Behar, Shahabad, Bhagulpoor, Goruckpoor, Dinagepoor, Puraniya, Rungpoor, and Assam, under the Orders of the Supreme Government, and lately published by M. Martin, Esq., in 3 vols. thick 8vo. London, 1838.

4. An Account of the Fishes found in the River Ganges and its Branches, with a volume of Plates. In royal 4to. Edinburgh, 1822.

5. Commentaries on the Herbarium Amboinense of Rumphius, published in the Transactions of the Wernerian Society of Edinburgh.

6. Commentaries on the Hortus Malabaricus of Rheede, published in the Transactions of the Linnean Society of London.

Dr. Wallich appointed Superintendent of the Calcutta Botanic Garden.

As Dr. B. Hamilton did not remain in India long after this, Dr. Wallich was, in 1815, appointed to succeed him, and still continues the distinguished superintendent of the Calcutta Botanic Garden. As we have shown that the resources of a country depend so much upon the vegetable kingdom, and as great extension of territory had taken place, it was desirable that the vegetable riches of the new acquisitions should be ascertained.

Parts of India visited, and investigated.

Dr. Wallich has effected this to a great extent, as in 1820 he made an excursion into Nepal, and on his return commenced publishing an account of the more conspicuous plants of that region, in a work which is remarkable, as presenting us with the first specimen of a Botanical work* with lithographic drawings, published in Calcutta. A severe illness having forced Dr. W. to seek benefit from a voyage to sea, he visited the islands of Penang and Singapore, and other places in the Straits of Malacca. In 1825 he was deputed by the Indian Government to inspect the Timber forests of the western provinces of Hindoostan, when he had a favourable opportunity for examining and collecting the plants of the kingdom of Oude, of the province of Rohilcund and the Deyra valley, &c. In 1826 and 1827 he accompanied a mission from the Supreme Government of British India to the court of Ava, and ascended

* Tentamen Floræ Nepalensis illustratæ. Folio. Calcutta, 1822.

the Irrawaddy as far as its capital, and the mountains in its vicinity; proceeding afterwards to the then lately acquired territories on the coasts of Martaban and of Tenasserim. Parts of India investigated.

Contributors and plant collectors in different parts of India.

Besides personal examination, Dr. Wallich has stated that he further enjoyed all the advantages belonging to the institution over which he presides, and which, for extent and importance, he believes to be unrivalled. These consist in the co-operation of many distinguished individuals residing in different parts of India, who are in the habit of transmitting every object of interest which the vegetable kingdom presents to their notice. Thus he received contributions from Penang, Singapore, and Bencoolen,* and from Nepal nearly to the banks of the Sutlej from the Himalayan mountains. Besides these a number of plant-collectors connected with the Garden are stationed in various parts of India, such as Silhet, Nepal, Kemaon, Penang, &c.

Living and dried plants collected.

From the strenuous and extended exertions which have been made, a very complete idea has necessarily been obtained of the vegetation of a great part of India. The number of indigenous plants cultivated in the Botanic Garden of Cal-

---

* Of the various contributors none deserve more notice than Mr. W. Jack, assistant surgeon at Bencoolen, who contributed much valuable information respecting the Botany of the Malayan Peninsula, in the "Malayan Miscellanies," re-published with a memoir and notice of his other writings, by Sir W. J. Hooker, in the Companion to the Botanical Magazine, p. 121.

Herbarium collected.

cutta was greatly increased in the course of a few years; and the Herbarium attached to it amounted to upwards of 8,000 species, comprising a vast number of duplicates, and coloured drawings were made of upwards of 2,000 species.

Drawings made.

Dr. Wallich's health having become impaired from repeated attacks of illness, he obtained permission to visit Europe, and to take with him the collections which had been made, in order that he might deliver them in person to the Court of Directors. On arrival, Dr. W. commenced publishing his magnificent folio work,* containing descriptions and coloured figures of a select number of unpublished East-Indian plants. Among these are included many of the most ornamental plants (such as the Amherstia nobilis), which the vegetable kingdom produces; and many curious for their structure, with others suited to form the ornaments of the Shrubberies and Forests of this country. Among those remarkable for their useful or dangerous properties, is the Aconite, yielding the famous *Bikh* or *Bish* poison, which is used in India as a medicine, and for nearly the same purposes as the Aconite of Europe; also the kind of Gentian of which the dried plant forms the Cheretta, so celebrated as a

Herbarium brought to England.

Descriptions and figures of new plants published.

Useful plants.

---

* Plantæ Asiaticæ Rariores, or Descriptions and Figures of a select number of unpublished East-Indian Plants, by N. Wallich, M.&Ph.D.&c., 297 coloured plates. London, vol. I. 1830; II. 1831; III. 1832; with a Map, which points out the places examined by the several naturalists.

bitter; likewise a substitute for the Ginseng of the Chinese, which, though produced in their own country, they also import from North America. Useful plants.

Besides these, the celebrated Prangos Hay plant is figured in pl. 205. This was discovered by Mr. Moorcroft, in Tibet, and found by him to be employed as winter fodder for sheep and goats, and frequently for neat cattle. Mr. M., writing from the neighbourhood of Droz, describes the Prangos Hay plant as producing fatness in a space of time singularly short, and likewise as being destructive to the Liver Fluke; he therefore justly concluded that it would be an invaluable acquisition to any country to the climate of which it was suited, "as its highly nutritious qualities, its vast yield, its easy culture, its great duration, its capability of flourishing on lands of the most inferior quality and wholly unadapted to tillage, impart to it a general character of probable utility unrivalled in the history of agricultural productions. When once in the possession of the ground, for which the preparation is easy, it requires no subsequent ploughing, weeding, manuring, or other operation, save that of cutting and of converting the foliage into Hay."—(Moorcroft in a letter to W. Butterworth Bayley, Esq., now Chairman of the Court of Directors.)

Prangos Hay Plant figured; discovered by Mr. Moorcroft; value of;

Various attempts have been made to introduce the Prangos Hay plant into Great Britain, but hitherto unsuccessfully; and yet it is probable it

Attempts to introduce it into Great Britain.

Prangos Hay Plant.

will only succeed, and be valuable in a climate similar to that where it is found indigenous.

Duplicates of Herbarium ordered to be distributed to museums

in Europe,

The duplicates of the vast collections which had been made and accumulated for a series of years, having been brought to this country, were ordered to be distributed to the various scientific societies of Europe by the Court of Directors. "That enlightened body," as Dr. Wallich has said, "with a munificence never equalled, and which has been already appreciated and gratefully acknowledged, not only in this country but throughout Europe, immediately directed me to proceed to the distribution of the duplicates among the principal public and private museums * in Europe and

* This novel and most liberal determination was one most unexpected by the nations of Europe, as each had hitherto accumulated such collections only for the benefit of its own subjects. But it was duly appreciated and acknowledged in the scientific publications of all nations. It may be sufficient to adduce one instance only, published in the *Bulletin Universel*, July 1829, Paris.

"C'est avec une vive satisfaction que nous communiquons à nos lecteurs une noble détermination que vient de prendre la Compagnie Anglaise des Indes orientales. . . . La Compagnie des Indes, jalouse de donner à ces découvertes toute l'utilité possible, a chargé M. Wallich de composer des collections de plantes rares cueillies en Asie, non-seulement pour les principaux établissemens scientifiques de la Grande-Bretagne, mais encore pour ceux du Continent Européen et des autres parties du monde. Cette belle et généreuse idée mérite la reconnaissance de toutes les nations, et la Compagnie des Indes s'honore infiniment en associant à ses spéculations commerciales un but aussi élevé que celui de concourir ainsi à la propagation

America. They were pleased to order a similar distribution of the herbariums of Indian Continental Plants in their Museum, made by Drs. Patrick Russell, Roxburgh, and Hamilton, the Tranquebar Missionaries, the late Mr. Finlayson, Dr. Wight, and myself."—(Preface to Pl. Asiat. Rar. p. ix.) and America.

The Herbarium itself, "the fruits of the researches of the last half century, comprising about 1,300 genera and about 8,500 species," and invaluable for consultation on all subjects relating to Indian Botany, was presented by the Court of Directors to the Linnean Society of London.* Original Herbarium presented to Linnean Society of London.

---

des connaissances. Comme toutes les choses humaines, sa prospérité actuelle peut passer; la politique de l'Angleterre elle-même peut amener de nouvelles combinaisons, qui changent ou modifient beaucoup la nature de ses relations dans l'Inde: aucun évènement ne peut lui ravir le mérite qu'elle devra à de pareilles communications."

* The correspondence which passed on this occasion, Dr. Wallich has published in the Postscript, vol. III. p. vii. of his great work.

Letter to the President of the Linnean Society :—

"East-India House, 19th June, 1832.

"My Lord,

"The Court of Directors of the East-India Company have, within the last four years, caused to be distributed to various bodies in this country and in Europe, interested in the promotion of science, between 7,000 and 8,000 species of plants, collected by celebrated naturalists in the Company's service during a series of years in India.

"The objects being attained for which the originals of these specimens have been placed with Dr. Wallich in Frith Street;

Herbarium. It is now, conveniently arranged, named, and deposited in an elegant cabinet in the same

---

the Court of Directors feel that this collection may not be an unacceptable addition to the museum of the Linnean Society of London, which already possesses the Herbarium of the celebrated Linnæus. We have therefore the honour, at the instance of the Court of Directors, and in the name of the East-India Company, to proffer, through your Lordship, for the acceptance of the Linnean Society, the collection in question: and should the Council of the Society be pleased to give effect to the intentions of the Court, the necessary directions will be given to Dr. Wallich to transfer the collection to the party who may be authorized by the Council to receive the same.

"We have the honour to be,
"My Lord,
"Your Lordship's most obedient humble servants,
(Signed) "JOHN G. RAVENSHAW,
"C. MARJORIBANKS."

"To the Viscount Stanley, M.P."

Address presented to the Honourable Court of Directors.

"The Council of the Linnean Society having had a letter laid before them by the President, addressed to his Lordship by the Chairman and Deputy Chairman of the Court of Directors of the East-India Company, in which that Honourable Court have been pleased to offer for the acceptance of the Society the extensive collection of dried plants preserved in the Museum of the India-House, take the earliest opportunity of expressing their high sense of the distinguished honour conferred upon the Society by this unexampled act of liberality.

"The Council, in behalf of the Society, accept with feelings of profound gratitude the Collection thus proffered to them, and beg to assure the Court that it shall be held as a trust for the general benefit of science.

room with the Herbarium of the immortal Linnæus and that of Sir J. E. Smith. Herbarium.

"The Council cannot avoid expressing their admiration of the enlightened policy shewn by the Honourable Court of Directors, with relation to their collections in Natural History, in extending the advantage to be derived from them, by the most liberal distribution of specimens throughout the scientific world, and by this memorable instance of their munificence, in placing the fruits of the labours of König, Roxburgh, Röttler, Russell, Klein, Hamilton, Heyne, Wight, Finlayson, and Wallich, along with those of the immortal Linnæus.

"The East-India Company, by extending its patronage to those distinguished naturalists who have cultivated science in Asia, so much to their own honour and the credit of the service to which they belonged, and by the generous use of the rich materials in its possession, has deeply impressed the members of every learned institution throughout Europe and America with feelings of admiration and respect: and the council of the Linnean Society can only re-echo the voice of general acknowledgment for the great services which the Honourable Company has thus rendered to the cause of science.

"An example of disinterestedness has been exhibited by the Company which has already reflected, and will continue to reflect, deserved honour upon them and upon the country, and which cannot fail to diffuse a spirit of emulation throughout the world.

(Signed) "STANLEY.

"A. B. LAMBERT, G. BENTHAM,
"W. G. MATON, W. NICHOLL,
"R. BROWN, R. H. SOLLY,
"E. FORSTER, W. YARRELL,
"T. HARDWICKE, F. BOOT."

"London, June 23d, 1832."

Coffee in India.

The Coffee Plant a native of Arabia,

Among the subjects of a practical nature to which Dr. Wallich turned his attention, was the cultivation of Coffee in Bengal. It is well known that the Coffee plant is a native of Yemen, in Arabia, whence it has been introduced into other parts of the world. All those in the West-Indies are supposed to have been produced from a single plant which was presented to Louis XIV. from the hot-houses of Amsterdam. The plant has long been introduced into India, and Coffee of a fine quality cultivated on the coast of Malabar; also to a considerable extent in Coimbatore, and the cultivation might, no doubt, be easily extended elsewhere. It was early tried in the Calcutta Botanic Garden, where it succeeded remarkably well under the shade of the Teak Plantation, and nothing could be more healthy looking, or in better bearing, than these Coffee plants when seen by the Author in 1823. Dr. Roxburgh had long previous to this ascertained that two middling plants, at the age of six or seven years, produced a crop in the Botanic Garden in one year, of seven pounds of the dry berries, which gave three pounds of clear Coffee, equal to the Jamaica produce.

introduced into West-Indies by the French;

cultivated in India on the Malabar coast;

in the Calcutta Botanic Garden.

Quality of this Coffee;

Dr. Wallich, in his evidence before the Select Committee of the House of Commons, described the Coffee as excellent in quality, or, as he graphically stated, " I will say for myself, I never used to drink good Coffee, except that produced in the Company's garden at Calcutta." The Coffee plant thrives well in the open air, and bears annually a few berries even one thousand miles further to the north-west, that is, in the Botanic Garden at Saharunpore, in 30° of north latitude. But the cold in winter is too great for this cultivation so far north, though it might probably be carried as far as the Rajmahl Hills, and into Assam and the Silhet Hills, or south into the Malayan Peninsula. A rocky substratum in a congenial climate would probably be found favourable for the production of fine-flavoured berries, as is the case with the Pimento, for "a rich soil and moist climate are said, both in Java and the West-Indies, to produce luxuriant vegetation, and a coarse-flavoured, though sufficiently abundant, crop of berries."

Coffee, goodness of; plant thrives all over India; southern parts alone suited to the culture of Coffee;

The cultivation of Coffee was commenced on a large scale by Dr. Wallich and Mr. Gordon, in the year 1823, when the Indian Government allowed Europeans to hold land on long leases. In the evidence of the former, he states, that in the year 1832, several plantations had been established by a number of mercantile houses, as well as private individuals, to the extent of about four thousand acres. But, in establishing untried cultures in new situations, and particularly those like the Coffee, which require several years to elapse before their success or failure can be ascertained, some assurance or probability of suc-

cultivation in Bengal commenced by Dr. Wallich and Mr. Gordon.

Coffee culture in Bengal.

cess must be obtained before capitalists will be induced to embark in the new undertaking. But in this case assurance was in some measure given, by the result of the experiments in the Company's Botanic Garden.

Discouragements to Indian Culture.

The disadvantages under which Indian-grown Coffee has to labour are still considerable, as Mr. Larpent, in his evidence before the Committee of the House of Lords, 4th March 1840, states, that Coffee from British possessions within the Company's limits pays 9d. per pound duty, while that from British possessions, such as Ceylon and the West-Indies, pays only 6d. Thus, Ceylon Coffee sells in London from 100s. to 112s. a cwt., and Malabar at 75s. to 86s. This would appear to be owing to inferiority of quality in the latter, but is, in fact, merely the difference of duty, as 3d. a pound, or 28s. additional duty, added to these prices, will make them 103s. and 114s., showing the Coffees to be of at least equal quality, though so different a price is obtained by the original importers. A still higher duty, or 1s. per pound, is levied if the Coffee be the produce of places within the Company's limits, such as Mysore, but which, though not strictly British possessions, are under British protection, and the affairs are managed by British officers. British manufactures, however, such as Cotton Piece Goods imported into India, at an *ad valorem* duty of only 3½ per cent., having once paid this duty, are free to pass into

Duty levied on Indian-grown Coffee;

all such territories which the British Government however chooses to consider as foreign, whenever it has to admit even the produce of their soil, in exchange for the British manufactures upon which so light a duty is levied.

Discouragements to Indian Culture.

Tobacco from Arracan.

Tobacco.

One of the results of Dr. Wallich's investigations was the bringing to notice some very superior Tobacco, which obtained the name of Martaban Tobacco. This the Author has already noticed in another work, in the following words: "Dr. Wallich states, that 'the sort is from Arracan and not from Martaban;' and describes it as having 'a fine silky leaf: tried by many people, it had been pronounced the very best they had ever tasted, equal to, nay surpassing, the finest imported from Turkey and Persia.' An extensive tobacconist says, 'a finer and better-flavoured Tobacco he never saw or tasted in his life.' One of the first brokers in the City says, 'the sample of leaf Tobacco is certainly of a very fine quality, and appears to have been produced from some peculiar seed and a greatly-improved cultivation and cure.' By many manufacturers 'it was supposed to be from the seed of Havannah or St. Domingo Tobacco.' For smoking, it is compared with Maryland Tobacco, having the same qualities, 'except the flavour, which is better, and

Some excellent Tobacco produced in Arracan;

opinion of brokers and dealers on its quality.

Arracan Tobacco, quality of.

more like Havannah.' The colour and leaf are moreover, pronounced excellent for cigar-making; 'but if anything is against it for that purpose, it is the largeness of the principal stalk, and coarseness of the small fibres in the leaf.' The commercial gentleman by whom the Tobacco was transmitted to the brokers pronounces it very superior, and the leaf as very fine, adding, that the price of *6d.* or *8d.* per lb., might readily be obtained, perhaps more, with the improvements suggested."*

Arracan and Shiraz Tobacco both produced near former settlements of Europeans.

As we purpose resuming this subject in the subsequent pages, it is at present only necessary to call attention to the remarkable fact of this Tobacco, cultivated by the Burmese, being so excellent in quality, while the only other Tobacco of those regions which has a European reputation is that of Shiraz, where the climate, it is important to remark, is not at all like that of Arracan. But in one point both places have enjoyed the same advantage, that is, they have had Europeans settled in their neighbourhood, by whom it is more than probable that the improved culture of Tobacco was taught. Shiraz we know is not far from Ormuz, so long occupied by the Portuguese, and Arracan was the seat of a Roman Catholic mission in the beginning of the seventeenth century.

* Illustrations of the Botany and other Branches of the Natural History of the Himalayan Mountains. London, 1839, p. 285.

Forests of Timber in India.

The reports of Dr. Wallich are particularly valuable respecting the Natural Forests, both of those within the British territories in India, and also those of the neighbouring Powers. In his visit to the Turai, or low and moist forest land skirting the base of the Himalayas, he particularly recommends a vast extent of Forest land in Oude, situated on the East side of the Kowreala river, as holding out the prospects of very valuable supplies in the course of ten or twelve years, provided that means are adopted for preventing wanton destruction, and of allowing the young plants to grow up, and supply the place of those which are cut down. Among the forests in our own provinces, Dr. W. adverts particularly to those occupying the Islands of the Gogra, commonly called Chandnee Choke. He represents them as extremely important, and in every way deserving of being preserved for the exclusive use of Government, and especially of being emancipated from the destructive depredations which are annually committed. The Sissoo and Saul forests of the Deyra Doon are also recommended to be preserved for the use of the service; though from these the facility of transportation is represented as not equal to that from the other quarters previously mentioned. But they are nevertheless as important for the stations in the north-west of India, as the forests of Oude and Gorukpore are for those in the south.

Natural Forests in India.

in Oude,

in Rohilcund,

in the Deyra Doon.

Natural Forests.

Destruction of forests by natives.

As considerable deficiencies of Timber, at least of those kinds usually employed, such as Saul and Sissoo, besides Bamboos, had been experienced, and as the deficiency every day increased, Dr. Wallich was induced to recommend that Government should interfere in the management of the forests: for the natives, from their extremely injudicious mode in felling forests, cut and carry away all that is easily accessible, both young and old plants, without planting anything new in their place, or encouraging the growth of the young seedlings. Another great defect in the native mode of managing timber, is their total neglect of any regular system of seasoning—timber ever being seasoned by them, depends entirely upon the proprietor not having been able to sell it.

Malabar forests of Teak.

The Coast of Malabar has long been famous for its forests, especially those of Teak, of which the timber has always been remarkable for its superiority to that of other places, and with which the dock-yards of Bombay, as well as of Calcutta, have been long supplied. The quantity, however, has of late diminished, from the forests being partially exhausted, and pains not having been taken to keep up a supply. The Teak was also long ago pointed out by Dr. Roxburgh as abounding on the mountainous parts of the Coromandel Coast and on the banks of the Godavery, above Rajamundry. It extends also far into Central India, though there it is very dwarfish in size. It was planted in the Calcutta Botanic Garden, and plantations were established at se-

Teak Forests of Circars.

veral places in the interior of the Bengal Presidency. A new supply was, however, laid open, on the acquisition of the territories along the East Coast of the Bay of Bengal. The forests to the eastward of the Saluen river, in Martaban, when visited by Dr. Wallich, were very favourably reported on, for the supply of splendid Bamboos as well as of Teak, for the extent of forests, the size of timber, and the facility of procuring it, as the timber could be procured within two miles of the river. Teak is not generally considered of so good a quality as that of Malabar, probably owing to its being produced on an alluvial soil, while the former is the produce of a mountain range.

Plantations in Bengal.

Teak Forests of Martaban.

Besides the timbers commonly employed, India produces a vast variety of trees which are possessed of every diversity of quality required in wood, and which may, whenever attention is paid to the subject, be applied to almost any purpose.*

* A very extensive collection of Indian Woods is contained in the Museum of the India House. One of 117 specimens was sent by Dr. Roxburgh, and one of 100 specimens from Java was presented by Dr. Horsfield. A collection of 456 kinds was also presented by Dr. Wallich, who gave the duplicates of this collection to the Society of Arts, of which they published a list in their "Transactions," vol. xlviii. p. 439.

A Collection was also presented to the same Society by Capt. Baker, late of the Bengal Artillery, who was Superintendent of the half-wrought Timber-yard in Calcutta.

Col.

PRACTICAL BENEFITS OF THE CALCUTTA BOTANIC GARDEN.

Practical benefits of Calcutta Botanic Garden.

Besides the scientific services of the several Superintendants, it is desirable to notice the practical benefits which have been derived from the Calcutta Botanic Garden; and for these we can refer to a report by Dr. Wallich, dated 1st December 1836. But we may commence with a few general observations on its peculiarities of climate, as these are applicable to the gardening in general of Bengal, as well as to the open culture of the plains.

Difficulties of culture in tropical climates.

In a tropical country, there exist few, and these very limited, means of reducing the temperature of the air during the hot season; and in the rains there is a still more unmanage-

Col. Frith, of the Madras service, sent to the United Service Museum, 1836, from the peninsula of India, 111 specimens of different kinds of wood in use in various parts of the country, and which were collected in the course of a tour partly undertaken for that purpose. The necessity of precision in the names of such substances is noticed in their letter of acknowment. "In returning you their thanks for your very interesting collection of woods, the Council have desired me to request as a particular favour, if attainable, a list of the botanical names, corresponding to the native names affixed: this would be of infinite value, as it would permanently identify the specimens which the native name may fail to do in future years. Such a list would be a most valuable document indeed for many purposes."—Wight's Illustrations of Indian Botany. Introd.

able combination of excessive heat with all-pervading moisture. The means of obviating excessive heat are confined to a cautious degree of shading, combined with the admission of as large a proportion as possible of the indirect rays of the sun. This is attainable under the shade of some tree, that does not too much interfere with the influence of night dews; or under that of some narrow but lofty shed, from which the plants must be removed when the sun has sunk beneath the horizon. **Means of obviating heat of climate.**

The cultivation of extra tropical plants depends therefore, on the combination of the maximum of light with the greatest reduction of heat; and it is hopeless for the purposes of Agriculture and Commerce, to cultivate shrubs and trees, the perennial plants of such climates. But annuals, which are exposed for a few months only, to the climate of a place, may be varied according to the seasons of the year. Hence we may see the plants of various countries cultivated in the same fields at different periods of the year. Thus in India, Rice, Indigo, and Cotton are cultivated during the hot weather and rains; and Wheat, Barley, and Millet in what are the winter months of European latitudes. **Principles of culture;**

Kitchen garden vegetables and other exotic annuals are perfectly cultivated in India, though frequent changes of seed have been required; partly because the climate is in some measure unsuitable, and partly because all the modifica- **Exotic Annuals;**

degeneration of exotic annuals in India; tions required in culture in their new situation have not been ascertained. Hence the plants have been said to degenerate. But, in fact, they return to the state in which they were found in nature, when the causes are removed which produced their artificial state; that is, as they are when in a high state of culture. When the mode of cultivation is better understood, deterioration does not take place, or, in other words, the acclimation; artificial state is retained. Dr. Wallich adduces Oats as a remarkable instance of this, as annual supplies used formerly to be imported from the Cape of Good Hope, but it may be said now to be acclimatized. Though in fact the present success is probably only a simple consequence of a better knowledge of its proper treatment, after oft-repeated trials.

Annuals for culture in India; It is practicable, therefore, in the Calcutta climate, and very successfully in the northern parts, of India to cultivate the annuals of European countries in the cold weather, and those of tropical ones in the hot and rainy seasons. Perennials for Calcutta, But the perennial plants of all parts of the Tropics, such as those of many of the tropical islands, of the countries from the Malayan Peninsula from hot countries. to the south of China, of the hot parts of Africa, as well as those of South America and of the West-Indies, are well suited to its climate.

Plants cultivated in Calcutta Botanic Garden. The Calcutta Botanic Garden, thus situated in a tropical climate which yields to none in its vegetable resources, has had for its first and permanent object, the accumulation of the greatest possible number of native Indian plants, and the subsequent dissemination, throughout the empire, of such of them as are in any degree useful for the purposes of Agriculture, Commerce, Medicine, the Technical Arts, and Horticulture, or can in any manner contribute to the comfort and even to the luxuries of domestic life.

Chief objects of Calcutta Botanic Garden.

The number of species in the Garden in 1836, was double the number of what it contained when the catalogue was published in 1814. The whole includes plants of the mountains and of the plains of India, besides others from the Malayan Archipelago, China, the Mauritius, and the south of Africa, with some from Europe and America. The number of species kept in cultivation for the purposes of general distribution exceeds 1,200, comprising buds, layers, and cuttings of the best sorts of fruits in the country, of valuable timber, or otherwise useful trees, and shrubs; also medicinal plants, with elegant flowering or ornamental trees, shrubs, and herbaceous plants. Commencing with the 12th June 1835, to the same date in 1836; that is, from the commencement of one rainy season (the chief period for moving plants) to the beginning of the next, sixteen thousand growing plants were gratuitously supplied to three hundred individuals, both European and native, residing in all parts of the country. Besides these, forty-two thousand Tea plants were raised in the Garden from Chi-

Number of species.

Countries whence obtained.

Extent of distribution;

about sixteen thousand plants annually;

Tea plants

raised and distributed; nese seeds, and forwarded to Upper Assam, Kemaon, Sirmore, and the Peninsula. From the 15th June to the 1st October 1836, nine thousand plants were distributed to 170 individuals.

also seeds. The difficulty of preserving seeds, combined with the facility with which growing plants are transported and preserved, during the rains and the cold weather, induces most applicants to prefer growing plants to seeds, though these are also abundantly supplied. During the above period sixteen thousand papers of seeds were distributed, independently of large quantities of seeds of timber trees and shrubs of extensive cultivation, such as Teak, Sissoo, Coffee, &c.

Importance of such distributions in a country without nursery gardens. The importance of such distributions may not be obvious to those accustomed to the existence of Botanic and Horticultural Gardens in every town, with Nursery Gardens and seedsmen in almost every village, by which the wants of the public are supplied with whatever is required either for Horticultural or Agricultural pursuits. But in a country where no such facilities exist, the services of the Government Institutions, labouring incessantly, and successfully, in supplying wants from which the country so materially benefits, are most important and indispensable.

Botanic Gardens n India perform the offices of Nursery Gardens. From the absence of the facilities which exist in Europe, the Botanic Gardens in India are obliged to unite in themselves the offices of Botanist, Gardener, Nurseryman, and Seedsman; and "the inhabitants have been in the habit of looking to the Calcutta Botanic Garden, and having their wants supplied during a period of fifty years, with a degree of liberality and attention worthy at once of the paternal care of the Government and of the magnitude of this garden."

Calcutta Botanic Garden looked to by the inhabitants for a supply of seeds and plants.

The result now is, that a complete change has been effected among the inhabitants of Bengal with respect to their gardening, the original state of which has been alluded to at p. 26. Country seats have risen in all directions, gardens have been attached to the houses in town, in the suburbs, and on the banks of the river, both among natives and Europeans, all replete with the choicest fruits and flowers. Similar improvements have taken place in many parts of the interior of the country. The share which belongs to the garden in producing this amelioration is evident from its records, which show that scarcely a garden exists in Bengal, certainly not within twenty or thirty miles from Calcutta, that has not received supplies of plants from it; besides large collections being transmitted to all parts of Hindostan. Such is the difference of feeling in this respect among the natives of the country that it is gratifying to find, that for one man who used in former times to ask for plants, there are now ten applicants; and these chiefly among the middling classes, both of Hindoos and Mahomedans.

Results of distribution of plants.

Gardens established everywhere.

Increased attention of natives.

Among the useful trees which have been distributed, many hundred thousand timber trees, some indigenous in the country, and others intro-

Useful trees.

Useful trees distributed.

duced from congenial climates, besides their seeds, may be enumerated. Amongst them, the Teak, Mahogany, Logwood, and Casuarina, hold a conspicuous place, and numbers of these may now be seen growing in great luxuriance in the northern provinces, at least as far as one thousand miles from Calcutta. The Teak is of slow growth, requiring from sixty to eighty years to attain the proper size and maturity for ship-building; but Dr. Wallich states, that the large trees in the Calcutta Garden, are equal in size to the generality of those of probably similar age, which he saw in the forests of Martaban, and little inferior to them in the quality of their wood. The Mahogany grows as well in Bengal as in its native country,* and though inferior in fineness of grain to the best kinds, it is at least equal in quality to that of Ja-

Teak;

Mahogany;

* As an instance of the imperceptible manner in which useful plants are introduced into, and distributed through a country, we may adduce the Mahogany, as Dr. Roxburgh in a paper presented to the Society of Arts in 1806, on the growth of Trees in the Botanic Garden at Calcutta, mentions of Mahogany, that two plants (and these were the first introduced into India,) were sent by the Honourable the Court of Directors to the Botanic Garden in 1795, and by the end of 1804, above five hundred plants had been reared from these two. It succeeds so perfectly well in the East Indies, that the tree will, without doubt in a few years, form a valuable acquisition to that country.—Soc. of Arts Trans. vol. xxiv. p. 154.—The tree is now common in the Northern as well as Southern India, yet so little is known of such subjects, that some seed was sent to India only last year by the overland mail.

maica. Of the native woods there are a great variety, and of every quality, which it is unnecessary here even to mention further. To bring as many as possible of these into general cultivation has been, and must always be, one of the primary objects of the institution. Mahogany.

The Garden has likewise been extensively beneficial to the country in the distribution of fruit trees; a fact best proved by comparing the quantities that are annually sent from thence, with the manifest improvement that has taken place in the fruit-markets and gardens. Not only have the indigenous plants been improved, but foreign fruits of various kinds have been introduced, as the Sapota, Otaheite Apple, Alligator Pear, Litchee, Loquat, Wampee, Mabolo. Besides, the Guava, Custard Apple, Soursop, Pumplemoose, Pine-apple, and others, introduced at earlier periods, with its own indigenous fruits, such as the Mangoe, Plantain, and Orange. But it is not to be expected, as some seem inclined to think, that with these, the Apple, Pear, Gooseberry, and Currant, will be found growing; as if Calcutta was a temperate climate. Many of the above fruit trees, such as all the Chinese and West-India fruits, were originally introduced into India by the Calcutta Botanic Garden, and all the others have been greatly improved.

Fruit trees; introduced into and distributed throughout India.

The Lansa, a Malayan fruit of very delicate flavour, has lately been multiplied for distribution; and even the Mangosteen and Bread fruit-trees have so far become accustomed to the cli-

Fruit trees distributed.

mate, as to endure the hot weather, and the fogs of the cold season, without injury. The Nutmeg, which during many years has existed in the Calcutta Garden, and even produced ripe fruit, has, by a slight modification of the treatment, become less impatient of the climate. The Cherimolia, a fruit of new Spain, which is described by Humboldt as being of very excellent quality, thrives well in Bengal; but though it flowers annually, it has not yet ripened its fruit.

Botanic Garden a place of resort for inhabitants of Calcutta.

As a magnificent garden, laid out in a beautiful manner and stored with the choicest vegetable productions, the Calcutta Garden has during many years been visited by all classes of people for the sake of harmless, rational, and useful recreation. Persons of all nations and ranks, both European and natives, resort to it, and are freely admitted, having liberty to walk over all the grounds, and to examine every plant and species of cultivation. The Garden is accordingly much frequented at all seasons of the year, but more particularly in the hot and cold seasons, during which on Sundays and Holydays, when public offices are shut, and no business is transacted, it is frequently crowded by individuals and families who come down to enjoy a day of coolness, pure air, and relaxation.*

* The substance of the above observations is extracted from the report mentioned at p. 192, on the practical benefits of the Calcutta Botanic Garden by Dr. Wallich, its present superintendent.

Establishment of the Saharunpore Botanic Garden.

In the preceding part of these observations, we have seen that Bengal and the south-eastern parts of India, where the great heat is tempered by the moisture of the climate, are suited to the culture of the Silk-worm. That the table land of India, and the tract along the north-western boundary, alone appear suited to the pasturing of Merino-bred Sheep, likely to be valuable for their Wool. While the Himalayas, already supporting a breed, valuable both for their carcass and for their fleece, seem from their abundant pasturage, and European, almost insular climate, to be better suited to support the valued breeds of England. These facts are sufficient to indicate the great extent and diversified nature of the British dominions in India. **British possessions in India; diversified nature of;**

We know that these possesions extend from 8° to 31° of north latitude; the long extended coasts washed by a tropical ocean, the wide plains stretching far to the north, the elevated table-land and hilly regions, and the range of the loftiest mountains in the world, rising from the tropical plains into elevated regions of the atmosphere, give us as great a variety and gradation of temperature as is met with in proceeding from the Equator to either Pole. **extent of; character of;**

But as the whole of British India is under the influence of the rainy season, a considerable

British Possessions in India, climate of; degree of uniformity of temperature and of moisture is produced throughout the country during their prevalence. The northern plains being dry and open, are both hotter in the summer and colder in the winter than the moist climate of Bengal; but they have the advantage, with their dryness and cold, of enjoying the latter for a longer period. This produces a very delightful and healthful climate from October to April, which allows of the cultivation with great ease during this season of the annuals of more temperate climates. Hence it is evident, that the horticultural experience of the garden situated near Calcutta, will in a great measure be inapplicable to the plains of Northern India, as the difficulties in culture of the one situation will often prove the most easy in the other. A different field, therefore, is required to ascertain the effects of physical agents on vegetation in the North, and to introduce suitable plants from other countries for subsequent distribution; so as to produce the same effects for the northern, as has been proved to have been the case in the southern provinces.

culture of northern different from that of southern provinces.

Public garden at Saharunpore;

To obviate the inconveniences of depending only on the results of an institution situated in a part of the country so distant, and in one which differs so much in climate, and to benefit by the advantages of one placed in the midst of the country which is to profit by it; there is fortunately a public Garden nearly at the most northern limit of the British territories, and in one of the most eligible situations for such a purpose. This was established by the Native Governments which preceded the British. Zabita Khan appropriated in 1779 the revenues of seven villages for its maintenance. Gholam Khadir, as well as the Mahratta princes after him, continued the same revenue until the time of Bapoo Scindia, who reduced the establishment to two villages. The Marquis of Hastings, on his visit to the Upper Provinces, determined, with the enlightened views for which he was distinguished, that what was established with the limited views of an Asiatic prince on such subjects, should contribute to the advancement of Science, at the same time that it increased the comforts of the people, and administered to the tastes of the most civilized European. He therefore recommended the institution to be formed into a Botanic Garden.*

Garden at Saharunpore established by natives;

formed into a botanic garden in 1817, by the E. I. Company.

---

* Extract from a Public General letter from the Honourable the Court of Directors, dated the 28th June 1820.

"86. We have perused with great pleasure the very interesting Memoir, by Dr. Govan, upon the advantages derivable from the Botanic Garden at Saharunpore, connected with the object of exploring the Natural History of the Himalayan Mountains, near the base of which the Garden is said to be situated.

"87. Although it appears that at its first formation, in 1779, a very liberal provision was made by the Maharattas for its maintenance, which was continued till 1801, and then reduced to a more moderate sum, yet there is but too much proof in the documents now before us of the Garden having gone into a

Dr. Govan appointed super intendent.

Dr. Govan was appointed the first Superintendent in June 1817. Many preliminary measures were required to be completed, before the Garden could be made available, either as a useful or a scientific institution. When first seen by the Marquis of Hastings, in 1816, it had degenerated pretty nearly into a grove of self-sown Mangoe trees; and in a few clear patches kitchen vegetables were cultivated. Much therefore remained to be done after the rooting out of numerous useless trees, before soil so exhausted could be renovated, or the interrupted succession of its valuable fruit trees restored by engrafting, and its proper objects, as a Botanical establishment, even entered upon. Many useful and ornamental Plants and Trees were introduced, from the Calcutta Botanic Garden, and from the Himalayan Mountains, which Dr. Govan had opportunities of occasionally visiting and examining.—Continued indisposition compelled him to leave India, and visit, first, the Cape of Good Hope,

Plants introduced from Calcutta and Himalayas.

---

state of rapid decay whilst under the immediate charge of the natives.

"88. As you entertain a strong impression from the various local advantages of the Garden, especially in regard to climate and soil, and the rich resources of the neighbouring countries, that with proper management considerable advantages would be derived, not only to science, but in the conduct of the affairs of the Company, we shall not withhold our sanction to any moderate expense which may be incurred in promoting the objects of so useful and laudable an institution."

and, subsequently, England, for the recovery of his health. While in Edinburgh he presented to the Royal Society there, a Memoir on the Natural History and Physical Geography of the Himalayas between the Sutlej and the Jumna, which is published in the second volume of Brewster's Journal of Science.*

Dr. Govan on Physical Geography of Himalayas.

* Dr. Govan, on his return to India in 1826, was attached to the Geographical and Minerological survey of the Himalayas, which had been instituted in 1823, under charge of Capt. Herbert, and was appointed to prosecute Botanical researches in the same region; that is from the Kali to the eastward, and the Sutlej to the westward, more especially with respect to the Geographical distribution of plants; respecting which he wrote—" The Geography of the plants and vegetable productions of the Himalayan districts, a subject equally worthy of attention, whether considered with reference to the foreign vegetable products capable of being introduced there to the manifest advantage and improvement of the districts themselves, and the direction of the industry of the population, to the development of those resources over which their varied clime and soil gives them power, or to the valuable shrubs and trees capable of being furnished from thence to our native Island, where I have been pleased to observe many of the Himalayan plants flourishing as in the native soil."

Dr. Wallich in reference to the same subject states, " It is not the mere investigation of vegetables with reference to the absolute number, their structure, the endless variety of their forms, their properties, their uses and artificial dissemination in other countries, it is also necessary to attend to the relations which the plants bear to the physical Geography of their respective stations, to mark their absolute and relative properties, to compare them with those of other regions, corresponding either in the nature of their formation, or in the similarity of their elevation or latitude, in one word, to fix their Geographical history."

Garden subsequently neglected.

Subsequent to Dr. Govan's departure, the Garden was left under the charge of the Medical Officer of the station, and of the head native gardener, who, being more solicitous respecting the culture of saleable produce in the Garden than of the ultimate objects of such an institution, neglected much of what had been introduced, and allowed it to return very nearly to the state in which it had been found by the Marquis of Hastings.

The Author appointed Superintendent;

succeeded by Dr. Falconer.

The Author was appointed Superintendent in 1823, and retained the appointment until the rainy season of 1831. He was succeeded by Dr. Falconer, who continues the present Superintendent. The plans adopted for making the institution efficient for the several purposes contemplated in its establishment, have been detailed in several reports, and are briefly recapitulated in one presented by the Author to Lord William Bentinck, then Governor-General, on his visiting and inspecting the Garden in March 1831. This was printed with a plan of the Garden in the Journal of the Asiatic Society of Calcutta for February 1832, and the results, in a Scientific and Botanical point of view, have been more fully dwelt upon in a work especially devoted to illustrating the Botany and other Branches of the Natural History of the Himalayan Mountains, and of the Flora of Cashmere.

Situation of Saharunpore.

The situation of Saharunpore, in point of latitude, its elevation, vicinity to the hills, the nearness of water to the surface, and facility of irrigation from the Doab Canal, make it particularly eligible for the purpose of a Botanic Garden. The parallel of latitude of 30°, or that which nearly passes through it, embraces in its course a greater variety of interesting country than any other, and as temperature is dependant upon latitude, and may be deduced by a formula, simple and sufficiently accurate for practical purposes, it will be found that the vegetable productions in the vicinity of this parallel, will have a considerable general resemblance to each other. For the vegetation of different countries depends in a great measure upon their climate, and the plants of one country will easily grow in another which possesses a similar climate.

Eligibility of Saharunpore for a Botanic Garden.

Besides the latitude and elevation, which is about 1000 feet, the climate of Saharunpore is particularly favourable for the introduction into India of the plants of more temperate countries. The temperature for nearly six months in the year is sufficiently European for the cultivation of most of the annuals of that part of the globe, while the cold is not sufficiently great, nor long enough continued, to destroy the plants of southern countries, with the exception only of such tropical ones as cannot bear any frost.

Climate;

Though there may be some earlier, the best crops of European vegetables and medicinal plants are those obtained from seed sown in November, about which time Wheat and Barley are sown. After this, the weather becomes steadily colder

Culture in cold weather months.

Climate of Saharunpore in cold weather; until Christmas, when some heavy rain usually occurs, but this is sometimes deferred to a later period: the mean temperature of the months of November, December, January, and February, being 64°, 55°, 52°, and 55°. During this season the growth of indigenous perennials is stopped, as well as of the herbaceous plants of warm countries. In March, a rapid rise takes place in the mean temperature of the month, and the increase amounting to 12°, is a sufficiently powerful stimulus, to accelerate rapidly the vegetation of the Spring. About the beginning or middle of April in hot weather; the hot winds begin to blow, and continue to do so until the middle of June, when the maximum of temperature, about 107°, is attained. The mean temperature of the months of March, April, May, and June, is 67°, 78°, 85°, 90°. About the 15th or and rainy season. 20th of June, the rainy season commences, the temperature is then moderated, the means of the months of July, August, September, and October, being 85°, 83°, 79°, 72°, but universal moisture, suitable to the culture of Tropical annuals, as Rice, &c., is diffused. The rains terminate about the middle or end of September, and according to this, the diminution of temperature which ushers in the cold weather, is late or early.

Desirableness of a nursery in the mountains. Though the temperature at Saharunpore is lower in winter, and the cool weather longer continued, than in the more southern parts of the Great Gangetic valley, yet the climate is essentially Indian, and as such is unsuited to the culture of many plants in their young state, which may yet be successfully introduced into the plains of India. These require to be taken care of when in a tender state, and to be brought by degrees to bear the extremes of temperature. It is therefore desirable to have the means of giving protection, or of producing an artificial climate, such as in Europe is effected by Green-houses and Hot-houses, or to have the power of making our experiments in a cooler climate, during the seasons when heat and dryness, or heat and moisture prevail in the plains. This, very fortunately, is easily attained, and in the most desirable manner, that is, by a natural instead of an artificial climate. The Saharunpore Garden being situated within thirty miles of the Himalayan Mountains, the elevation of which affords us the same diminution of temperature which we obtain by proceeding to higher latitudes, whether in the northern or the southern hemisphere.

Climate of Saharunpore unsuited to many plants; cooler clima desirable; attainable in the mountains.

The advantages of such a situation were too obvious to be lost sight of; very soon, therefore after the establishment of the garden at Saharunpore, a site for a nursery was selected by Dr. Govan on the Suen Range to the northward of Nahn. Though eligible in point of climate and from facility of irrigation, it had the disadvantage of having a large river like the Jumna intervening between it and the Superintendence at Saharunpore. This impeded the ready communication which is so necessary, from the impos-

Nursery established by Dr. Govan on Suen range.

Nursery established by the Author on Mussooree range.

sibility of insuring the exertions of natives when removed from inspection and control. The range of the Himalayas which extends between the Ganges and Jumna rivers, and which rises immediately above the Deyra Doon, having in late years become better known and more accessible, afforded all the advantages, without the disadvantages, of the former site. A new site, therefore, was selected in the year 1826 by the Author, for a nursery, in the neighbourhood of the stations in the Himalayas, now so well known as Mussooree and Landour.

Advantages to inhabitants of Himalayas;

The results of experiments made in such a situation would be of trifling consequence, if considered merely in reference to the Garden, of which it is an accessory; but they become of considerable importance, when viewed as the source whence plants and seeds suitable to the soil and climate are to be distributed to the inhabited parts of the Himalayan Mountains. The inhabitants of these, being enabled in their cool climate to produce more of the useful articles of northern latitudes, which are in request in the plains, would have the means, as they now have the inclination, to purchase more of those products which are analogous to, or identical with, those of tropical countries in general, and which are grown in the plains of India.

elevation of from 6 to 7,000 feet;

The above range, at an elevation of from six to seven thousand feet, enjoys a delightful climate. From the middle of November, and during the winter months of December, January, and February, the cold is moderate, that is, the thermometer seldom sinks below the freezing point, and the mean temperature of these four months is 50°, 45°, 42°, and 45°. The season of cultivation is from March to October, the dry weather continuing until the middle of June, about which time the greatest heat (80°) occurs. The mean temperature of the months of March, April, May, and June, is 53°, 59°, 66°, and 67°. The accession of the rainy season causes little diminution of temperature, and it continues remarkably equable; the mean temperature of the months of July, August, and September, being 67°, 66°, 64°, and that of October 57°. During the latter month, or at the conclusion of the rainy season, the sky is clear and serene, the air mild and still, and the climate very delightful.

Mussoorce range; climate of; mean temperature of. dry weather. rainy season.

In the Plains, the rainy season is, of course, that in which Rice and other tropical grains and vegetables may be sown. Some of them, as Rice itself, may also be sown and attain perfection in the mountains during the same period of the year. The moderate temperature in the plains, however, extends from November to March, and in the mountains from March till the middle of June, and with rain from that to October. We may take advantage of the months adapted for cultivation in the hills and plains, and obtain a complete year of moderate climate, suited to the germination of seeds, and for the growth

Plains of N. India. rainy season of; moderate temperatures of; also of hills; year of moderate climate obtained.

Plants thus introduced into Saharunpore Garden.

of the plants of temperate climates, of every part of the globe. In fact, many plants were thus actually introduced and preserved in the Saharunpore Garden, which, if confined to either situation, while young, would have been destroyed by the hot winds of the plains, or killed in the mountains, by the frost of winter.

Plans adopted for improving the Garden;

On the Author taking charge of the Garden, it required, first, to be cleared of much exuberant vegetation, and then the plans upon which it was laid out to be much modified, so as to adapt it to the English style of gardening. The surface was levelled or sloped, a free communication effected with every part by means of new roads; and as irrigation is the object of primary importance in the north of India — as it is in the

wells sunk;

south of Europe—additional wells were sunk, and the Persian wheel introduced, to facilitate the raising of water. These were all afterwards in a great measure superseded, a cut from the Doab

cut from Doab Canal;

Canal being obtained, which, running through the garden, much facilitated the almost constant irrigation, that at some seasons of the year is indispensable to the existence even of herbaceous vegetation in the upper provinces. Pieces of water were also formed for aquatic plants. The uncultivated parts of the garden were laid in

ground trenched;

Doob grass, and the cultivated parts, as well as the borders of the roads, were trenched to the depth of two feet. By this means the clayey substratum became well mixed with the sandy surface, when the whole was improved and enriched by the addition of vegetable and animal manure. Some English tools were introduced, and the use of wheelbarrows made general. A conservatory was also built, where the plants of warm countries could be protected from the cold of winter, and those introduced from the hills, equally saved from the scorching effects of solar radiation, during the months of the hot weather.

Saharunpore Garden.

English tools introduced.

Conservatory built.

In order to ensure due attention being paid to the respective objects contemplated in the institution of the garden, it was divided into several departments. In one, plants were arranged as objects of Botanical investigation. In another, those devoted to Agricultural experiments, and in a third, to Horticultural purposes. Of the plants introduced from the Himalayas, some were planted in nurseries, others in an artificial rock work, and some in flower-pots in the conservatory; but in all the soil was enriched by the addition of decayed vegetable matter. Nurseries were likewise made for Fruit, and Ornamental Trees, and for Shrubs for general distribution. A portion of the garden was allotted for the Experimental Medicinal garden, and another as a Nursery of Timber trees for the Delhi and Doab canals.

Garden divided into departments,

Botanical,

Agricultural,

and Horticultural.

Nurseries formed, for Hill plants, Fruit trees, Ornamental shrubs, Medicinal plants, and Timber trees.

As the climate has been shown, at different seasons of the year, to partake of the nature both of tropical and of temperate parts of the world, so it will be found that the vegetation,

Saharunpore. climate.

Saharunpore. Correspondence of climate, vegetation, and cultivation.

natural to the country, partakes of the same double characteristic. We shall therefore be less surprised at finding the cultivation participating also in this double nature, and that the northern like the southern part of India, enjoys two crops during the year, the one called the *khureef*, or rain crop, sown in June, and reaped in October, the other sown in October, and reaped in March and April, called the *rubbee* crop. The latter, embracing the months which approximate in temperature to that of the seasons of cultivation in colder countries, corresponds with them also in the nature of the plants cultivated, as for instance, Wheat, Barley, Oats, and Millet, Peas, Beans, Vetch, Tares, Chick-peas, Pigeon-peas, and Lentils; Tobacco, Safflower, and Succory; Flax, and plants allied to Mustard and Rape, as Oil Seeds; Carrot, Coriander, Cummin, and other seeds of a similar kind, as *ajwain*, *sonf*, *soya*, *aneeson*. Hemp exists in abundance in a wild state, but is only used for making an intoxicating drug. Almost all the esculent vegetables of European countries succeed remarkably well in the cold weather in India.

Khureef, or rain crop; *Rubbee* crop. Plants cultivated in cold weather; in rainy season.

In the rainy season, a totally different set of plants engages the agriculturist's attention, as Rice, Cotton, Indigo, and Maize, with Sorghum, joar, koda, most of the tropical legumes, as well as several of the Cucumber and Gourd tribe, together with the Sesamum for Oil, and the varieties of the Egg plant, as a vegetable.

The Sun and Sunnee, two cordage plants, are also cultivated at this season.

As exemplifications of what has already been effected in the naturalization of plants, and as guides in the course which it would appear proper to follow, it may be useful to indicate some of the plants of different countries which have already been naturalized in the open air in the Saharunpore Garden. We may now see there, many of the plants and trees of very different countries, as of India, China, Cabool, Europe, and America collected together, and naturalized in the open air. *Plants of different countries naturalized in Saharunpore Botanic Garden;*

Of those of southern latitudes, for which the cold of the Saharunpore climate is not too severe, we may mention the Plantain, Shaddock, Orange, Lemon, Mango, Tamarind, Jack fruit, with the Cinnamon, Sweet Laurel, and many others. *of southern latitudes;*

Of those from more northern climates, such as Cabool and Cashmere, for which the parching heats of May and June, and the tepid moisture of the rains have not been so unfavourable but to allow of their naturalization in the Saharunpore climate, may be mentioned the Almond, Peach, Nectarine, Plum, Pomegranate, Walnut, Apple, Quince, Grape Vine, Mulberry, and Fig. Of Chinese fruits, the Leechee, Loquat, Longan, Wampee, Flat Peach, and digitated Citron are perfectly naturalized. Where these plants not only grow but flourish and perfect their fruit, *of northern climates.*

Plants of northern climates.

there can be no difficulty in introducing others from the same localities.

Acclimation of Himalayan plants.

But the greatest variety of plants which have been acclimated are those which have been procured from the Himalayas, and this does not proceed from their more easy naturalization, but from the greater facility of communication. The difference between the climate of the hills and that of the plains is much greater than what occurs in places differing only in latitude, for not only the temperature of the atmosphere, but also its pressure and density differ, as do likewise the quantity of light, and the variations between dryness and moisture. The success has, notwithstanding, been very considerable, and may, no doubt, be much extended, as far as plants from six and seven thousand feet of elevation are concerned.

TREES AND SHRUBS.

Oak	Dogwood	Juniper
Fir	Service tree	Yew and Box
Maple	Horse Chesnut	Buck thorn
Holly	Black thorn	Spindle tree

FRUITS.

Apple	Apricot	Walnut
Pear	Cherry	Barberry

FLOWERS.

Primula	Potentilla	Thyme
Viola	Geum	Gentian
Clematis	Delphinium	Hypericum
Anemone	Aconitum	Spiræa

Climate of hills.

As the climate of the hills resembles that of European countries, the transition is easy, from consideration of the plants of the former to that of those of the latter. The success in acclimating in the plains of the north of India many of the perennial plants of the south of Europe, or what botanists call the Mediterranean region, would, no doubt, be considerable. But Saharunpore is remote from the sea, the means of obtaining European plants are few and difficult, and seeds in a vegetative state arrive but seldom. The introduction, however, of the various European kitchen garden vegetables, and the successful cultivation of many of the flowers, as well as of the Medicinal plants of Europe, affords the most rational prospect of the eventual success, being only limited by the means afforded for insuring it.

Cultivation of plants of Europe in northern India.

In proceeding westward in the latitude of Saharunpore, the countries of which it is most desirable to acclimate the productions, are Arabia, Egypt, and the lower parts of Persia. As there is a considerable resemblance between the botany of these and that of the upper provinces of India, and as some of their fruits have already been introduced, while others, as well as many of their vegetable and useful productions are the same as those of India, there is no doubt that a considerable proportion of their valuable products, as Assafœtida, Ammoniacum, Galbanum, Sagapenum, Opoponax, Myrrh, Aloes, and others might be naturalized at Saharunpore, or between it and its mountain nursery, as the Coffee plant flou-

Plants of Persia, Arabia, and Egypt.

Plants of Mexico and North America in Himalayas.

rishes, and Senna is produced in the fullest perfection in the former.

From the similarity in the temperature of parts of Mexico, as also of North America, and the correspondence, in a general point of view, in vegetation, between them and the Mussooree range, it would be quite possible to acclimate in the nursery there, many of the natural productions of the western world. Some of the plants of America, though from very different parts of the continent, have already succeeded remarkably well in the Saharunpore Botanic Garden, such as the Mahogany, Logwood, Sapota, Pimento or Allspice, Cherimolia, and Ash-leaved Maple. It would, therefore, be easy to naturalize many others.

Of Cape of Good Hope and New Holland.

The countries in the southern hemisphere, which have the nearest approximation in latitude and temperature to northern India, are the Cape of Good Hope and New Holland; the most populous parts of which are about the thirty-fourth parallel of latitude. Though the vegetation of each is distinguished from that of the other, by possessing a number of genera peculiar to itself, yet there is the closest affinity between that of the two countries, and a marked difference from that of every other. They possess indeed but few plants in common, yet we must not, from this circumstance, conclude that the plants of the Cape and of New Holland will not succeed in India. We must rather consider the similarity of these countries in latitude and temperature, with the northern parts of India; and that having possessed themselves of every kind of vegetable and many fruit trees known in other parts of the world, some of which are natives of, and the greater number flourish in, India; so their own peculiar or useful productions may, no doubt, be as easily transferred to the latter country. Those which have been already attempted, in the open air, in the Saharunpore Botanic Garden, have completely succeeded, such as species of Aloes, Pelargonium, Stapelia, Amaryllis, Casuarina, and Melaleuca Cajeputi, or Kayapootee plant. Plants of Cape and New Holland.

In the Agricultural department less has been done than perhaps might have been effected, but here the chief difficulty to be contended with, is the want of a population, ready to take advantage of any objects of culture that are introduced. Still, much good may be effected by introducing improved kinds of the seeds which the natives themselves are in the habit of sowing, as from this they might be led to adopt new and untried cultures. The finest kind of wheat now in the Delhi market is said to have been introduced by an European gentleman stationed at Bareilly. The number of articles cultivated in the open fields is very great; the most important have been already enumerated, but the majority of them are little known, and are usually included under the term of small grains and pulses. Agricultural experiments.

As instances of what may be effected, it may be Oats;

Introduction of Oats;

mentioned, that Oats were originally cultivated by Dr. Govan in the Saharunpore Garden, and were spread both in the district and in the hill provinces, but a few gentlemen only employed them for feeding their horses. The Barley of the Himalayas, from ten thousand feet of elevation, was introduced by the Author into the Saharunpore Garden, and produced finer crops than any of that cultivated in the neighbouring plains. The species from an equal elevation, on the northern face, so remarkable for its permanent monstrosity of form, was also cultivated, though less successfully. Of plants affording fodder for cattle which were introduced, and grown with success, were the Guinea and Fiorin grasses, as well as Lucern, Clover, and Succory. The three last are particularly valuable, as affording green food when there is little or no grass in the country.

arley;

Fodder grasses.

Further experiments by Dr. Falconer.

Dr. Falconer has since introduced the numerous and fine varieties of Rice cultivated in the Himalayas. Of these, some of the best sorts were at his suggestion distributed to cultivators along the Doab canal. Other grains, peculiar to the Himalayas and the Tibetan region, have also been grown, as well as the remarkable kind of Wheat, mentioned by Mr. Elphinstone as the Huzara Wheat, of which the seeds were obtained by Sir A. Burnes. The Otaheite, or Mauritius Sugar-cane, has also been introduced, grown most successfully, and distributed in the

Rice.

Huzara wheat.

Otaheite Sugar Cane.

Saharunpore and neighbouring districts. A sugar-mill, also, after the construction used in the West-Indies, and turned by a water-wheel, was erected, and kept some time in operation, and trouble was taken to have it extensively shown, with the object of enlightening the natives, and removing the prejudice which they entertained against the cultivation of this new variety of cane. Sugar-mill erected.

Attempts were also made by the Author, about 1829, to improve the cultivation of Cotton, by experiments with the Bourbon Cotton, and also with the Tree Cotton of India (Gossypium arboreum), which is much esteemed by the natives, for some of the finer kinds of muslin. Samples of both having been submitted to Mr. Saunders, Commercial Resident at Calpee, he pronounced the staple of the Bourbon Cotton to be better than that of the common Cotton of the country (G. indicum), which was also sent, and which he considered to be of very excellent quality. The Cotton of the Tree species, however, from its staple and texture being both good, he considered to be the best description of Cotton. But it is doubtful whether this species would be profitable for culture, and the soil of the garden was too good for the Bourbon Cotton, as it always grew to a large size, and, notwithstanding much cutting down, ran very much into leaf. Cotton—experiments on; Bourbon Cotton; India Cotton; Tree Cotton;

Dr. Falconer has since had opportunities of continuing the experiments with other kinds of cotton seed which have been introduced into India, by Dr. Falconer.

Upland Georgia; Peruvian; as the Upland Georgia, the Egyptian, some fresh Barbadoes, and the Peruvian. "The Upland Georgia," he states, "would most undoubtedly be very successful" in the upper provinces, as it ripens its seed before the Bourbon Cotton even flowers. Egyptian. The Egyptian Cotton, also, seemed likely to thrive; for though seed only reached him on the 15th July, six weeks at least too late, and it did not all ripen before the frosts came on, yet what did so was long, fine, and strong in the staple, with large bolls.

Other subjects worthy of attention. There are many other subjects of great importance which might be mentioned as worthy the attention of the agriculturist, because yielding products likely to become of commercial importance; but we shall restrict our notice only to those which have been introduced, and which are likely to succeed.

Saffron. Saffron is a substance of high commercial value in India, and consumed to the full extent which the supply, even at the present high prices, can be brought to, and a great portion of the Hindoo population of India are debarred from its use, though a favourite seasoning in all their dishes, by the advanced price of the article. It is now imported into India both from Persia and Cashmere; into the north-western parts of India from the latter only, whence the Author introduced the bulbs which flowered in the Botanic Garden. Dr. Falconer, who has since visited Cashmere, is of opinion that Saffron could be successfully cultivated in the Himalayas, at heights varying from six thousand to six thousand five hundred feet above the sea, and that if it were once brought into the market, the demand for it would be almost unlimited. Saffron might be cultivated in Himalayas.

Assafœtida is a substance which, though used chiefly as a medicine in Europe, is of immense consumption in India. Both Hindoos and Musselmans use it as a seasoning to food, and it is brought down in very large quantities to the fair at Hurdwar. A species was found by Dr. Falconer on the most western part of the course of the Indus within the mountains. Plants and seeds having been introduced, he thinks it may be brought into cultivation in the Himalayas. Assafœtida,

In the price currents of Bombay, Calcutta, and Canton, an article is constantly seen under the name of *Putchuk*, as an import into the last, and an export from the two former places. Of the Putchuk, 6697¾ bazar maunds, of the value of 99,903 rupees, were exported from Calcutta in the year 1837-38; it would appear, therefore, that it is a product of some part of the Indian territory. The Author, in comparing specimens of Putchuk procured in Calcutta, with those of a substance which in the northern provinces was called Orris-root by some Europeans, and *koot* by the natives, found that they were identical. When in the northern provinces he had learnt that *koot* was imported from Lahore. Subsequently he was informed by Mr. Becket, who was long en- Putchuk, or Koot.

Koot. gaged in mercantile transactions at Allyghur, that what he bought in northern India by the name of *koot*, was sold in Calcutta as *putchuk*. On consulting the works now in use among the natives in northern India, it was seen that *koot* was without doubt the Costus of the Ancients. This was highly esteemed by the latter, burnt as incense on their altars, and described by them as being procured from India; affording a remarkable confirmation, with many others, of the knowledge which they possessed of the useful products of even remote parts of India.

Costus of the Ancients

discovered in Cashmere;

On Dr. Falconer's proceeding on his journey to Cashmere, the Author requested him to make inquiries respecting this substance, and he discovered that it was exported from the valley in large quantities to the Punjab, whence it finds its way to Bombay and Calcutta: and that it is sold in China at an advance of about three thousand per cent. on the price at which it is gathered in Cashmere. Dr. F. subsequently found it growing in great abundance all round the elevated summits of Cashmere. From the plants with which it is associated, and the circumstances under which the Koot grows, being one of the Compositæ, or Thistle tribe, with feathered seed, of which, when once established, the dissemination becomes easy; Dr. F. has no hesitation in thinking that it could be produced to an unlimited extent, of the best quality, in the Himalayas at elevations of from seven thousand five hundred

introduced into Himalayas.

to nine thousand feet above the sea, and that the Choor mountain alone might be brought in a few years to produce thousands of maunds of it. Preparatory to diffusing the Koot, or Costus, he has introduced it into the Mussooree nursery. **Koot, or Costus of the Ancients.**

Prangos Hay Plant. The Prangos is another vegetable product highly valued in the cold and arid region of Tibet, where it is indigenous, and which Mr. Moorcroft (v. p.179) thought would be valuable as fodder for sheep and cattle in European countries. Dr. F. found it in Tibet, and also most abundantly on Ahatoong, a low trap hill in the valley of Cashmere; but here it was not so vigorous as in its Tibetan habitat. Though abundant in various directions, the Cashmerians do not esteem it of any value, and Dr. F. is of opinion that its importance has been much over-estimated, in consequence of its being the only food in many of the bleak and barren tracts of Tibet. In Cashmere, where, far from a deficiency of herbage, there is actually a superabundance of pasture grasses, it is necessarily much less esteemed. The Prangos will, therefore, most probably be a valuable acquisition only in countries devoid of good natural pasturage, and of which the climate is favourable to its growth.

Fruit trees and Vegetables. Fruit trees and vegetables, though of considerable importance in European countries, are still more so in such as derive much of their subsistence from the vegetable kingdom. Some of the former also, are likewise important, as form-

Fruits, commerce of, in Europe; ing articles of commerce. We know that fruits which are now cultivated in England, were formerly imported from France. Even at the present time, besides dried fruits, we have a considerable commerce in Oranges from the Azores, and Apples are now imported from New York. So in India; there are great importations of Cocoa and Betel Nuts from more southern countries into India. From the northward also, which is so much cooler in climate, there are importations of those very fruits which have been naturalized in Europe, from the same parts of the world, such as Grapes, Apples, and Quinces: besides others which we receive from the south, as Raisins, Figs, Almonds, Pistachio, and Pine-Nuts.

Fruits cultivated in Saharunpore Garden; of India and Himalayas, China and America; Cabool and Cashmere. The fruit trees of the country, of the finest sorts, were introduced, improved, and distributed, as well as those of the Himalayas; also those of China and America, procured originally from the Calcutta Botanic Garden. Some of the fruits of Cabool and Cashmere were obtained by sowing the seeds; others were introduced by sending, in 1828, gardeners belonging to the Saharunpore establishment with the northern merchants who bring down fruit for sale. In this way living bulbs of the Saffron of commerce were obtained, as well as of the plant furnishing the true Salep; together with many fruit trees of Fruit trees of Cashmere introduced into Mussooree Nursery; Cashmere, such as the Apple, Pear, Peach, Nectarine, Plum, Cherry, Walnut, and Grape-Vine. Attempts were also made to obtain some of the fruit trees of England, which were at that time annually imported by the Agricultural and Horticultural Society of Calcutta. But the distances are so great, and the modes of transport were so little understood, that only one apple tree arrived alive at Saharunpore, and thus cost no less than £70. It was planted, as well as the Cashmere plants, in the Mussooree Nursery.

Fruit trees introduced into the Mussooree nursery.

Dr. Falconer, in his visit to Cashmere, had the best opportunities for obtaining a complete assortment of the Fruit trees of that valley. These he did not fail to introduce into the Saharunpore Garden and Mussooree Nursery. He has continued the experiments on the improvement of fruits, introduced additional methods of grafting, and more extensively adopted the indigenous trees of the country as Stocks, such as the Himalayan Pear for European Apples and Pears. He has also made arrangements for an exchange of the more rare plants of the garden, for the fruit trees of Europe. Dr. F. observes, as, indeed, the Author has also observed, that large quantities of Apples, Pears, and other fruits are annually imported into all the north-western parts of Hindoostan from Cabool and Cashmere. It admits of little doubt that these fruits could be cultivated to perfection in the Himalayan mountains, at altitudes of from six thousand to seven thousand feet above the sea, and an advantageous traffic in them established in the hills. An increased supply would lead to cheaper prices,

Further importations by Dr. Falconer,

and improvements.

Commerce in fruits

might be extended between hills and plains.

Commerce of fruits might be established.

and beget a greater demand, so that the consumption might be augmented to many multiples of what it is at present. The speediest mode of accomplishing this desirable end would be by the introduction of all the best cultivated varieties of the Apples, Pears, &c. of England.

Horticulture, in the rainy season, tropical in nature;

As far as Annual plants are concerned, the Horticulture, like the Agriculture, partakes both of a European and of a Tropical nature. In the rainy season great equability of warmth and moisture being diffused over the whole of the plains of India, the same vegetables may then be cultivated at Saharunpore, as in the most southern parts of India. These are all necessarily of a tropical nature, and pains have been taken to bring together as many as possible of such as are cultivated in different parts of the country.

in the cold weather, like that of European countries.

In the cold weather, the temperature, as we have seen, approximating in a great measure to that of European countries, most of the vegetables which are common in England, and many of which were introduced by means of the Garden, are cultivated with almost equal success: in the plains of Northern India during the cold weather, but in the Himalayas in the same months as in Europe.

Potatoes.

The Potatoe, that most useful product, may be mentioned as being produced as fine as in any other part of the world, both in the plains and mountains. It was first introduced into the latter by Lieut. Col. Young, who induced the Hill people to cultivate this new produce by taking it in part payment of their land-tax. He afterwards found a sale for them, among the Europeans in the stations of Deyra, Saharunpore, Kurnaul, and Meerut. It is fortunate also, both for cultivators and purchasers, that the Potatoes of the Hills come into use about the time that those in the Plains are going out of season. As the Potatoe ripens its seed in the mountains with great facility, advantage has frequently been taken to grow seedling plants, which in the second year have produced very fine and very large potatoes.

Potatoes introduced into the Himalayas.

Though the subject is hardly less important, it would lead into too much detail to notice particularly the many other useful kinds of plants which are cultivated in the Saharunpore Garden, though many general observations are equally applicable to those of the Garden at Calcutta. It may be briefly stated, that there are few of the proximate principles of vegetables which are not secreted in large quantities, and of the purest quality, by many of the plants cultivated in both gardens, and from thence distributed throughout the country. The products of such plants are not only useful for the arts and manufactures of the country, but also for those of other parts of the world to which they are exported, and thus serve to give an impulse to the commerce of India.

Useful plants cultivated in Saharunpore Garden.

proximate principles of Vegetables;

useful in arts, and form articles of commerce.

Taking these according to the nature of their

Plants yielding Mucilage. principles, we have whole tribes of plants, in which Mucilage abounds, and which may be used as substitutes for such plants as the Mallow and Linseed. The fine Sugar for which the Saharunpore district is celebrated, is chiefly refined by the aid of two plants which are found in most parts of India, these are Kydia calycina, and Hibiscus Abel Moschus. A number of trees yield Gum, which is used in India for a variety of purposes, and is likewise exported to foreign countries; but from the careless way in which the natives collect it, as well as from their mixing together the produce of several different trees, the East India Gums are not so much valued in the market as they otherwise would be. The more common trees yielding Gum, are species of Acacia, as the Babool and Seriss, with the Sem, the Toon, and many others.

Gum;

Fecula, or Starch;

Of plants which yield fecula or Starch, besides Wheat, Barley, Rice, Maize, and the small grains, there are several others with tuberous roots or Root-stocks, which, like the Potatoe, abound in this principle, as the Curcuma or Arrow-root of India; the Yam, Sweet Potatoe, and species of Arum and Dioscorea, as well as the stems of species of Phœnix. The Sago Palm and the true West India Maranta have been introduced into Calcutta, and very excellent Arrow-root prepared there; and the Tapioca or Cassava plant is now common in Gardens in most parts of India. Those which abound in Saccharine

Arrow-root;

Sago;

principle are of less importance, as the Sugar Cane is so easily cultivated, and with care, excellent sugar is produced almost every where. In Bengal, large quantities of Sugar are prepared from the wild Date tree of India, and might be obtained from other species of Palms. Very good Salep is yielded by a plant of the Kheree jungle in the neighbourhood of Saharunpore, and the true Salep plant was introduced from near Cashmere into the Mussooree Nursery.

Sugar Cane; Date—sugar of; Salep;

A multitude of plants yield fixed oils by expression of their seeds; of these, some are well known, as Sesamum, Poppy, and Linseed, with substitutes for Mustard and Rape. The seeds of Safflower, Sunflower, and Jerusalem Artichoke also yield oil in large quantities. That of the Apricot of the Himalayas, which is cheap and abundant, was sent down to Calcutta, and highly approved of, and the oil of Prinsepia utilis is also of fine quality. Some plants yield a fatty substance, of the consistence of butter, as the Phulwa or Gheetree of Almora. Of Volatile oils, the number is nearly as great as that of the plants which have odorous flowers or leaves, though but few of them are employed for obtaining the oils in a separate state; yet the attar of the rose is distilled almost every where. The Kayapootee succeeds in gardens, even as far north as Saharunpore, and the Spikenard oil grass is common in the jungles of the neighbourhood.

Fatty oils; Volatile oils.

The Himalayan Pines almost all abound in

Turpentine.

Turpentine: Tar; turpentine, and yield tar. One species of these, Pinus longifolia, succeeds equally well in the plains, and yields turpentine of a very fine quality, from which an excellent Oil of Turpentine may be distilled; an equally good Resin is left as a residue. Besides this, there are many other Resins; trees which yield resins valuable for the different arts; amongst these, that of the Saul tree, and the Olibanum of Boswellia thurifera, are Gum Resins; even imported into Europe. Of gum resins, there is the Bdellium, which may be described as an inferior kind of Myrrh.

Dyes; Many of the plants are used as dyes, as the flowers of the Dhak, of the Nyctanthes, Safflower, and Toon. Also Turmeric, Pomegranate rind, Myrobolans, Marking Nut, Acacia bark, Lodh, the roots of Al and Munjeet, the Lichen called Tanning materials; Chulchelira, and others. Several in tanning, as species of Acacia, Conocarpus, the gum of the Alkali; Dhak and others. The ashes of almost all will yield Potash, though that of the Plantain seems Acids; most valued by the Natives. Acetic acid may be procured from the fermentation of a variety of vegetables. The Lemons and Limes are abundant enough to yield a prolific supply of Citric acid; the Tartaric may be obtained from the juice of the grape, and the Oxalic from a species of Rumex, as well as from the stalks of the gram or Cicer Arietinum.

Cordage plants. Many plants are valued for their woody fibre, when this is strong and flexible enough to be used for cordage; as the Hemp, Flax, Sun and Sunnee, (the two latter are called Indian Hemp), Chonch, and Isbund, of which the fibre is commonly called Jute. The Maljhun, Bihul, Koombhee, Dhak, are all used for such purposes, as well as the Bhabhur, Dab, and Surkura, kinds of Sedge and of Grass. The Maljhun, Simbhaloo, Jhuo, and Furash, with a species of Willow, have their osiers employed in making baskets, and the leaves and leafstalks of Palms for making fans, &c. Among the timber trees the Saul, Sissoo, and Bamboo are the most valuable, and the most extensively used; but the Toon, Seriss, Jamoon, Mulberry, and Babool are also much employed. The Teak, Maple, and Casuarina, have become so completely naturalized, that they are extensively planted along the Doab canal, and are distributed throughout the upper provinces.

Hemp, Flax, and cordage plants.

Timber trees.

The system introduced into the Calcutta Botanic Garden of distributing plants and seeds to whoever applies for them, for the purpose of planting, whether Europeans or Natives, is also practised in the Company's Garden at Saharunpore. It may be interesting to observe the numbers distributed from a smaller establishment, and in a district less populous, though some of the dispatches were to distant stations, as Deyra, Nahn, Sabathoo, Kurnaul, Meerut, Loodhiana, Delhi, Hansi, Allygurh. In the year 1829, 3214 fruit trees and plants were distributed. In 1830, 4064, with 10,307 timber trees, to the Doab Canal,

Plants distributed.

Numbers of fruit-timber, and other trees and plants.

Fruit trees and Plants distributed.

during the months of July and August. In the year 1831, 1509 fruit trees and 6025 other plants and timber trees. In 1837, 1269 fruit trees and 7367 other plants, besides numerous parcels of seeds at all times.

Medicines Grown or Prepared in the Saharunpore Garden or its Hill Nursery.

Medicinal plants cultivated.

"In the list of Medicinal Plants* will be observed many which form the most powerful articles of the European Materia Medica, while others, per-

* This passage is quoted from the report of 1831 (v. p. 206.) The attention of the Author was more particularly directed to the subject of the Materia Medica of India, at the request of the Medical Board of Bengal. He proceeded to investigate the subject, by having several Persian works on the subject, collated, and in order to get acquainted with things instead of words, made a collection of every article he was able to procure in the bazars, whether used in Medicine or in the Arts. To the Asiatic synonymes he added the Natural History names, so as to connect the science of the West with the products of the East. A rough catalogue of a portion of his Collection was published in the Journal of the Asiatic Society, vol. I., Calcutta 1832, and the Medical and Physical Society of Calcutta adopted the Author's suggestion to form a collection of native Materia Medica, to which he contributed the first one hundred specimens. The subject has since been attended to, by many of the medical officers of the Establishment, and copious lists published in the Medical Journals of Calcutta, and great progress is making towards an accurate knowledge of Indian Materia Medica, by the chemical analyses of various substances by Dr. O'Shaughnessy.

haps not less valuable, are known only to native hakeems. So much time has been occupied in preliminary investigations that it is not easy to give an idea of the results that may finally be obtained ; but it may at present be stated in general terms, that the Materia Medica in use among the natives of India is very extensive in the number of its articles. These, according as the knowledge of them has been derived from the Greeks, through the Arabs and Persians, or from ancient Hindoo works, are the produce either of European or of Asiatic countries. To one unacquainted with the subject, it would appear surprising to be told that the natives of India are in the habit of administering, or rather of prescribing, such medicines as Hemlock, Hellebore, Henbane, and Colchicum."

Indian Materia Medica very extensive.

" But, having derived much of their knowledge of Medicine from the Greeks, they are naturally anxious to prescribe that which they find praised in their works. Most of the articles, however, being of European growth, and the distances which they have to travel great, the adulterations are proportionally numerous ; and the natives, both physicians and patients, are too ignorant of the original article to be able to detect the falsification. As considerable anxiety, however, is now displayed, and expense incurred, by the Government in the instruction of native doctors for the public service, the benefit of this must eventually ex-

Some knowledge of it derived from Greeks.

Desirable to examine native drugs, and grow others in India.

tend to the class of practitioners who administer to the mass of the population. It would appear the part of a wise and provident foresight, that, as a more correct knowledge of medicine is imparted, and as the art of detecting the impostures in drugs is acquired, means should be adopted for more genuine articles being provided. This might be effected by first investigating the true value of genuine Indian medicines, and then naturalizing in the hills or plains such articles as they are deficient in, or which are now of foreign growth."

Difficulties in growing and preparing medicines.

"That the success would be considerable, I feel warranted in assuming, from the results of the experiments I have already made, even in introducing medicines for the use of the public service. These have borne the test of comparative trials with the best from European depôts. The difficulties to be surmounted may not be so obvious, except to those who have made similar attempts. But, if it be considered that not only the seed or plant is first to be procured, and grown with all the care of an exotic, then extended into a crop, and converted into a form fit for exhibition as a medicine, and, lastly, proved equal in medical virtues, and at the same time cheaper than those already in use, the attempt will not appear so easy. It must also be remembered that not an oil can be distilled without first making a still, nor an extract prepared without first constructing an apparatus for expressing the juice, and then evaporating it to a proper consistence in an apparatus of steam." Preparation of Medicines in India.

"Among the articles which have been introduced, and reported upon by Mr. Twining, after experiments made at the General Hospital, it appears, that 'the cultivation of Rhubarb at the Mussooree Tibba is expected to afford a very valuable remedy, which is less disagreeable to take than the best Turkey Rhubarb, nearly equally efficacious as a purge, and very superior in small doses as a tonic, and astringent in profluvia;' and Mr. Twining concludes his report with saying, that 'the acquisition of this remedy to the Materia Medica of this country will be of the utmost importance.' The medicine has been introduced, and 115 lbs. supplied to the depôts. The Oil of Turpentine, distilled from the Turpentine of the common long-leaved Fir, is considered, in a letter from Mr. Hutchinson, to be of 'very superior quality.' The extract of Henbane has been pronounced by many, from its freshness, to be superior to that imported from Europe, and by Mr. Twining to be of 'most excellent quality.' It has even been sent to Madras; 190 lbs. have been sent to the depôts, and the supply discontinued from Europe. Senna has only this year been introduced into practice. The Medical Board, after the trials made at the General Hospital, express their gratification at the result, and direct that its cultivation be extended as

Rhubarb. Oil of Turpentine. Henbane. Senna.

Medicines prepared in India.

much as possible for the public service. Mr. Twining pronounces the Senna cultivated at Saharunpore very superior to that commonly supplied for hospital use, possessing in a high degree the peculiar aroma of the best Senna; and after forty-five trials considers it equal to the best Senna he has ever seen." The other articles which were cultivated or prepared for hospital use were exhibited in the catalogue, which formed an appendix to the report.

Eligibility of growing Medicinal Plants in India.

"In considering the cultivation of medicines in India in an economical point of view, it may be safely assumed, that by cultivating a sufficient number of articles to keep in full employment whatever establishment may be entertained, a very considerable saving will eventually be effected. For the cost of the production of medicines, must, like every other product of the soil in India, be less than what they can be produced in, and exported from Europe for; particularly if some machinery be employed for the grinding of powders, and the expressing of oils and extracts, which might easily be done by the water-mill in the garden."

Scientific Objects attended to in the Saharunpore Garden.

In our notice of the Botanic Garden of Calcutta an account was given both of the services rendered to Science, and of the practical results. These are important, because they are applicable to the general culture of the provinces which approximate to it in soil and climate. The practical results obtained at the Saharunpore Garden have been detailed before the scientific investigations: though the latter preceded the former. They are valuable, not only for the above reasons, but also because the two gardens being placed at the extreme limits of an extended territory, many of the results are applicable to much of the intermediate tract of country.

Advantages of results obtained in the Government Gardens.

Practical application of scientific investigations.

As the experiments in a scientific institution require to be conducted on principle, instead of according to the chance system which is usually adopted, so in a new country many preliminary inquiries require to be completed before any practically useful experiments can be instituted. These preliminary investigations, consisting of the identification of old, and the description of new species of plants, with a notice of the soil and climate in which they are found, are considered by many as useless for practical purposes. The very same individuals would probably consider it essential that any one wishing to improve the breed of horses, of cattle, or of sheep should

Experiments require to be made on principle.

Experiments made in conformity to principles.

be able to distinguish a horse from an ass, or a sheep from a goat. In what respect the systematic investigation of plants differs, it would not be easy to describe. We know that they are more numerous, and less obviously different from each other, and, consequently, require much time and care accurately to distinguish.

Blunders often committed.

That as great blunders have been committed with plants, as if a breeder were to mistake a camel or a buffalo for a cow, will be evident to any one who will examine the accounts given by several otherwise intelligent gentlemen, of their attempts to cultivate various vegetables in different parts of the world. In India, when it was desired to cultivate the Hemp plant, several plants were so called, which had no greater resemblance to one another than that each yielded fibre fit for cordage, as if all woods were oak, or the flesh of all herbivorous animals was beef or mutton. So, a very intelligent merchant, as the Author has elsewhere mentioned, wishing to improve the culture of Rice, actually sent out to India some American Rice, which in the process of cleaning, had had the embryo removed, for which, in the process of germination, the rest of the grain is intended as nourishment, and which therefore was not more capable of growing, than is pearl barley or kiln-dried hops.

Errors committed from want of scientific principles.

Measures adopted for combining principle with practice.

For the purpose of obtaining as perfect a knowledge as possible of the vegetation of the countries in the neighbourhood of which the Garden was situated, a Herbarium was formed of the plants of the plains of the northern provinces, of the Himalayan mountains, of Kunawur on the northern face of those mountains, and of the valley of Cashmere; amounting in all to about four thousand species. Of the more remarkable of these about five hundred drawings were made by the East-India Company's establishment of painters. A set of specimens was left with Dr. Falconer at Saharunpore, and the duplicates have been presented by the Court of Directors of the East-India Company to the Linnean Society of London, for general distribution, in the same manner that the former East-India collections were distributed.

Herbarium formed.

Drawings made.

Duplicates presented by Court of Directors to the Linnean Society.

The usual course with a collection of Natural History, has been to examine accurately, and to describe with more or less minuteness, the several objects of which it consists, arranging them at the same time systematically in one or other of the systems of classification in use among naturalists. Botanists used, till of late years, chiefly to employ the artificial system of Linnæus, in which the stamens and pistils are employed for the purpose of forming a simple, and, like the alphabetical arrangement of words in a dictionary, in many respects a convenient method of classification. In a general point of view, however, this method has the defect of bringing together many plants which have no resemblance to each other, either in appearance or in structure,

Modes of arranging objects of Natural History.

Artificial method.

Mode of arranging plants.

and the still greater objection of separating some, such as grasses, which are most intimately related to one another. In the Natural classification, on the contrary, the characters are taken from as great a number as possible of the parts of plants, and resemblance is observed, therefore, not only in the organs of re-production, but also in those of nutrition. Hence we find among plants of the same family a similarity of structure, and also a similarity both of constitution and in the secretions which they prepare; so that it is not surprising to find plants of the same family delighting in the same soil, flourishing in the same climate, and abounding in the same products. This mode of classification is therefore not only advantageous as presenting a philosophical method of arrangement, but also as affording many important practical results.

Natural classification; philosophical and practical.

Means adopted for attaining its advantages for India.

To obtain the advantages of the natural classification, it was necessary, though requiring a good deal of time and labour, to arrange not only the plants in the Author's collection, but also those which had been collected by Dr. Roxburgh and other botanists, in order to be able to compare the vegetation of the Northern with that of the Southern parts of India;* also of both, with that of other hot countries having similar climates, as some parts of Africa and America. The

* In this labour the Author has been much assisted, since his return to this country, by the lithographed Catalogue formed by Dr. Wallich, of the East-India Herbarium, v. p. 178.

mountains, also, having at successive elevations a different climate, from the reduction in temperature as we ascend, have also a gradual change of vegetation, and the occurrence of forms similar to such as are found in Europe, China, Japan, Siberia, and North America, is observed. Vegetation of India compared with that of other parts of the world;

To show the connection, therefore, between the different branches of Natural History, and their dependence on the Physical features, Soil, and Climate of the country, the Author, in his work* illustrating the Botany and other Branches of the Natural History of the Himalayan Mountains, divided it into two parts. The introductory portion treats of the Physical Geography of the Plains and Mountains of India, and is followed by a view of their Geological structure. The Meteorology is next treated of, and the climate of the Tropics compared with that of India and of the Himalayas. Tabular views are given of the monthly and diurnal range of the barometer and thermometer in the former. The characteristics of Himalayan climate, consisting of mildness and equability of temperature and of pressure, are next treated of, especially at such elevations as Simla and Mussooree, resorted to by European officers and their families for the recovery of health. method adopted by the Author. Physical Geography. Geology as connected with soils. Meteorology with climate.

The physical features, soil, and climate, hav-

* Illustrations of the Botany and other Branches of the Natural History of the Himalayan Mountains, and of the Flora of Cashmere. London, 1833-1839.

Geographical distribution of plants and animals. ing been noticed, a general view of the Geographical distribution of the Plants and Animals which these are calculated to support, is treated of in connection with the Cultivation, both in the plains, and in the mountains at different elevations, as well in the cold weather as in the rainy season.

Cultivation in plains and mountains.

Vegetation according to soil and climate; The account of the vegetation is then detailed, according to the natural method of arrangement, under the head of two hundred and seven families of plants. The observations on each family consist of a notice of its geographical distribution in different parts of the world, an enumeration of the genera and remarkable species found either in the plains and hot vallies, or in the mountains of India, and the vegetation natural to different parts of India is compared with that of other countries enjoying similar climates. This plan was adopted in consequence of its affording, as has been stated, the most interesting and important general results, and naturally leading to a just appreciation of the influence of physical agents on vegetation, and as elucidating those principles which require to be attended to, not only in the culture of new plants, but also in the improvement of that of old plants in new situations. After an examination of the Geographical distribution of the Natural Families to which they belong, the Useful Plants of other parts of the world are usually noticed immediately after the Properties and Uses of the family have been given,

as found in India and other parts of the world.

Influenced by physical agents.

Practical results.

Useful plants of other countries suited to India.

and the particular parts of India pointed out, to which, from such considerations, they appear suited. This method thus affords great facilities in treating of the properties of plants, as connected with structure, and for showing the immense resources of British-India, and the probable means of still further increasing them.

Resources of British India.

Scientific investigations objected to, as not practical;

A detailed account has been given of the method adopted in publishing the results of the investigations made at the Saharunpore Botanic Garden, in consequence of the prevalent notion, among many otherwise well informed people, of the inutility for practical purposes of scientific investigations; while, in fact, they are the only means we possess of obtaining any principles for our guidance in experimenting on the improvement of old products, or in the introduction of new ones into the culture of a country, and by which we can have anything like certainty in the results we are likely to obtain. The absence of such guides in the numerous experiments which have been made in India may explain the almost constant want of success; the experimentalist having been unable to explain either the causes of the sometimes partial success, or of the far more ordinary total failure. He also was incapacitated from perceiving that a modification of treatment, to which he might easily have been led by a consideration of the influence of physical agents on vegetation, would certainly have produced very different, and at the same time the very results he desired.

are in fact the only ones which give principles and successful practice.

India capable of growing the useful products of most parts of the globe.

After an extended consideration of the peculiarities of Climate and of Vegetation, the Author has no doubt that the Plants of almost every botanical region may be grown in some one, or more, of the diversified soils and climates of India and its mountains, and that the useful products of most parts of the world may be profitably cultivated there for the benefit every where of the people. Also for the establishment of much enlarged means of profitable interchange between the nearest as well as the most distant provinces, and likewise for affording materials for a very widely diffused external commerce.

Countries of which the plants may be grown in different parts of India.

Reserving the right, when time will permit, to go into the necessary details for the comparison of the climate and vegetation in each country, and to make any modifications in the following suggestions, it may be stated that the plants of the following countries may be successfully grown in those parts of India placed opposite them in the accompanying table. It cannot be expected that all such plants, if attempted, will be cultivated with equal success; for even to ensure that success which certainly is attainable with many, it would be necessary to enter into the details of their respective peculiarities. The statement must at present therefore be considered only as a general one.

Tropical and East-Indian Islands, Tropical Africa, Brazil, Guiana, West-Indies, and Florida.	Travancore, Cochin, Malabar, Ceylon, Malayan Peninsula, Chittagong, Bengal, Lower Assam.

Countries of which the plants will grow in the different parts of India.

East and West coast of Africa.	Coromandel Coast, Northern Circars, Concan.
Southern States of North America, Egypt, north of Africa, Syria.	Gujerat, Behar, Doab, Delhi, Malwa.
Mexican Highlands, Lower Mountains of Spain.	Mysore, Hilly ranges in Deccan, Rajpootana.
South of Africa, Extra-Tropical New Holland, South America beyond 23½° S. lat.	Saharunpore and Northern Doab.
Mediterranean Region.	Deyra Doon, and Himalayan Valleys to moderate elevations.
Chino-Japanese region, Middle Andes, Peru, and Mountains of Brazil.	Neilgherries, Upper Assam, Himalayan Mountains.
North of Europe, North of Asia, and North America.	Himalayan Mountains, Region of Oaks and Pines.
Arctic regions, Mountains of Europe, Elevated Andes.	Himalayas above Region of Forest.

Plants to be arranged as suited to seasons of different parts.

From these different regions, we may proceed to import their various seeds or plants, and introduce them with considerable confidence into the analogous parts of India. For practical purposes we may arrange the plants according to their capability of bearing the extremes of climate in different localities—as

Tropical Perennials suited to the southern parts of India.

Tropical Annuals suited to the rainy season of every part of the plains, and even of some of the mountains of India.

Annuals fit for cultivation in the plains of India during the cold weather, and in the Himalayas during the summer months.

Perennials suited to the drier and more northern parts of India.

Perennials suited to the summer, and able to withstand the cold of the Himalayan winter.

Practical inferences.

From these considerations, therefore, the Author has inferred, that in the southern parts of India, especially in the neighbourhood of mountains, many valuable products of the New World, such as the Cinchona, Ipecacuanha, Brazil Wood, and others enumerated in the Appendix, might be successfully grown. So in the higher latitudes of the north-western provinces, the Carob and Olive trees, the Cork tree, and some others of the south of Europe Oaks might be easily cultivated. In the hill provinces many of the Fruit and Timber trees of northern Europe and of North America might be naturalized: these also being mentioned in the Appendix, it is unnecessary further to detail.

Some of the plants which might be grown in India; in southern parts; in northern parts; in the hills.

Cultivation in India of Tobacco, Tea, and Cotton.

From a consideration of the geographical distribution of the families to which they belong, as well as the vegetation with which they are associated, considering also the soil and climate they require, the Author inferred that India was capable of producing of the best quality in its wide-spread plains, Tobacco during the cold weather months, and Cotton in the rainy season; and that the mountains would afford suitable localities for the cultivation of the Tea plant.

Culture of Tobacco in India.

Tobacco, it is well known, is a produce of the New World, which was introduced into Europe soon after the discovery of America. The largest quantities are now imported from Maryland and Virginia, and the finest qualities from Cuba and Cumana. Good Tobacco is not, however, confined to America, as some Turkish and German Tobaccos bring higher prices than the great mass of that which is imported from the United States. The Tobacco plant was introduced into India in the year 1605, during the reign of Akbar. It is now cultivated there in every part, and must be so, to a considerable extent, as it is smoked by almost all classes throughout that thickly-peopled country. As a commercial article, however, Indian Tobacco holds a very inferior place, being frequently unsaleable, and bringing only the lowest prices. It fetches only one-third of the price of the American, selling from 1d. to 2d. a pound. It is complained of as being too high-dried, or as all stalk and powder, and fit only for the inferior kinds of snuff, or for re-exportation to the continent.

Tobacco native of New World; introduced into India;

Tobacco being so extensively consumed in India, it is probable that the best which the country produces is never exported; though the inconveniences of its imperfect preparation cannot be

extensively consumed.

felt there as in other countries, in consequence of its being always smoked in the hooqqa, after being beaten up with conserves or molasses.

Some good Tobacco produced in India; Chunar; Bhilsa;

That India however can and does produce some good Tobacco, may easily be proved. That of Chunar, on the Ganges, and more especially that of Bhilsa, near Nagpore, are celebrated throughout India, while Dr. Ainslie states, that "the finest kinds in India, and perhaps in the world, are grown near the village of Woodanum, in the Northern Circars, and in some of those low sandy islands formed at the mouth of the river Krishna, (from this is made the famous Masulipatam snuff,) also in the Delta of the Godavery, where the soil is peculiarly rich and fertile." But as the commercial value of these has not been ascertained, they might be found very inferior to American Tobaccos. Mr. Ritchie, however, in his Evidence before the Committee of the House of Commons, in 1831, states, that Tobacco of very fine quality is produced extensively in Guzerat, and the northern districts of the Bombay Presidency. One bale imported, sold higher than any American, as it brought 6d. when the latter was sold for 5d. a pound; but the average of an experimental exportation was found to be defective in the curing, and did not pay. Besides this, we have seen, that excellent Tobacco is grown at Sandaway, in Arracan, (p. 187,) and that this when brought to London was valued at from 6d.

Masulipatam; Guzerat; Sandaway, in Arracan;

to 8d. a pound. Mr. Piddington mentions the Tobacco of Singour, in Burdwan, near Chandernagur, as selling at the price of the Arracan sort, though of the same species as that cultivated in the surrounding country; and that the best Bengal tobacco is grown at and about Haiglee, in the Kishnagar district. All these were specimens of Tobacco grown and cured by natives from seed of plants which have no doubt been long introduced into these countries.

Tobacco of Singour; Bengal.

The above specimens of Tobacco having been pronounced to be of good quality by the best judges in London, is sufficient evidence that India is capable of producing Tobacco very supérior to what is usually imported from that country. The facts are still more important as having been results produced by the natives themselves, and without the aid of any foreign seed; and are of yet greater consequence, if we consider the very distant situations, and the very different climates of Arracan, Bengal, the Northern Circars, Nagpore, and Guzerat, in which they were produced.

India capable of growing good Tobacco.

About the year 1829, the Court of Directors of the East-India Company sent out Tobacco seed, procured both from Maryland and Virginia, and a Paper on the culture of Tobacco in Virginia, sent by their Agent along with the seeds. These were distributed to Calcutta, Madras, and Bombay. The Agricultural Society of Calcutta were the first to obtain successful results. Having

American Tobacco seed sent out by East India Company.

Tobacco cultivated by Agricultural Society of Calcutta; cultivated and prepared the Tobacco according to the American method, they sent specimens to England, which were submitted by the Court of Directors to dealers and manufacturers in London, who pronounced it to be "the best sample of Indian Tobacco they had ever seen. In flavour and general appearance of the leaf, it approaches the descriptions which are usually selected here for manufacturing into cigars, and for smoking in a pipe, *viz.*, Havannah, St. Domingo, and Amersforth, and which command high prices in relation to other kinds of leaf tobacco." It was considered equivalent in value to 6d. or 8d. a pound.

excellent in quality;

grown in Madras Presidency;

In the Madras Presidency, several experimentalists endeavoured to grow good Tobacco from the American seed. But the situations they selected were evidently unfavourable; either from unsuitableness, or over-richness of soil, or too great moisture of climate, or perhaps from too highly manured and close cultivation. The faults appeared to be those of over-luxuriance, for the stalks and fibres had attained great size and coarseness. The tobaccos had, moreover, been badly packed, and worse cured, and were pronounced by the brokers to be "not marketable," and "of no value;" and of the best, it was said, that some from Holland, of much better quality, had been sold under 2d. per pound.

inferior in quality;

The Author having had an opportunity, through the kindness of Mr. W. Johnson, of examining the documents, and inspecting the experimental specimens of Tobacco in the India House, had no doubt that good Tobacco might be grown in India, in spite even of the mass of unsuccessful experiments. The faults, being those of rankness in flavour, and over-luxuriance of growth, might evidently in a poorer soil and drier atmosphere, with equal attention in other respects to the culture and curing, be most easily remedied. The Author was highly gratified in being shortly afterwards informed by Mr. Johnson, that one of the very experimentalists who had so signally failed before, on having the causes of failure pointed out to him, made fresh experiments, and grew his tobacco, as was understood, in a more elevated situation, and prepared it in so superior a manner that it actually sold in the London market for 8d. a pound.

Tobacco might be grown in India;

faults are luxuriance and rankness;

later attempts successful in Madras Presidency.

These successful results with American seed, especially when considered in connection with the superior Tobaccos which are already produced in several very widely-separated parts of India, are sufficient proofs that the country is capable of growing the best kinds of Tobacco. So there is no doubt that, if cultivators will pay attention, not only to the selection of the soil and of the seed, and to careful culture, but also to the subsequent preparation and packing of the tobacco, that it may be grown in India with as much certainty of success as any other crop in any other country. At present, though rich soils

Points to be attended to in culture of Tobacco.

Defects in Indian culture.

are usually selected in the neighbourhood of villages, and a good deal of attention is paid to the culture, yet the ground is not sufficiently weeded nor worked. Neither is the plant prevented from shooting too much into stalk, nor are the superfluous leaves taken off, so that the remainder may expand and produce size with softness, and fine flavour from full exposure to air and light. But the subsequent preparation is much more defective than the culture of the plant. Nothing seems to be done but to expose Tobacco when gathered to the full influence of a very powerful sun, which with the drying effects of a parching and dusty wind, makes it not surprising that the Tobacco is complained of here, if not all stalk, as being over-dried, and ready to crumble into dust.

Tobacco—kinds of cultivated;

The kinds of Tobacco cultivated, no doubt vary according to situation and the mode of culture. Some distinct species are also cultivated in different countries, but Nicotiana Tabacum and its varieties are so, most extensively. N. rustica is chiefly cultivated in western Africa and Egypt, also near Salonica and Latakia, and likewise in some parts of Europe. Dr. Lindley considers the Persian Tobacco to be a distinct species, which he has named N. persica. The seed of these several species is well worthy of trial in different parts of India, as well as seed from those places which are already celebrated for their tobacco, as the Author has already recommended in his article on this subject.

The soil for Tobacco in North America, and also in European latitudes, requires to be of the richest nature, but it is doubtful whether this would be necessary to the same extent in a warmer climate, and more moist atmosphere. In Virginia, "the light red, or chocolate-coloured, mountain lands, the light black soil in the coves of mountains, and the richest low grounds" are particularly specified. Mr. Piddington states that the Tobacco soils of the Havannah, as well as those of Manilla, are red sorts, and that the red and reddish brown soils contain most of their iron in the state of peroxide, or the reddish brown oxide of iron, while the light grey soils contain it only in the state of protoxide, or the black oxide of iron. He believes the quality of the tobacco to depend mainly on the state and quantity of the iron in the soil.* Tobacco, soil suited to;

The climate of India is no doubt suitable, as good Tobacco, we have seen, is produced in very different parts of that empire, and the mean temperature of the cold weather months there, is about equal to that of the summer temperature of those other countries where good Tobacco is grown. But the temperature of other places, as of climate suited to;

* We shall probably soon have more accurate information respecting the Tobacco and Sugar soils of America, as the China and East-India Association have applied to Lord John Russell, Secretary for the Colonies, to obtain specimens of the above soils from the West Indies and America in the same way

Havannah, Cumana, &c. is modified by local peculiarities of climate.

Preparation in America ;

In America, the greatest care is taken with the gathering of the plants, when the leaves are what is considered fully ripe ; and then only those which are so, are individually selected. The largest plants are split down the centre, that the air may be more freely admitted to every part of the leaves during the process of drying. The plants when sufficiently pliable to bear handling, are removed to and hung up in large barns, or tobacco houses, the sides of which are left partially open to allow of a free circulation of air, where they remain for four or five weeks. The leaves are then separated from the stalks, and thrown together in heaps, where they undergo the process of sweating, after which, when in case, equal pains are bestowed on the packing.

might be well grown and prepared in India.

If any one will compare this careful culture and preparation with that practised in India, they will not be surprised that the Tobacco of the latter country should bear so little comparison with that of the former, where so much pains is taken with every part of the process. There is little doubt that if any one practically acquainted with every thing that is requisite, were seriously to

---

that the Cotton soils had been procured by Lord Palmerston for the Royal Asiatic Society ; the Court of Directors of the East-India Company having been applied to for payment of the expenses, authorized a sum adequate to the purpose.

turn his attention to the culture of Tobacco in India, that he would obtain the most successful results, and be able to grow the best Tobacco. He might also realize the full profit, and obtain the highest prices if he could send his goods to the open markets of England, instead of depending on the more limited competition of the Presidencies, where the buyers are all interested in keeping down the prices of Indian produce. It must never be forgotten (vide p. 43) that American Tobacco did not attain its pre-eminence, until after years of unremitting attention both on the part of the Government and of the Cultivators of Virginia.

Tobacco of the best quality might be grown in India.

Culture of Tea in the Himalayas.

The Tea plant is one of those which has long attracted public attention, both, as giving us the means of forming a most grateful beverage, which has detached nations almost from the use of intoxicating liquors, and from its being the produce of a country, which, though anciently civilized, we know so little, that great curiosity is attached to all its productions. Tea is not more remarkable for being a source of profit to the Chinese, by whom it is cultivated, than for the extent to which it has yielded profit to the merchants and revenue to the Governments of those nations who have imported it.

Tea plant of great interest

as source of revenue.

Tea plant thought to be confined in distribution.

The Tea plant has usually been considered very peculiar in its nature, and, like the Cinnamon, Nutmeg, Clove, and Mangosteen, very confined in its distribution, and therefore very difficult of cultivation in other countries. The

The Author conceives it might be cultivated in the Himalayas;

Author, when investigating the vegetation of the Himalayas in the general manner which has been described, and studying the practical application of the scientific information he had obtained, long ago conceived that, from the peculiarity of climate and of vegetation of the Himalayan Mountains, it was possible there, at certain elevations, and in suitable localities, to cultivate the Tea plant successfully as a commercial article. This also, so as to retain the present proportion of astringent and of stimulant properties which makes the infusion of its leaves so grateful as a beverage.

recommends it to the Government.

Towards the end of the year 1827, in a report to the Indian Government, the Author recommended the culture of Tea in the north-western portion of the Himalayas, because included within the British territories, and stated, that the Tea plant "does not appear by any means so delicate or so limited in geographical distribution as

Natural localities of Tea plant.

is generally supposed. It is said to delight particularly in sheltered vallies, the declivities of hills, or the banks of rivers, where it enjoys a southern exposure to the sun. These warm situations do not, however, appear to be essential to its welfare, as it is found to grow on the rugged tops of mountains; and, although it appears to attain the greatest perfection in the mild climate about Nankin, yet it flourishes in the northern latitude of Pekin and in Japan, as well as about Canton; and thus appears to be confined within the parallels of 20° and 40° of north latitude."

Tea plant—natural localities of.

That this opinion respecting the practicability of cultivating the Tea plant in the Himalayas was not accidental, but the result of deliberate conviction, is evident from the Author recurring to it in his report to the Governor-general, Lord William Bentinck, when he visited the Saharunpore Garden in March 1831. This was published in the Journal of the Asiatic Society of Calcutta in February 1832. Again, in 1833, in the introductory chapter to the "Illustrations of the Botany of the Himalayan Mountains," he adverted to this; and stated, p. 5, "Somewhere in the vallies at the foot of these hills, or at moderate elevations, the more generally useful productions of European countries might be successfully introduced." "Here, also, as I have recommended in a report to Government, there is considerable prospect of success in the cultivation of the Tea plant, for the different elevations allow of every variety of climate being selected, and the geographical distribution of this plant is sufficiently extended, and the natural sites sufficiently varied, to warrant its being beneficially cultivated."

Cultivation of, frequently recommended by the Author.

The Author, not having had any favourable opportunity for giving in detail his reasons for

Reasons for the opinion.

Essay on the cultivation of Tea in the Himalayas.

the opinion he had so frequently promulgated, did so in the "Illustrations," p. 107, published in September 1834, on the occasion of his treating of the natural family of Ternstrœmiaceæ, to which the Tea plant is usually referred; of this, the genera Cleyera and Eurya are common to China, Japan, and the Himalayas. The Camellieæ form a tribe of Ternstrœmiaceæ, and are sometimes called Theaceæ, and considered a distinct family.

Geographical distribution of the Tea family of plants.

In the first place, it was shown that the species of the above family are found in the warm parts of Asia and America, but that the Asiatic species are chiefly confined to China and the mountains which divide it from India. The Camellias, for instance, were originally found only in China and Japan, but afterwards in the Indian mountains, from Munnipoor, in about 25° N. lat., to those which surround the valley of Nepal, between 27° and 28° N. lat. The genus Thea had then been found only in China and Japan, chiefly in a cultivated state, but had been supposed, as stated in the above Essay, p. 109, to be indigenous in the mountains which separate China from the Burmese territories. Dr. Wallich had also seen a Tea plant ten feet high at Katmandoo in Nepal, where it had been growing for many years in the open air. That is, at an elevation of 4,784 feet above Bengal, in 27° 42′ of N. latitude, and in a mean temperature of 64° of Fahr.

Cultivation recommended by Dr. Wallich.

Dr. Wallich, in 1832, presented a paper to the Committee of the House of Commons on the

Affairs of India, recommending the cultivation of Tea in the Himalayan Mountains, in the districts of Kemaon, Gurhwal, and Sirmore. Cultivation in British Himalayas.

So much had already been proposed, when the Author proceeded to point out in detail the parts of the Himalayas where he had so frequently stated that the Tea plant might be successfully cultivated. These did not appear the only, or the most favourable localities, for such a purpose; for in that case the valley of Nepal, where the Tea plant was already growing, would have been the most eligible for the first experiment, but this is not included within the British territories.

The Himalayan Mountains extend from near Cashmere in a south-east, and afterwards in an easterly direction, to Bootan (forming between 27° and 28° the northern boundary of Assam): thence one branch crossing the Chinese province of Yunan, penetrates to Fokien, opposite to which the island of Formosa may be considered the termination of the chain. The late Mr. Calder, in a letter, written after his return from China, to the Author, stated that the geological structure of this termination was the same as that of the Himalayas. Taking the extreme limits, we have the chain extending over 45° of longitude, but not making more than 10° of northing in its whole extent. Though variation in longitude, no doubt, produces differences in Climate, yet, as this is chiefly influenced by latitude and elevation, it is evident that along the whole extent of this mountainous country there must be many locali-

Extent of Himalayas; a branch extending into China; similarity of this in geological structure; probable similarity in climate.

Extent of Himalayas.

ties which differ but little in latitude and in elevation, and which must consequently resemble each other in Climate, and therefore, probably, also in Vegetation.

Information obtained from Mr. Reeves.

From the foregoing notice respecting the various localities in which the Tea plant is found to flourish, it is evident that it can bear considerable differences of dryness and of moisture, as well as of heat and of cold. Being in the metropolis, the Author endeavoured to obtain, as far as was possible, the fullest and most correct information on so important a subject. He was fortunate in being favoured by Mr. Reeves with some new information, the result of inquiries obtained from the Chinese, and when in the employment of the East-India Company at Canton.

Valuable from the attention he paid to Natural History.

This was the more valuable from the attention which Mr. Reeves had paid, when there, to subjects of Natural History, as may be seen from the result of his labours in the library of the Horticultural Society. From him the Author learnt

One kind of Tea plant more hardy than the other.

that one of the kinds of Tea plant was able to bear a greater degree of cold than he had previously supposed. This was confirmed by the experience of Messrs. Loddiges in their Nursery grounds, and by the testimony of Sir W. J. Hooker, and of Mr. George Loddiges.

Species and varieties of Tea plant.

Before proceeding in the inquiry, it would be desirable to ascertain whether one or several species of Thea yield the several varieties of tea; as this might explain some of the discrepancies in the accounts respecting the soil and climate required for its cultivation. Some authors consider that all the varieties of tea may be prepared from the same plant, and that the differences are therefore due to the age of the leaf and the mode of preparation. Others are of opinion that they are dependent on variations in soil and climate, as well as on distinctness in the plant, whether this be a species or a permanent variety. Species and varieties of Tea.

Dr. Abel, when passing through the country, had little doubt of there being two species of Tea plant, and mentions that the plants from the *black* and *green* tea districts differ in the form, colour, and texture of their leaves; those of the green tea being larger, thinner, and of a lighter colour than those of the black, though growing in the same soil. These characters may be seen in the plants in the Kew or Chiswick Gardens, or in that of the Messrs. Loddiges, and known as the green and black tea plants in this country. Both have been figured and described by Sir W. J. Hooker and by Mr. Loddiges. Green and Black Tea plants distinct. Dr. Abel's opinion.

Mr. Reeves expresses his surprise, "that any person who has been in China, or, indeed, any one who has seen the difference in the colour of the infusion of black and green tea, could suppose for a moment that they were the produce of the same plants, differing only in the mode of curing; particularly as they do not grow in the neighbourhood of each other;" and he further says that the Chinese manufacturers do not, and they say they cannot, make black tea into green, Mr. Reeves's.

and *vice versa*; and this I believe to be true: indeed, the colour of the infusion is alone sufficient evidence." Mr. Pigou, on the contrary, adduces the evidence of a Chinese, as stating that "Bohea may be cured as Hyson, and Hyson as Bohea." The discrepancy in the information Mr. Reeves explains by adding, that "there is a species of tea grown in the province of Canton, of a pale-coloured leaf (occasionally mixed with Congou tea, to make the tea imported under the name of Bohea), and this tea can be coloured and made up to imitate various qualities of green tea, and large quantities are yearly thus made; but still it is only an appearance that can be given: the deception is detected as soon as it is put into water." (Illustrations, p. 111.)

Green and Black Teas stated to be from the same plant.

Discrepancy explained by Mr. Reeves.

As there are several acknowledged species of Thea, there seems no reason why more than one species may not be employed in manufacturing into tea. There is no doubt that the plants known here as green and black tea plants retain permanently their characteristics, and that their leaves respectively resemble those obtained after infusing good specimens of green and of black tea. The green tea plant is, moreover, much more hardy than the black tea plant; one of the former lived for twenty years in the open air, nailed against the common wall of the garden in Mr. Loddiges' Nursery grounds at Hackney, and was only killed in the very severe winter of 1837-8, when the thermometer fell to 4½° Fahr., which proved fatal to

Green Tea plant more hardy than the Black.

so many of the old established trees and shrubs of our gardens. From the fact of artificial means being adopted, to change the colour of the common tea from black to green, we might infer that there is naturally a kind of tea which this was intended to resemble. A gentleman, well known in London, for his knowledge acquired when at Canton, of the teas of China, has been in the habit of showing, by experiment, in one vessel divided by a partition, how the black may be converted into green tea.*

Black Tea converted into Green artificially.

From the great extent of territory over which, and the variety of situations in which, tea is produced, there can be little doubt that it is grown in a variety of soils, though there are, no doubt, certain physical states which are best suited to the production of the *finest flavoured* teas. The principal cultivation of teas for the foreign trade is between 27° and 31° of N. lat. Dr. Abel was of opinion that the tea plant succeeds best on the sides of mountains, where there can be little accumulation of vegetable mould. The plantations which he saw were in a kind of gravelly soil, formed either of disintegrated sandstone or primary rocks. "Judging from specimens," says Dr. A., "collected in our route through the province

Soils suited to the Tea plant.

* Mr. Bruce has lately described the process, which, besides an extra degree of preparation, requires the addition of indigo and of sulphate of lime. He is of opinion that the different kinds of tea are prepared from the same plant.

Soil of Tea districts.

of Keang-nan, whence the green tea is procured, its rocks consist chiefly of sandstone, schistus and granite;" and he was inclined to think that those of Fokien must be similar. This coincides also with the testimony of others. (Illustrations, p. 113.)

Extent of cultivation of Tea in China.

The tea plant is cultivated in China over a very large extent of territory. Dr. Wallich mentions it in Cochin-China in N. lat. 17°, and in China in the southern provinces of Yunan and of Quang-tung. Mr. Reeves informed the Author that, in a Chinese Herbal, tea is said to be produced, among other places to the northward of 31°, in nine places in Hoo-Quang, three places in Ho-nan, one place in Shensi, and two places in Shan-tung; one of these latter, and the most northward of the whole, is Tang-chow-Foo, in 36° 30′ N. lat.—and in the Japan islands, which extend from 30° to 41° of N. lat., Dr. Abel states having found it in an apparently wild state at See-chou, in the province of Kiang-see, about N. lat. 26°, where the hills were covered with pines. The Author has, since the publication of his observations, seen an excellent specimen in flower in the British Museum, collected by another botanist (Mr. Cunningham) near Cheusan, which is in 30° of N. lat., and where, he say, it delights on the tops of mountains like the Pine.*

From 17° to 36° 30′ N. lat.

At Cheusan, 30° N. lat. on Mountains.

The information which we possess respecting

* This specimen was pointed out to the Author by Mr. R. Brown, distinguished as the first botanist of the day. The

the climate of the tea districts is, like that of the soil, rather of an inferential than of a positive nature; so the Author adopted the plan of taking the extremes of that of Canton and of Pekin, and considering that of the tea districts as a medium between them. The mean annual temperature at Canton is about 69° 7.; the greatest cold, 29°, occurs in January, and the greatest heat, 94°, in July. At Pekin, in N. lat. 39° 54′, the mean temperature of the three winter months is 26° 42, that is below the freezing-point, as at Copenhagen, while the summer is as warm as that at Naples, with a mean temperature of 82° 58.—(Vide Humboldt on Isothermal lines, or Illustrations, p. 113, where some of the details are given.)

Climate of Tea districts.

Of Canton.

Of Pekin.

The Author then proceeded to give an abstract of the observations of the thermometer, made in the progress of the British Embassy, from the 8th September to the 24th of November, from Tiensing, near lat. 39°, to Nanchangfoo, about lat. 28° 40′. During this time, 44° was the lowest, and 80° the highest temperature observed.

Thermometric Observations by British Embassy.

Mr. Reeves, moreover, informed the Author, that "snow has been on the ground for days together upon the green teas, and the manufacturers of the black tea complain of the coldness

Coldness of Tea districts.

---

note attached to it is in the hand-writing of Cunningham. "Tea frutex flore albo rosaceo summitatibus montium gaudens uti Pinus."—Herb. Mus., vol. xciii., fol. 146.

Climate of China.

of their country at times."—The extremes of temperature are, however, well known to be considerable in all the parts of China with which we are acquainted when compared either with India or with Europe, as indicated in the "Illustrations," p. 116. Humboldt has observed: "The whole of Europe, compared with the eastern and western parts of America and Asia, has an insular climate. Also, that the northern part of China, like the Atlantic region of the United States, exhibits *excessive climates*, as Buffon indicated, and seasons strongly contrasted, while the coasts of New California and the embouchure of the Columbia, have winters and summers almost equally temperate." This great contrast of climates between summer and winter is most conspicuous in the north, and diminishes, probably by degrees, as we proceed to the south. If we compare the climate of Canton with that of Calcutta, which is not a degree to the southward, we shall find that the latter, with a maximum temperature of 93° 6, being 3°.6 above that recorded at Canton, has a minimum of only 56°. 8, which is 27°.8 above that at Canton. The annual range of the thermometer at Calcutta, therefore, is about 36°; that at Canton being upwards of 60°, and characteristic of an excessive climate.

Great contrasts of its winter and summer temperature.

Comparison of the climates of Canton and of Calcutta.

Difference between Indian and Chinese climate.

The greatest difference between the climate of India and that of China is, probably, in the absence in the latter of a regular rainy season, which fertilizes the former during one period of the year.

Climate of China. rain; at Macao; in Tea districts.

The northern parts of China enjoy upon the whole a very dry climate; but the months of June, July, and August, are stated to be often very rainy, and the average of rainy days to be fifty-eight. At Macao the quantity of rain on an average of eighteen years is about 69½ inches annually; or 107 inches is the largest, and 49 inches the smallest quantity which fell in any year. Mr. Reeves informed the Author that he has known the black tea manufacturers complain "that their first picking, in May and June, often suffers from rains and cold easterly winds." This indicates frequent but not periodical rains.

Tea districts—vegetation of, Perennial and Annual. Perennials of southern provinces; resemble those of tropical countries;

Having noticed the extent of distribution, and, as far as practicable, the soil and climate, of the tea districts, it is desirable to ascertain the vegetation natural to the same regions. This may be distinguished into that which is Perennial, and that which is Annual; and into the former as characterizing both the southern and the northern provinces. The Perennial plants of the southern provinces are exposed to no great extremes of temperature as great or long-continued cold is not to be expected in the latitude, and excess of heat is moderated by the greater moisture. There is, therefore, considerable resemblance to the vegetation of tropical countries in general, and to the southern parts of India in particular.

Perennials of northern provinces;

The Perennials of mountainous situations, as well as of the northern provinces of China, being exposed to the extreme severity of the winter of

Perennials of northern provinces.

that country (notwithstanding that they have to bear the heats of summer), have a resemblance to the plants of northern latitudes, and to such as are found on the slope of the Himalayas. Some genera are associated with these, of which the species are most prevalent about the centre of the temperate zone, and to which great extremes of temperature may be supposed to be obnoxious. With these occur some other genera, the species of which are chiefly diffused through tropical countries: "but of these only single species have in general been enumerated in the northern provinces of China, in the same way that we have seen species of the same genera extending to the most northern parts of India, and ascending up the sides of the Himalayas within the thick covering of jungle and forest, when they could not exist in the moderate cold even of the open plains of northern India."—Illustrations, p. 120.

resemble those of Himalayas.

A few tropical species found as far north as in India.

Comparison of Flora of China with that of other countries.

Great resemblance of the Flora of the north of China to that of Europe, of Tartary and Siberia, likewise to that of Japan, and in some genera to that of North America, is also observed. But the analogy is the greatest between the Flora of the Himalayas and that of China, and some species even, which were first discovered in the Himalayas, are now enumerated in the Flora of China, while others, which were only known as Chinese and Japan plants, are found in abundance within the Himalayas.

Annuals of China.

Though congenial with the vegetation of

southern latitudes, we are far from expecting with the shrubby and arboreous vegetation of the northern provinces, the prevalence of many Annuals, or of such cultivation as we expect only in tropical countries. But the temperature of rainy countries, or of moist situations, varies less than that of dry ones, even when their latitudes differ to a considerable extent. The summer maximum of temperature also increases with the latitude to a certain extent, owing to the greater dryness of the countries immediately beyond the influence of moisture and the rains. Thus Bruce, in Abyssinia, found the climate, on account of the rain, was 12° cooler when the sun was over head than when he was 36° to the southward. So, in India, the mean temperature of the hot weather exceeds that of the rainy season months, though the latter extend over those months which in drier countries are the hottest in the year, that is, from the middle of June to the middle of September. The temperature of the warmest months at Canton is 83°.6, and at Pekin as high as 82°.58, that is less by only 1°.02, though it is 15° more north in latitude. **Modifying effects of rain and moisture on temperature.**

Hence, we may find the lakes abounding in the same vegetation in the northern as in the southern provinces of China, as we may see some of the plants of England in the vicinity of water in India. In a regularly warm and steady climate, therefore, if water be applied artificially, as by irrigation, whether from wells, **Vegetation and Cultivation dependent on water.**

Effects of water on cultivation.

rivers, or canals, so that it be sufficiently abundant, the same plants may be as successfully cultivated as in tropical countries. Therefore we have all along the canals of China the cultivation of Rice, Sorghum, &c. in the summer months, as we observe in India during the rainy season.

Cold weather cultivation of China.

The similarity in culture is still greater, for at the termination of the Rice and Millet crop we find wheat, barley, buckwheat, peas, beans, lucerne, and tobacco are grown. But we must not from this conclude that there is identity of climate, for the openness of the extended coast, backed by ranges of hills, must give it the advantage of having its climate modified by sea breezes and more frequent showers of rain. The latter are well known to be absent from India for many months, almost from October to June, with the exception of some rain at Christmas. The difference of climate is, however, strikingly manifest in the more northern latitudes to which the Silk culture is extended in China, while in India it is confined to the province of Bengal, where moisture modifies the great heat.

The Author recommends experiments in the Himalayas.

Such being the extent of distribution, soil, climate, and vegetation associated with the Tea plant, and the similarity in these respects to what is found in the Himalayas being considerable, the Author proceeded to recommend that experiments should be made to cultivate Tea in suitable situations in these mountains.

The British territories in the Himalayas,

Extent of British possessions in Himalayas; temperature; soil.

such as Kemaon, or those which are under British protection, as Gurhwal and Sirmore, extend from 28° to 31½° of N. lat., and present every diversity of climate and vegetation from their tropical bases to their snow-clad summits. But as the same latitudes are warmer in India than in China, we must go further north, or ascend higher, to obtain a similar temperature. With regard to soil, since that derived from the disintegration of primary rocks, or what is meagre in nature, is said to be suitable to the tea plant, (or, as according to one Author, "leaves of a fine flower are only produced in light stony ground,") there would be no difficulty in finding such as is suitable in the primary-structured Himalayas.

Temperature, requisite for Tea culture. Localities pointed out as desirable by Author.

Dr. Wallich has stated, that a temperature between 30° and 80° (meaning that with a summer heat of 80° there should not be a greater degree of cold than 30° in winter) is requisite. This the Author was disposed to coincide in; he therefore mentioned that Deyra, at the foot of the Himalayas, in 30° of N. lat. has a range of the thermometer of from 37° to 101°, while Mussooree, nearly immediately above, but at the top of the range, and about 4,500 feet more elevated, one from 27° to 80°; but that Jurreepanee, about midway between the two, seemed the most eligible situation, from having a favourable climate beyond the hot winds, facility of irrigation, and a decided change in the vegetation. A moist and warm situation, near the lake called Bheemtal,

Localities pointed out as desirable for Tea cultivation

another in the valley of Hawulbagh, and a third at Almora, elevated 5,400 feet, were recommended in Kemaon. Further to the north-west, one in the garden of Shalimar in the Pinjore valley, and two others at Nahn and Sabathoo, both elevated about four thousand feet.

varied in situation and climate.

The whole of these situations being spread along the tract above described as within British influence, gave as great an extent of latitude as was then attainable (Assam being unknown, except as abounding in jungles), and a sufficient variety of elevation and of climate. So that with the requisite attention to selection of open and of shady, moist or dry localities, &c. at these several places, a sufficient number of results would be insured as data for future cultivation.

Probability of success.

The Author concluded by stating, that from the latitude, elevation, soil, climate, and the course of the seasons in the Himalayas, as well as from the considerable identity of the vegetation, with that of China, there could not be a doubt of success in introducing the cultivation of tea, with the strongest probability of all its properties remaining unchanged, as every requisite is so similar to what it experiences in its native country.

Same tracts recommended by Dr. Wallich.

Such was the state of information, and such the results to which it led. Dr. Wallich having recommended, in February 1832, the same tract of the Himalayas which the Author had pointed out in 1827, and which, after entering more fully into the details of the subject, and after obtaining the best information that was procurable in this country, besides consulting those who had resided in China, he again recommended in 1834. Tracts for Tea culture.

Lord W. Bentinck, with the sanction of the Court of Directors, had, in the beginning of 1834, determined upon attempting the cultivation of Tea in India. A Committee was appointed for the purpose of submitting to government a plan for the accomplishment of this object. Determination to attempt Tea culture in India. Committee established.

The first conclusion to which the Committee came was, that "the proposed experiment may be made, with great probability of success, in the lower hills and vallies of the Himalayan range. Next to them, those of our Eastern frontier offer the best prospects, and after them, the Neilgherry and other lofty mountains in Southern and Central India." "To the former part of this conclusion they were led," according to their report, "by a very able and interesting letter of Dr. Falconer on the subject," and also by the fact, "that in the mountainous tracts of our northern and eastern frontier, several species of plants are found indigenous, which are also natives of China, and are not met with in other parts of the world." Localities recommended for experiments.

Circulars, with specific inquiries, respecting climate, soil, &c., were addressed in March 1834 to several gentlemen. Mr. Gordon, the secretary, was directed to proceed to China, to procure plants, seeds, and Chinese cultivators, to carry on the experiment. Dr. Wallich offered his gratuitous services as secretary. It was then stated, that "after Inquiries respecting climate and soil. Mr. Gordon deputed to China.

Tea culture when successful may be left to private enterprize.

the practicability of producing Tea fit for commercial purposes shall have been ascertained, it may safely be left to the enterprise of individuals to pursue the business as an object of speculation."

Tea districts visited by Messrs. Gordon and Gutzlaff.

Ankoy Tea Hills.

Mr. Gordon left Calcutta in June 1834, and in his progress obtained some account of the tea cultivation in Java. After his arrival in China he was accompanied by Mr. Gutzlaff, with whom he visited the Ankoy tea hills. In their account it is related they had to ascend a pass of 1,200 feet of elevation, and to descend again about 1,000 feet on the other side. The plantations were mostly at the foot of, and on hills 700 feet high; and the tea plants were found forming small bushes, in a sandy soil, without shade, and not irrigated. They learnt also that hoar frost is common in the locality, and that snow falls occasionally to the thickness of three or four inches, but does not lie long on the ground, and that the plant is sufficiently hardy to bear any degree of dry cold. Messrs. Gordon and Gutzlaff also made an unsuccessful attempt to reach the Bohea tea hills, and they intended to endeavour to reach the Green tea districts, but the former was recalled to Bengal in consequence of the finding of the tea plant in the British Indian province of Assam. (Journ. Asiatic Soc., vol. iv., pp. 95, 553.)

Bohea Tea Hills.

Seeds of Bohea Tea plants obtained.

Mr. Gordon, however, obtained abundance of seed, of the Bohea tea plants. These arrived in Calcutta in January 1835, and being sown, produced numerous plants, which were distributed to the several districts thought to offer favourable localities for the growth of the tea plant.

Young Tea plants distributed to Madras Presidency.

Twenty boxes of seedling plants were sent to Madras, and thence still further distributed; six boxes being sent to the Neilgherries, to Coorg, and to Mysore, and two to the Agricultural and Horticultural Society of Madras. Respecting all these, we learn by a letter from the chief secretary to the Government of Fort St. George, dated 22d August 1836, that "the experiment has almost entirely failed; with the exception of a few plants on the Neilgherry hills, and in the Nuggur country, the rest have withered away." The causes of failure, however, whether owing to soil, climate, or imperfect culture, are not assigned in any of the letters.

failure of many;

A few, apparently, of the same plants, which did not succeed in the Neilgherries, were given by the officer commanding there to Captain Minchin, who was stationed at Mannantoddy in Wynaad, a district of the western Ghauts belonging to the province of Malabar. These have been described to thrive, and become bushy and fine plants, and as coming out in full bloom in June. It is probable, therefore, that some of the districts possessing the same soil and climate will be able to grow the tea plant; but whether so as to retain the same degree of astringent and stimulant property as the tea of China, can only be ascertained by experiment.

success in Wynaad.

Seeds and young plants were also sent to the

Seeds and young plants sent to the North-western part of the Himalayas.

north-western parts of the Bengal presidency. These were at one time thought to be the only favourable places for the cultivation of the tea plant, and they had been frequently recommended by the Author, as well as by Dr. Falconer,* in a report (Tea papers, p. 21,) which is remarkable for coincidence in argument and in opinion with that of the Author, though the two Essays crossed each other in their passage to and from India.

Tea nurseries established in Kemaon, Gurhwal, and Sirmore.

Chejooree, Rama Serai, and Koth, at elevations of 4,000, 5,000, and 5,300 feet, the first having a northerly and the two latter a south-west aspect, were selected for experiment in Gurhwal by Dr. Falconer. A few plants were, moreover, tried above the Chejoorie nursery, at an elevation of 6,400 feet. Rama Serai presented the advantages or disadvantages of being a flat and open valley, which, though elevated, is extremely hot in the summer months. Two situations were selected in Sirmore, one at Ruroo, 5,400 feet, and the other at 5,100 feet of elevation, the former with an east-south-east and the latter with a southerly aspect.

Result of first experiments.

Since the institution of the experimental tea nurseries, Dr. Falconer has been deputed to investigate the natural history of Cashmere and Tibet, and no report has yet been published on the result

* The Author has since learnt, that the same tract had been recommended by Dr. Govan in 1815, and at a much earlier period by Sir Joseph Banks. All botanists know that the latter had within his reach the best advice on botanical subjects.

of the Tea experiments. In a letter to the Author, dated the 1st of December 1838, he says that "the tea plant was thriving vigorously in two, and had flowered in three, of the above nurseries;" and in another, dated the 18th of May, he writes—"I have now plants growing at Saharunpore, the produce of seeds from the Koth nursery. This is no contemptible progress. They have not yet got a step further in Assam, with the materials afforded by the tea committee. The tea which has gone home is the leaf of the Assam jungle stock."

Result of experiments in the Himalayas.

Of the replies to the circular of the 3rd March, the most important for its information, and in its consequences, was that of Capt. Jenkins, agent to the Governor-general on the north-eastern frontier, dated 7th May 1834. In this he recommends the district of Assam for the cultivation of tea. He mentions that "the part directly under us ranges from six thousand to eight thousand feet: and that further east the mountains attain a height of ten thousand feet, and the vallies and beds of streams are from two thousand five hundred to four thousand feet above the sea." "Camellias are found in every part of this hill country; and within our jurisdiction, in the Singpho district of Beesa, a coarse variety of the tea plant is, as I am informed, undoubtedly indigenous." He further informs us, that "a plant was given to him at Suddiya, which he had reason to suppose was a genuine tea tree."

Reply of Capt. Jenkins.

Recommends Assam for the Tea culture;

states that a Tea plant is indigenous.

Lieut. Charlton writes, on the 17th May, that

Letter of Lieutenant Charlton on the discovery of the Tea plant in Upper Assam.

he had been informed three years previously of the tea plant growing wild near Bheesa, whence, indeed, he obtained three or four young trees, which he gave to Dr. John Tytler, to be planted in the Government Botanical Garden. But these arrived in a sickly state, were thought to be Camellias, and soon died. Lieutenant C. further writes, that on the Putkoye range of hills, which divide the waters of the Burhampooter from those of the Kuendwan, "the trees are said to grow in abundance, and are described to reach the size of small forest trees or very large shrubs."

Sends seeds and leaves to Calcutta.

On the 8th November, he sent to Calcutta some seeds and leaves of the tea tree of Assam, which were forwarded on the 24th December to the Government by the Tea Committee, who announced that "the tea shrub is beyond all doubt indigenous in Upper Assam, being found there, through an extent of country of one month's march within the Honourable Company's territories, from Suddiya and Beesa to the Chinese frontier province of Yunnan, where the shrub is cultivated for the sake of its leaf."

Assam Tea known in 1826 to Mr. D. Scott.

So far back, however, as 1826, the zealous and ingenious Mr. D. Scott sent from Munnipore, to Mr. G. Swinton, then chief secretary to the India Government, specimens of the leaves of a shrub which he insisted was a real tea. These we find were first discovered by Mr. Bruce, who was then in command at Suddiya. He sent tea seeds and plants to Mr. Scott, having been previously in-

discovered by Mr. Bruce.

formed of their existence by his brother, the late Major Bruce; and he subsequently, in 1833, brought it to the notice of Capt. Jenkins.—(Tea Cultivation in India, p. 91.)

Existence of Tea in Assam known to Major Bruce.

The history of this discovery is instructive, as showing how long facts of the most important nature often remain unnoticed, even among those most interested in the information. If the evidence were not so conclusive, it would hardly be credited as occurring with a commercial people like the English, that Tea and Caoutchouc, should both have so long remained neglected after having been discovered in British India. Nor was there any thing very remarkable in the tea plant being found in Upper Assam; as it is mentioned by some authors as indigenous in the mountains which separate Burma from China.

Remarks on discovery of Tea and Caoutchouc in Assam.

In consequence of this important discovery, a scientific deputation was, at the recommendation of the Tea Committee, sent by the Indian Government, for the investigation of Upper Assam, and for the collecting on the spot the greatest variety of botanical, geological, and other details; as such preliminary information was absolutely necessary before ulterior measures could be successfully taken with regard to the cultivation of the tea shrub of that country. Seldom has a deputation been better qualified for the task it had to perform, as Dr. Wallich was aided by Mr. Griffith, already distinguished as a Botanist, and by Mr M'Clelland, who had paid great attention to, and

A scientific deputation sent to Upper Assam.

Scientific deputation to Upper Assam.

published a work on, the Geology of Kemaon. They were met and accompanied in their visit to the tea localities by Mr. Bruce, who was subsequently appointed Superintendent of the Tea Plantations in Assam.

Description of the Tea and its sites in Upper Assam by Dr. Wallich.

Descriptions have been published by these gentlemen of the several tea tracts which they had at that time an opportunity of examining. These, according to Dr. Wallich, were five in number,—Koojo and Niggroo, among the Singpho, Nuddooa (Noadwar) and Tengrae, in the Muttuck country, and Gubroo, at the foot of the Naga Hills, in the territories of Rajah Purundur Singh. The last, Dr. Wallich supposes, is connected with others to the southward, and with the tea plant originally announced as existing in Munnipore, and this, he says, may have originated from the plant at Hookum, and that all may have "originally travelled from the frontiers of China," where we know that a kind of tea is cultivated in the province of Yunan. Dr. Wallich describes the boundary of these tea tracts as very irregular, and their surface as much undulated; the plants as generally overwhelmed by a thick jungle of shrubs, climbers, &c., and amongst them numerous bamboos, with large trees overtopping the whole. The tea plants, he says, are remarkably healthy and vigorous, and of all ages, between quite young seedlings and tall shrubs of twelve, sixteen, to twenty feet in height, with stems mostly under an inch in diameter,

Supposes it has travelled from China.

and in no instance reaching beyond two inches. When seen in February, almost all the full grown plants had abundance of seed-buds; a few had still some flowers on them. The older foliage was large, and of a fine dark-green colour.

Description of Assam Tea plants by Dr. Wallich.

It was observed that where the forest trees had been felled, the tea plants, by exposure to a sudden excess of light and heat, had the colour of their leaves changed from a dark, to a pale, somewhat yellowish green colour. In many instances, where tea plants had been cut down, vigorous and frequent shoots were observed at the base and top of the stumps that had been left standing on the ground. Dr. Wallich concluded, that though the Assam forests hold out the fairest prospects of being "made to yield a very valuable supply of good and potable tea," yet he suspects that "we shall have to ascend much higher elevations than those where the tea has been hitherto seen in Assam, to meet with localities subject to a decided winter of six weeks or two months' duration, before we can expect to find the more valued and superior sorts of teas, and that it is to such localities that we must chiefly direct our attention in the establishment of our new plantations."—(Papers, Tea Culture in India, pp. 58 and 67.)

Effects of light;

of cutting on Tea plants.

Dr. Wallich's opinion that greater elevation and cold are necessary for the higher flavoured Teas.

Reports by Mr. Bruce.

Mr. Bruce, in his communication 1st October 1836, describes the tea tracts as consisting of little mounds or hillocks of earth, on which large trees had grown, whose roots alone appeared to save them from being washed away. One

Report by Mr. Bruce on Tea of Upper Assam; fondness for water;

thing he observes as worthy of notice, that all the Assam tea grows near water, of which it appears to be very fond, for wherever there is a small stream or jheel, tea is sure to be there. He describes also the results of cutting down the tea plant with the other trees of the forest, when the ground was cleared from weeds and hoed in January for the purpose of sowing rice in February. This came up, ripened, and was cut down; after which, the tea sprung up, and displayed numerous young leaves in March, which had rather a yellowish appearance; but in October the plants had grown from three to ten feet high, and the leaves were of a fine healthy green. Those tea plants which had only been cut down to about four feet from the ground had abundant shoots springing up a little below the part that had been cut, and some of them were full of flower-buds. All those that had been cut on a level with the ground threw out more shoots and leaves than those that had been allowed to remain four feet high. This experiment, though accidental, and to a small extent, Mr. B. concludes, was "quite sufficient to show us that the experiments so long desired (to know whether these trees would grow in the sun or not) have been crowned with the greatest success."

effects of exposure and cutting down.

Completely successful.

Report of Tea Committee.

The Tea Committee report to the Government in January 1837, that "the plant is now found to be much more generally diffused over the Muttuck country than he (Mr. Bruce) had supposed, seven new spots having been brought to

Mr. Bruce's notice during his last trip; and further observation has served fully to establish the expediency of clearing away the jungle, and cutting down the tea trees close to the ground, in order to improve the quality of the foliage. From the new shoots of plants that had been thus treated, Mr. Bruce has prepared five boxes of tea, a sample of which he has forwarded to Capt. Jenkins, for despatch to Calcutta."—(Papers, Tea Cultivation, p. 85.)

Mr. Bruce's reports on Tea plant of Assam.

Tea prepared, and sent to Calcutta.

Mr. Bruce, in his latest account, published in August 1839, in the Journ. Asiatic Society, gives an account of the further discovery of tea tracts, which then amounted to no less than "one hundred and twenty, some of them very extensive, both on the hills, and in the plains." The hills on which tea has been found by Mr. Bruce are the Naga Hills, and those of Gubroo and Tipum. "The flowers of the tea on these hills (Gubroo) are of a pleasant, delicate fragrance, unlike the smell of our other tea plants; but the leaves and fruit appear the same." The tea was described to Mr. B. as having been brought from Munkum to the Tipum Hills, and that the plant was cut down every third year to get the young leaves. On a hill, three hundred feet high behind Jaipore, a tea tract two or three miles in length was found: the trees were in most parts as thick as they could grow, and the tea seeds (smaller than what Mr. Bruce had seen before), fine and fresh, literally covered the ground. This was in the middle of

Tea plant found on the hills in Assam; account of.

Mr. Bruce's reports on Tea plant of Assam hills.

November, and the trees had abundance of fruit and flower on them. One of the largest trees he found to be two cubits in circumference, and full forty cubits in height. The Namsong tract, on the Naga Hills, Mr. B. describes as the largest that has yet been seen, and its extent as not having been yet ascertained.—(Report, p. 8.)

Productiveness of high or low grounds.

"With respect to the tea plant being most productive on high or low ground, I cannot well say, as all our tracts are on the plains; but from what little I have seen of the hill tracts, I should suppose they were not more productive. In China, the hill tracts produce the *best* teas, and they may do the same here." With regard to the tracts in the plains, Mr. Bruce believes they are equally productive, "although if I leaned towards any side with my limited experience, I should say that the low land, such as at Kahung, which is not so low as ever to be inundated by the strongest rise in the river, is the best. The plants seem to love and court moisture, not from stagnant pools, but running streams."

Effects of Sun on Tea plants.

Mr. Bruce further observes, that "the sun has a material effect on the leaves; for as soon as the trees that shade the plants are removed, the leaf, from a fine deep green, begins to turn into a yellowish colour, which it retains for some months, and then again gradually changes to a healthy green, but now becomes thicker, and the plant throws out far more numerous leaves than when in the shade. The more the leaves are plucked, the greater number of them are produced: if the leaves of the first crop were not gathered, you might look in vain for the leaves of the second crop. The tea made from the leaves in the shade is not near so good as that from leaves exposed to the sun. These also are much earlier in season, and give out a less watery liquid when rolled. When the leaves of either are rolled on a sunny day, they emit less of this liquid than on a rainy day. This juice decreases as the season advances. The plants in the sun have flowers and fruit much earlier than those in the shade, and are far more numerous; they have flowers and seeds in July, and fruit in November. The rain also greatly affects the leaves, for some sorts of tea cannot be made on a rainy day. The Chinese dislike gathering leaves on a rainy day for any description of tea, and never will do so, unless necessity requires it. Some pretend to distinguish the teas made on a rainy and on a sunny day, much in the same manner as they can distinguish the shady from the sunny teas—by their inferiority. The season for making tea in Assam generally commences about the middle of March; the second crop in the middle of May; the third crop about the 1st of July; but the time varies according to the rains setting in, sooner or later."—(Report of 1839, pp. 10 and 11.)

Effects on the Tea plant of plucking its leaves; of shade and of sun; of rain.

Teas made on rainy days inferior.

Seasons for making Teas in Assam.

In both the reports which Mr. B. has published valuable details are given respecting the modes of preparation of the different kinds of tea; many

Mr. Bruce on the manufacture of Teas.

of them are dependent on the age of the tea leaves, others on the mode of preparation. He says, that "the leaves of the green tea are not plucked the same as the black, although the tree or plant is one and the same, which has been proved beyond a shadow of doubt; for I am now plucking leaves for both green and black from the same tract and from the same plants; the difference lies in the manufacture, and nothing else." It may be so; but a question which has been so long disputed at Canton, is not likely to be satisfactorily settled, and at once, in Assam. As the question will always occur to every one acquainted with the history of the subject, is this the mode of making the real high-flavoured green tea, or is it that of preparing the substitute which Mr. Reeves describes (p. 264) as yearly made in large quantities in the province of Canton, and in the manufacture of which the people there are such proficients?

Black and green Teas from the same plant.

The real green Tea, or the substitute?

Coloured by indigo and sulphate of lime.

Mr. Bruce briefly states, that "in the latter part of the process a mixture of sulphate of lime and indigo, very finely pulverized, and sifted through fine muslin, in the proportion of three of the former to one of the latter, is added to a pan of tea, containing about seven pounds; about half a tea spoonful of this mixture is put, and rubbed and rolled along with the tea in the pan about one hour." This is not added for the purpose of improving "the flavour of the tea, but merely to give it a uniform colour and appearance, as without it some of the tea would be light and some dark."

The preparation of Green Tea considered.

It does not seem reconcilable with our knowledge of the effects of heat, that increased exposure to high temperature should elicit finer flavour, and more stimulant properties, which we know to be characteristic of green tea. But this would be of no weight in opposition to positive testimony from China. Mr. Bruce's is decisive respecting the mode of manufacturing it in Assam, and seems to be corroborated by reports from India respecting the good quality of the green tea which has been prepared there. In the absence of trustworthy testimony from the green tea district of China, it will propably be possible by means of chemical tests, to detect the difference between the best green tea of China, and that of Assam, if they should be differently prepared. Mr. Reeves' opinion is so positive respecting the substitute prepared at Canton; the leaves of the best green and black teas of commerce are so different from each other; each so like the plant known by its name in this country, and the green is so much more hardy than the black tea plant, that we cannot consider the question decided, and must wait for more positive information than we have yet had, from the green tea district of China.

If Green Tea be coloured artificially, may be detected by chemical tests.

Probabilities against Black and Green Tea being from the same plant.

Mr. M'Clelland on the geology, &c. of Assam.

Mr. M'Clelland has furnished a very valuable report on the geological features and the climate of Assam, as well as minute observations on the chemical analysis of the soils, in which the

Geology of. tea plant was found in a flourishing condition, in the five tracts or patches which were visited by the deputation. Kassia—mountains. In ascending the Kassia mountains, he found, at an elevation of one thousand five hundred feet, the well marked remains of a raised beach, characterized by a deposit of marine tertiary shells. Mountains on the north and south of Assam. The valley of Assam, he represents, is interposed between two distinct systems of mountains. Porphyry, Primitive Limestone, Serpentine, Granite, and Talcose slates, compose the mountains on the northern side of the valley, while Tertiary sandstones, Shell limestones, and Coal, in conjunction with Metamorphosed Gneiss, Green stone, and Syenite, compose the southern group. Breadth of the valley of Assam. The valley contracts towards its outlet, to a breadth of only twenty miles in Lower Assam; but is extended to a breadth of fifty miles in Upper Assam, where it forms an extensive alluvial plain, Upper Assam an alluvial plain; about eighty miles in length, elevated about 650 feet, surrounded by lofty mountains, and watered by four enormous rivers, beside six or seven smaller ones, the least of which is as large as the greatest river in England.

geological structure of, With respect to the formation of Upper Assam, Mr. M'Clelland observes, that the lowest deposit is a reddish yellow clay, which lies in contact with the rocky masses in Lower Assam, forming the surface of that part of the country. A short distance above Bishnath, this clay dips beneath the alluvial deposits. These succeed each other in the following order from below upwards; first, fine clays; second, sandy clay, containing gravel; and thirdly, sand and gravel. Upper Assam.

The climate of Upper Assam is characterized by equability, in consequence of its moisture as well as of its cloudiness in the cold weather. The former diminishing the summer heat, and the latter, combined with the effect of its forest-covered surface, the cold of winter. The wind in Assam is north-east at all seasons, and the whole valley lies in the direction of its current. It would appear, that 82° Fahr. at Suddya is considered as excessive as 96° in Calcutta, while the greatest cold of winter seems to be from 42° to 38°; (but a temperature of 32° and of 92° have been observed. Vide p. 301.) The absence of any season of perfect drought, and an excessively humid atmosphere, are the peculiar features of the climate. Throughout the cold season, dense vapours arise, and form mists, which have a tendency to occupy the south side of the valley. climate of. Range of Thermometer. Moisture.

The observations of Mr. M'Clelland on the soil in which the tea plant is found in Assam are particularly valuable. At the Kujoo tea tract, he describes the soil as "perfectly loose, and sinking under the feet with a certain degree of elasticity, derived from dense meshes of succulent fibres, prolonged in every direction from various roots. Its colour is light gray, perfectly dry and dusty, although the surrounding country was still wet, from the effects of rain that had fallen for several days immediately prior to our visit." He Soil of Tea plant, dry and sandy at Knjoo, soil dry and sandy at Kujoo; further found the peculiarities of the soil disappear with the tea plant itself, beyond the extent of a circular space of about three hundred yards in diameter. At Nigroo, the plants were found to disappear towards the brow of the mound, the soil becoming gray and sandy—"a fact which

less so where drainage more perfect.

first suggested the idea, that where the drainage is more powerful on the summit of an elevation, the plant requires a different soil from that in which it flourishes in low ground." At Gubroo, the elevation is sandy on which the tea plant is found, but it is surrounded with inundation. At

At Tingrai in a dark soil.

Tingrai, the first plants were seen in a dark soil. "The number of young plants found in this soil affords an encouraging instance of the disposition of the plant to accommodate itself to any soil, as far at least as its vegetative powers are concerned." But the plants were found to increase in size and number as they approached the light sandy soil.

Upper Assam Tea soil.

In the analysis of the soils, Mr. M'Clelland found that at Kujoo, the tea soil in the state in which it exists in nature contained only $18\frac{1}{2}$ per cent., while the common soil contained 26 per cent. of water. The Kujoo tea soil contained in 200 parts — water, 37; fresh fibres, 1; vegetable

Chemical analysis of

matter, $5\frac{1}{2}$; silex, 135; alumina, 11; oxide of iron, $4\frac{1}{3}$. The black soil contained less silex, and more water and vegetable matter; some of the latter was in the form of extractive, which "operates by affording coherency and solidity to the surface, while a portion of the vegetable matter, united with the extractive, assists in retaining moisture at the surface." Where the vegetable matter is greatest, alumina, the common absorbent principle of soils, is least, and the quantity of alumina is also in proportion to the degree of insulation of the soil with regard to moisture, and the greater drainage to which it is exposed: whence Mr. M'C. concludes that "the narrowest inference we can draw from this is, that the same soil would not be suitable to the plant in every situation." Upper Assam Tea soil.

An examination of some soil in which the tea plant is cultivated in China, yielded in 200 parts —of silex, 135; alumina, 36; carbonate of magnesia, 6; carbonate of lime, 4; oxide of iron, 13; roots and fibres of plants, 2; water of absorption, 4. But in the recent state, this soil no doubt contained a larger proportion of water. Tea soil from China.

In conclusion, Mr. M'Clelland observes, with respect to the soils and situations, that the tea plant is found in Assam, first, on the level plain, and second, on mounds somewhat raised above the plain.* The first situations are distinguished from the rest of the plain by a porous structure, and the peculiar character of maintaining a dry surface under exposure to excessive moisture; the second, by a structure less porous than the first. In both, the plants are situated above the range of inundations which prevail during the greater portion of the year on the adjoining lands. Soils and situations of Tea plant in Upper Assam.

---

* Since then many localities of the tea plant have been discovered by Mr. Bruce on the hills in Upper Assam, *vide* p. 285.

Sites secured from excess of moisture by their porous nature.

"The important peculiarity of these sites is, that they are less secure from inundations by their elevations than by their structure. Indeed, the lower sites are scarcely raised more than a yard above the adjoining flat plains, which are exposed to inundations, not merely during falls of rain, but also from the overflowings of the great rivers. But these circumstances, which are sources of fertility to the adjoining lands, appear to produce an opposite effect on the sites of the tea plant, thus causing the peculiar condition on which the presence of the plant in some measure depends. Protected in Assam under the shades of dense forests, and a gloomy and excessively humid atmosphere, the tea plant flourishes in its barren soil along the verge of rivers, lakes, and marshy lands."

Tea plant found in a barren soil and moist climate.

Mr. Griffith's report.

Mr. Griffith has also published a valuable report on the tea plant of Upper Assam*, in which the movements of the Deputation, the enume-

---

* Transactions Agricultural Society of Calcutta, vol. v., p. xcvi., 1838 Mr. G. has also published several profound papers on the structure of different families of plants in the Transactions of the Asiatic and Linnean Societies, and will, no doubt, enrich science with many more. The Herbarium collected by him in his different journies on which he has been employed by the Indian Government since 1836 has arrived at the India House in excellent order. The collections are—from the Khasiya Mountains, 1,756 species, Assam, 1,763, Mishmee Mountains, 1,186, Bootan, 1,595, Naga Mountains and Burma 1,200; in all, 7,500 species. But Mr. G. states that the amount will have to be considerably reduced when a general catalogue of the whole is formed.

ration of the Tea localities, and the appearance of the Tea plants are described. Comparisons are also made on the Vegetation associated with the tea plant in Assam and in China, as well as between the climate of Upper Assam and that of the tea provinces of Central China. Many of the observations are necessarily the same in the several reports, as the different observers describe the same things at the same time. But we find a difference in their opinions respecting the localities of the tea plant in China, and consequently as to what situations are best suited to the tea culture in India. Dr. Wallich, as we have seen, (p. 283) considers higher elevations to be necessary in Assam for the cultivation of the superior kinds of tea. Mr. Bruce, from the results of his experience, advocates greater exposure to light and sun, which will necessarily subject the plants to greater vicissitudes of temperature. For open places we know are warmer in summer from the unchecked absorption of the solar rays, while they are colder in winter from the more free radiation. This is checked in shady situations and cloudy nights, and therefore the cold is not so great.

Mr. Griffith's report.

Difference of opinion among observers in Assam respecting best sites for Tea culture.

Dr. Wallich recommends greater elevation.

Mr. Bruce advocates exposure to light and sun.

It is unfortunate that we have so little positive information respecting the principal tea tracts of China, and are unacquainted with the nature of their localities, their climate and the vegetation associated with the tea plant. Mr. M'Clelland considers the notions erroneous regarding the mountain habit of the plant; and Mr. Griffith

Messrs. M'Clelland and Griffith consider the opinion erroneous re-

specting the mountain habit of the Tea plant.

says, p. 52, that "all the evidence points out the visionary nature of the views of the aptitude of the Himalayas, &c. for the cultivation of the tea plant;" though at p. 83 he also states, "that the tea plant may succeed in certain portions of the Himalayas is probable enough." If it did not require more time and space than can be spared on the present occasion, it would be curious to trace how these views, if erroneous, should have been entertained by all those who have written on the subject, previous to these two gentlemen, and how so many botanists, without any communication with one another, should have recommended the same part of the Himalayas for the culture of tea. Also why Dr. Abel, after passing through China, should say, "it appears from every account given of the tea plant, that it succeeds best on the sides of mountains, where there can be but little accumulation of vegetable mould;" and why he should have recommended "Table Mountain at the Cape of Good Hope as a particularly eligible situation."

Most Botanists have recommended the Himalayas.

Dr. Abel recommended Table mountain for the culture of Tea.

Extent of distribution of Tea plant.

If we contemplate the extent over which tea is cultivated, we see with Mr. Griffith that "it grows in great abundance in Cochin-China, between 10° and 16° of N. lat.," and that Mr. M'Clelland admits that it is indigenous over 28° of latitude. "But in order to avoid exaggeration, I will confine my observations (he says) to the limits within which it is known to be cultivated with success, that is, from Fokien in 24° N. lat. to Meaco in the Isles of Japan, in about 35° N. lat." Mr. Reeves has, however, informed the Author that the most northern place at which tea is cultivated in China is Tang-chow-Foo, in 36° 30′ N. lat. These extreme limits, Mr. G. considers "only interesting, as pointing out the hardy nature of the plant;" while Mr. M'C. says, "we may suppose temperature to have little influence on its distribution." The Tea being thus cultivated over so great an extent of territory, must necessarily be able to bear considerable vicissitudes of temperature, and probably also of moisture. It is not remarkable, therefore, that flourishing in 10° and 36° of latitude, it should also be found intermediately in low and comparatively moist situations, and that it should be seen only in such, by British embassies travelling along Chinese canals. This has, however, been long well known, and eight years before the tea deputation visited Assam, the Author had stated that the tea plant delights in "sheltered vallies, the declivities of hills and the banks of rivers." (Vide p. 258.) That it may also succeed on the mountains of the same latitudes is not more remarkable; for if it is capable of bearing the extremes of temperature of still more northern plains, such as 36°, it will very easily be able to bear those of moderate elevations in lower latitudes, such as from 24° to 31°. On these the range of the thermometer will be found to be less than in the plains at their base, for the cold of winter is not in proportion to the

Distribution of Tea plant.

Able to withstand heat and cold,

may therefore be found in low and moist situations.

Tea plant may also be found on mountains.

Tea plant of China.

coolness of summer, as the Author has endeavoured briefly to show in his Observations on the Meteorology of the Plains and Mountains of North-western India, in "Illustrations of Himalayan Botany," p. xxx.

Found on mountains by Dr. Abel and Mr. Cunningham.

That the tea plant is found on mountains as well as in plains in China, there can be no doubt, as all the accounts we have concur in placing the tea districts in the midst of hills; and though Dr. Abel may not have seen the tea plant in all the situations he has mentioned in his book, yet he seems only to have adhered to the general impression on the subject when he ascribed hilly situations as most favourable to its culture; and at See-chow, about 26° N. lat., where he did see it, it was on hills which were covered with pines. Mr. Cunningham, the only other botanist who has given us his personal testimony on the subject, states, that it delights "summitatibus montium," in 30° N. lat. So the information obtained by Mr. Reeves, also by Mr. Gordon from Mr. Daniell and others, all point to hills and hilly situations. Mr. Gordon himself visited the Ankoy tea hills, where he found it on the top and sides of some that are seven hundred feet high; and attempted unsuccessfully to reach the Bohea tea hills. But in Assam itself the tea plant has been found to a great extent on the hills of Naga, Gubroo, and Tipum since the tea deputation left the country. (Vide p. 285.)

Information obtained by Mr. Reeves, Mr. Gordon, &c.

No one has attempted to assign the elevation at

which the tea is, or may be, cultivated in China, for we have no positive information on the subject. But it has been argued, and argued justly, that the hilly districts are alone suited to its culture in India. Assam itself is one of the vallies included within these mountains, and partaking as much of their characteristic climate, as of that of the plains. (Vide p. 302.) Hills of even moderate elevation offer certain peculiarities, which may or may not be suited to particular plants. They present diminished temperature in proportion to their elevation; with a moderate degree of equability. There is a certain degree of moisture, in consequence of the more frequent showers of rain, accompanied with more free drainage, and usually greater poverty of soil than on flat plains. There is exposure to the sun and light, and more free circulation of air, which though they may restrain the plant shooting up, as in Assam, yet will favour the production of finer flavoured leaves. Mr. M'Clelland has thought that the moisture of many of the situations in China may be useful, from the equalizing effects of water on temperature. If so, it will be found that being surrounded by the atmosphere, is fully as effectual, and will therefore be equally beneficial.

Height of Chinese mountains unknown.

Peculiarities of climate on hills.

The most important consideration with respect to the sites which have been recommended for the cultivation of tea, is not, what is the latitude or the elevation, but what is the climate, including temperature and moisture, of these

The climate of sites recommended for Tea culture,

The climate of sites recommended for Tea culture.

situations, and what the vegetation they support. As we have no precise information on these points respecting the tea districts of China, the method was adopted of taking Pekin and Canton as extreme points, and drawing inferences from these and the few facts we possess, respecting the climate and vegetation of the tea districts, by the passage near them of the British embassies. But as this method is liable to the objection that different writers have come to different and almost opposite conclusions, we may for the present take the climate of Assam where the tea-plant has actually been found growing, and compare this with that of some of the situations where it was recommended that tea should be cultivated, before it was known that it existed in Upper Assam.

compared with that of Upper Assam.

Tea districts of China.

The principal tea districts of China are situated between the parallels of 27° and 31° N. lat.

Tea district of Assam.

The tea district of Upper Assam is scarcely a degree of latitude in breadth, and is situated between 26° 45′ and 27° 35′ N. lat. (Griffith, p. 45). The tract recommended by the author included the British territories in the Himalayas from 28° to 31½° of N. latitude; so that there is identity of latitude with the tea districts of China, and no great excess over that of Upper Assam. As so much was inferred, rather than known, respecting the physical condition of the tea plant in China, no precise locality was dogmatically fixed upon within the above tract; but several were pointed out, be-

British Himalayas from 28° to 31½° N. lat.

cause experiments might be conveniently made in them, in consequence of the vicinity of European stations.

Sites pointed out within the Himalayas.

Of the situations pointed out, Bheemtal, Hawulbagh, Deyra Doon, and Pinjore were in vallies. Almora, Jurreepanee, Nahn, and Sabathoo, at elevations of from four thousand to five thousand feet, and one locality, Mussooree, where the nursery of the Saharunpore Garden is established, at six thousand five hundred of elevation, in 30° of N. latitude. It might be thought desirable to have mentioned some places in the plains, but the Botanic Garden was too obvious to be included in the above enumeration, as had any one who had charge of the experiment in the hills, omitted sending seeds or plants, Dr. Falconer is too zealous to have omitted applying for them. But those who are acquainted with the great heat, dry atmosphere, and hot winds of the plains of India, will perceive it would be hopeless without the aid of copious irrigation to grow the tea-plant in them. The above localities were pointed out, as enabling the advantages of various elevations to be ascertained, though the author was of opinion that an elevation of about five thousand feet, as at Jurreepanee, (*running water*) was most desirable.

Plains too hot and dry for Tea culture.

Neither time nor space permit that we compare the climate of all these localities with that of Upper Assam. But to give the objectors the full advantage of the argument, we will compare the extremes of temperature observed in Upper

The climate of the highest, and therefore the coldest, of these sites compared with that of Upper Assam.

Assam, with those of the most elevated, and therefore the coldest of the positions pointed out by the author. The observations on the Mussooree range during several years, give a range of the thermometer of 53° from a maximum of 80° to a minimum of 27°, giving a mean of 53°·5, which is 3°·5 lower than 57°·04, the mean temperature deduced from all the observations. How much higher is the mean temperature at Nankin?

Climate of Upper Assam.

The greatest degree of cold which has been recorded at Suddya was by Major White, who observed it on one occasion, at 6 A. M., to be so low as 32°. On another occasion it fell to 37°, but 42° is not uncommon. The highest range during the hot months was 92°, in 1836. At Gowahatty it was never observed above 90° by Captain Jenkins, (Griffith, p. 47). Taking the extremes, we have an annual range of the thermometer of 60°, which is 7° more than that at Mussoorree; the mean is 62°, which is 5°·2 less than the mean 67°·2 of all the observations, which is only 10° higher than at Mussooree.

Temperatures of Suddya, Canton, Deyra, and Mussooree compared.

Mr. Griffith has compared the mean annual temperature, as well as that of the four warmest, and of the four coldest months of Suddya and of Canton, which is about 4½° more to the Southward. To the means which he has adduced, we add similar ones for Deyra and Mussooree, in 30° of N. latitude; the former elevated about two thousand, and the latter six thousand five hundred feet. The climate of Jureepanee, elevated five thousand feet, and midway between the two, and which the author thought eligible for the experiment, as well as easily accessible, may be inferred from that of the upper and lower stations. Temperatures of Suddya, Canton, Deyra, and Mussooree compared.

	Canton.	Suddya.	Deyra.	Mussooree.
Mean Annual Temperature	70	67.2	70.65	57.04
„ of four hottest months	82.2	80	82.75	66.72
„ of four coldest months	54	57.8	56.45	45.45

If the object had been to find a climate similar to that of Canton, N. lat. 23° 8′, we could hardly have found any thing to correspond with it more closely than does that of Deyra, compared, at least, in this method. But the author was well aware that it was absolutely necessary for all purposes of culture to give the extremes, as well as the means of temperature, as one night's frost, or a few days of hot winds, might destroy the labours of a year of careful cultivation. Canton is some degrees south of the principal tea districts, and yet the minimum of the thermometer there is 29°, or 3° below the freezing point. If we suppose the rate of diminution of temperature to be equal to what takes place in the cold weather in India, we should have it sometimes several degrees below 29°, in N. lat. 31°, or 8° further north. But we have every reason to believe that the whole of the coast of China, like that of North America, participates, in degree, in what is so strikingly characteristic of the northern parts of China, that is, a climate strongly contrasted, or where there are hot sum- Deyra most like that of Canton. Canton, cold of. Cold of China in winter.

Cold of Canton in comparison with that of Calcutta.

mers with very cold winters. That this characteristic extends even as far south as Canton is evident, if we compare its minimum 29° with that of Calcutta, 56° ·8, which is only a degree to the southward, and yet we have a difference in their lowest temperatures of 27° ·8. In such a country, therefore, there is nothing incredible in there being frost in 31° of latitude, as there is in the plains of India in winter. Also, as there is, no doubt, a good deal of moisture, that this should occasionally descend in the form of snow. That this indeed is the case, we have the united testimony of several accounts, which state that snow storms occur in the green tea districts, and this we can easily believe, from the cold which that plant is capable of withstanding in this country even as far north as Forfar.

Humidity of Mountain climate.

Next to temperature, and, perhaps, equally important, is the humidity of the climate of the mountains. In this it might be thought by those unacquainted with the Himalayas that there would be some deficiency. But the author, when writing upon the subject, thought that its excess would be the chief point of difficulty, He was satisfied only after considering that the baneful effects of excessive moisture would be less felt, where evaporation was favoured by the rarity of the atmosphere: also after ascertaining that rain was frequent in Canton, and extended to the tea districts, especially of Fokien.

Assam may be considered as enjoying the

maximum of humidity. The rains are of long continuance; they commence in March, and last till about the middle of October. November and January are the only months throughout the year on which tolerable reliance can be placed for a continuance of fine weather, as rain always falls about the middle of December (Griffith, p.49). Moisture of Assam.

Contrast this with what Dr. Falconer wrote, respecting the Himalayan climate, long before the tea deputation reached Assam: "The climate of the Himalayas is decidedly damp," and "as a general fact it may be stated, what with rain, snow, and dew, that moisture, in one shape or other, falls abundantly every unclouded day during the year; and the cloudy days without rain do not amount to a week in the year," (Tea Report, p. 25). We have no data concerning the humidity of the tea districts of China, but Mr. M'Clelland has shown the great probability of there being considerable humidity in some of them, and that this may in some degree modify the temperature. Moisture of Himalayas.

The vegetation of the Himalayas was compared by the author with that of China, as far as materials were procurable. The same has been done by Mr. Griffith with regard to that of Upper Assam. The vegetation is, no doubt, chiefly tropical, all along the base of the Himalayas from Assam to the Deyra Doon. Mr. Griffith states that neither latitude nor elevation account for the northern forms in Assam. But the moisture and equability of the climate seem to explain this Comparison of the vegetation of the Himalayas, and of Upper Assam with that of China.

Climate of Assam moist and equable, supports a variety of vegetable forms.

satisfactorily. The valley being surrounded by mountains, and covered with dense forests, watered by large rivers, and also kept damp by numerous showers, as well as by the cloudiness of the atmosphere, resembles, in a great measure, to compare great things with small, Mr. Ward's mode of growing plants in glass cases, in which we may often see both Tropical and European plants growing nearly equally well in the same case. To the climate, therefore, it is probably owing that many of the peculiar genera and species of the Himalayas and of China are found in Assam, in the forest-covered vallies, but which in the Himalayas can only exist, especially in the northern parts, at considerable elevations; in consequence of the heat and dryness of the vallies there at some seasons of the year.

Northern vallies hot and dry.

Assam more moist than Tea districts of China.

The climate of Assam in the uncleared parts is undoubtedly much more moist than that of the tea districts of China, as is evident from the great height which many of the Tea plants attain, having slender stems, of often forty to fifty feet, with leaves four to eight inches in length. The China tea makers expressed their astonishment on seeing them. Mr. Bruce describes the great difference, by stating, "that our trees or plants are certainly more than four or five times the size of theirs, and must consequently yield so many times more produce—theirs is the dwarf, ours the giant tea." The Chinamen, moreover, on seeing the plants which

Tea plants of Assam much larger than those of China.

had been produced from Chinese seeds, " declared that the China plants now at Deenjoy would never have attained half the perfection they now have, under ten years in their own country." Even in Assam those growing on hills attain less height, as even the kind found originally at Gubroo, though only on a hillock forty or fifty feet high, "exists only as a moderate sized shrub, and was hence pointed out as a new variety, and was even dignified with the name of dwarf tea." Those obtained from the Nigroo Hill tracts, Mr. Bruce thinks will never attain any size, but be dwarfish like the China plants; but it is probable that if they were planted in the shady tea tracts of the Assam plains, they would attain the same height as the others, as their difference in size probably depends upon the influence of physical agents. That excessive moisture, both of soil and atmosphere, is not suitable, is evident by the preference the Tea plant has for sandy and porous soil, and for mounds in the moist climate of Assam, but which would probably not be requisite in a drier climate.

Great size of China Tea plants in Assam.

Assam Tea smaller on hills.

The foregoing examination of the habits of the tea plant in Upper Assam, and of the peculiarities of the climate and vegetation of that province, and of the Himalayas, show the resemblance of both in these points to the tea districts of China. Whether this is to the extent desirable, can only be ascertained when we have positive information from thence. But it might be said that things

Comparison of Upper Assam with Himalayas.

Resemblance between climate of Upper Assam and that of mid region of Himalayas.

which are equal to the same thing, are equal to one another. The mid region of the Himalayas and Upper Assam differ much less than might have been anticipated, considering that the one has an open and the other a close climate, and from the difference in latitude and elevation. From the heat and dryness of the plains and vallies of north-western India, from March to the middle of June, the influence of the hot winds extends much higher than in more southern latitudes; where, in fact, they are absent even from the plains. Hence we have to ascend above their utmost limits to obtain a cool climate and congenial moisture; or where "the air, charged with moisture in the heated vallies, in rising may deposit it on the mountains, when it reaches an elevation where it is cooled below the point of saturation."

Tea from Assam.

Tea, however, it is now well known has been manufactured of a good and sound quality from the tea plants of Assam; and it has been very favourably reported on by experienced judges in this country. From the great curiosity which was excited on the subject, it, however, sold at such high prices, that it is difficult to form a very correct judgment on its true value when compared with the teas of China. The Court of Directors and the Government of India having brought this important experiment to so successful an issue, have handed over its further extension to a private company, who will no doubt carry it forward with the requisite vigour, and we

The culture taken up by the Assam Company.

shall see Assam tea imported in large quantities into this country, and as the requisites for the culture of the plant are better understood, of a still higher flavour. *Tea culture in Upper Assam.*

From the facts we have enumerated, there is, however, no necessity that the tea culture should be restricted to the province of Assam. A tea plant has for many years lived in the open air in Nepal, and Dr. Falconer, who has had to carry the experiment into execution, so far from objecting, had, like the Author, formed an opinion that Tea could be cultivated in the Himalayas. He has in fact, already, at elevations of five thousand feet, obtained seedlings (*vide* p. 279) from the Chinese plants which were introduced into the Gurhwal and Sirmore nurseries. Those of Kemaon have also been placed under his charge. We might wait patiently, therefore, for the result of the experiments; but as he has expressed his confidence in the success of the culture in these northern parts of the Himalayas, several hundred miles from Upper Assam, and that of the Author remains undiminished, we may confidently look forward to having tea cultivated all along these mountains. Thus affording profitable employment to the inhabitants, and to them as well as to the dwellers in the plains, the means of obtaining a cheap and refreshing beverage, which they already highly esteem; and by this means giving an impulse to the Commerce and Agriculture both of the Plains and of the Mountains. *Tea may also be cultivated all along the Himalayas.*

The Committee of the House of Lords on the Tea culture in India.

The Court of Directors of the East-India Company will have the high gratification of having fostered in its infancy a culture which in its maturity will benefit to an incalculable extent the country and people committed to their charge, or as the Committee of the House of Lords on the petition of the East-India Company for relief express it, "The Government of India appear to have exercised a sound discretion in giving facilities to an experiment which, if successful, would make an important addition to the commercial resources of India, and confer a national benefit upon the consumers of tea in the United Kingdom." —2d March 1840.*

* The deductions derivable from the Botany of the Himalayas, of Upper Assam, and of China, though omitted in the foregoing observations, are not less important. Mr. Griffith has united Thea with the genus Camellia, and there is no good reason for keeping them separate. With regard to the Green, Black, and Assam Tea plants being distinct species or permament varieties of one species, it is impossible to give a decided opinion. The Assam Tea plant may be seen in Messrs. Loddiges' hot houses, and the others in their green houses, or in the open air in summer. The author was disposed to consider the Green and Black Teas as distinct species, and has not yet seen sufficient to change his opinion. The Assam Tea plant resembles the Green Tea in the size and form of its leaves, but they are thicker, and darker coloured. They are very much larger than the leaves of the Tea plant collected by Mr. Cunningham in China. (Vide p. 266.) The question can only be decided by those competent to the task in China, or by submitting the plants known as such to experiment in

the tea nurseries of Assam and the Himalayas. Of the genera of Ternstrœmiaceæ, to which the Camellias and Tea belong, Cochlospermum is found on the Hills of the Sewalic range. A Saurauja is found at the foot, and Eurya at the top of the Mussoree range. Cleyera is found in Nepal and the Khasiya range. The Camellias are found on the Khasiya and Naga hills, in the vallies and hills of Assam, and extend to Nepal, where C. Kissi is found at 4,600 feet of elevation. It is remarkable that so many genera and species, which are characteristic of the flora of China, and which were found by the Author at 6,500 feet of elevation, in 30° of N. lat., occur in Assam in the valley. These are Eurya, Stauntonia, Kadsura, or Sphœrostemma, and Hovenia; so also of genera more generally diffused, Coriaria, Cerasus, one of the Chrysobalaneæ, and Sabia, Lonicera, Viburnum, Sambucus, Æsculus, Engelhardtia, and Oaks. The other genera characteristic of China mentioned by the Author, as found all along the Himalayas, (Illustrations, p. 123, &c.), are Deutzia, Abelia, Marlea, Houttuynia, Chloranthus, Incarvillea, Hiptage, Euphoria, and Pardanthus. Illicium and Goniocarpus have been found by Mr. Griffith, the former on the Khasiya Hills at five thousand feet in shady, damp places, and the latter at Churia Pungee. Salamonia also has been found on the Khasiya Hills and the Tenasserim Coast, as well in Nepal, and about Canton. Hammamelideæ, widely diffused, were found in China by Dr. Abel, and by Mr. Griffith in Assam, Khasiya, and Mishmee Hills; but a species has also been found by Dr. Falconer, as far north as Cashmere. The botanical results confirm those deduced from the climate, that the tea plant may be cultivated as well in the mid region of the Himalayas, as in Upper Assam. The growth will no doubt be more slow, but the leaves will probably not be less high flavoured.

Cultivation of Cotton in India.

Cotton, a Native of India,

Cotton, we have seen, p.75, has been produced in India from the most remote antiquity; that it is naturally of a good quality is evident from the fine muslins which were manufactured with it, as well as from the durability of the Indian cotton piece-goods, now driven out of the markets, not only of Europe but even of India itself, by the cheaper manufactures of English cotton mills.

also of America,

Cotton is also a natural product of America; it has been found in the ancient Peruvian tombs, together with specimens of their early manufactures. That American cotton is also of excellent quality is evident from the high prices which it sells for in the English market; at the same time that the Indian cotton brings only very inferior prices, notwithstanding that the Indian manufacturer is able to prepare with it such superior fabrics.

Faults of Indian Cotton.

The chief faults of the Indian cotton are great carelessness in collection, and shortness of staple, in consequence of very imperfect culture. By this carelessness, from the quantity of dirt which is allowed to intermix with it, it is presented to the manufacturer in a less perfect state than that in which it was produced. There is reason also to believe that the cotton itself deteriorates in quality from the imperfect drying it receives, after being collected. The imperfect culture allowing the plants to run too much into stalk and leaf, and thus diminishing the supply of sap to the flowers and seeds, consequently curtails, not only the quantity of cotton, but also the length and strength of its staple. Thus everything combines to diminish the value of the produce, as well as its quantity per acre, and to keep down the profits of the planter. Indian Cotton, defects in its culture.

Localities of commercial Cottons. The cottons which bring the highest prices in the market are produced over a wide expanse of territory, in different parts of the world, from 0° to 34°, and in particular situations, even to 40° of latitude; and also in the mountains of South America and of Mexico at considerable elevations.

Extent of British India and sites suited to Cotton. The British territories in India, extending from 8° to 31° of north latitude, and including the loftiest mountains in the world, afford every diversity of soil and climate that is attainable elsewhere. In fact, cotton is produced in every part of British India, and complaint is made more against the mode in which it is brought to market than against the cotton itself.

Difference of Soil suited to the growth of Cotton. The soils in which the best cottons grow differ much more both in physical and chemical nature than is generally supposed. This is evident if we examine the soil of the Sea-Island cotton, and compare it with that of the sandy cotton farms of Georgia; or both with the rich alluvial deposits of the Mississippi, or the prairie lands of Southern Alabama. The difference is not greater, however, than that which we observe be-

Cotton Soils. tween the granite soil of the Coromandel coast and the black cotton soil of central India, or than that between the rich alluvium of Bengal and the sandy plains of North-western India.

Climate of India suited to growth of Cotton. The climate of India is congenial throughout to the growth of cotton. In the most northern provinces, frost sometimes destroys the young branches before the whole of the crop of cotton has been collected, but this is useful to some of the species as a kind of natural pruning.

Temperature. Moisture. The temperature being sufficient, the next most important consideration is the degree of moisture, both of the soil and of the atmosphere; as on this, in a congenial soil and climate, will depend the more or less rapid development of the stems, branches, and leaves, and, if not carried to excess, an healthy state of the plant for the abundant production of flowers and of fruit, as well as of cotton.

Difficulties of Culture. Too great richness of the soil, combined with extreme moisture of the atmosphere, are frequently in excess in India. The season of cultivation is during the rains, and the methods consisting in a mixture of crops, close sowing, and unchecked growth of the plant, all assist in developing leaves instead of flowers.

Why is not better Cotton grown in India? The soil and climate of so large a tract of country being favourable to the growth of a plant, which is indeed indigenous in the country, it does appear unaccoutable why the cotton of Indian growth should be so low in esteem. Also if the circumstances are so favourable, why, it may be asked, is not better cotton grown? We see it is obviously the interest of the planter to improve an article, for the production of which the extra expense and labour will bear but a small proportion to the increased produce, and to the high price which it will bring.

Why is not better Cotton grown in India?

Various causes have been assigned for this; some are not true, others are contradictory, and the whole combined to the extent assumed, would have some effect, but are quite insufficient to account for the continued inferiority of Indian cotton, and the slight effect produced by the experiments instituted for its improvement. The native cultivators, cramped by the usurious rates of money-lenders, are satisfied with the culture taught them by their forefathers, and have too little knowledge of the results which would follow from any change in the practice, to adopt others, with the sacrifice of their prejudices.

Causes assigned.

Natives satisfied with the present culture.

Few Europeans until lately have attempted the culture of cotton, probably because indigo and other products offered them more profitable employment. The merchants have found that the cotton of India would be bought both in China and England, and yield a profit without the risk of making larger advances on an uncertain result. The planters in the interior have thus had little encouragement to bestow extra labour and expense, on improving a produce which they find the buyers at the Presidencies only purchase

Few Europeans have attempted to improve it.

Planters have received little encouragement from merchants

at the ordinary prices of that which, though inferior, is at the same time produced by the natives at less expense. Yet considerable results have been obtained in the Bengal Presidency, chiefly by the energy of amateur experimentalists, and in Bombay and Madras by the Government farms.

Results produced by Government cotton farms.

Experimentalists often ignorant of practice and inattentive to principles.

In the experiments which have been instituted on the improvement of the culture, it is extraordinary to observe how little attention has been paid, or, at least, how little information is given us respecting the attention that was paid, to all the points essential to insure success in culture and improvement in produce. Also, how seldom any attempts are made, or reasons given, to explain the causes of failure. We find, as was to be expected, a general want of knowledge in the practical details of culture, but also, which was not to be expected, equal inattention to, if not ignorance of, principles. The majority also appear wise only after personal experience, and paying little attention to that of their predecessors. For we find that the same course is followed, the same faults are committed, the same results are obtained and continue to be announced as new, though we have had them on record for a series of years.

Plants, living bodies influenced by physical agents.

It seems to be forgotten, that plants are living bodies, influenced by the media in which they are placed; having their roots in the soil, and their leaves in the atmosphere, taking in watery fluid holding various substances in solution by the one, and both absorbing and giving off aqueous vapour and gaseous elements by the other. Growing also more or less vigorously, and producing better or inferior seeds or fruit, according as they are affected by the richness or poverty, moisture or dryness, warmth or coldness, of the medium in which they are placed, as well as by the influence of light and the action of the atmosphere.

Plants influenced by physical agents.

In the animal kingdom it is considered essential for those who have to recommend measures for the preservation of the health, or for the treatment of the diseases of man, that they should study both the structure and the functions of animals in general, and of the species in particular, as well as the peculiarities of constitution in the individual. Plants are equally living beings, and equally require attention, both to principles and to practice, in their treatment, whether we wish to ascertain how they will succeed in a new soil or situation, or how we are to remedy any defects which are produced. Also what measures are to be adopted, when we wish to increase the size or particular qualities of the parts of vegetation, that is, what refers to the individual; or what should be done, when we desire only the perfection of the seed and fruit, which, we know, are required for the propagation of the species.

Treatment of animals requires knowledge of structure and of functions.

Equally necessary with plants.

As the Author endeavoured to grow cotton, though on a small scale, in the Saharunpore Botanic Garden, paying attention at the same

Experiments on culture of Cotton.

time to the practices of the natives, he early conceived that the chief causes of failure were of a physical nature; and that the culture was to be remedied only by attention to principles. These he endeavoured to elucidate in an Essay on the Culture of Cotton in India;* where, after noticing the native country and early history of cotton, as well as the various places in which it is at present cultivated, both in respect to latitude and climate, he compared these with the extent and varied climate of British India. He then examined into the influence of physical agents as affecting the production of cotton; and first conceived, that the chief faults in India had been over-production of the parts of vegetation at the expense of those of fructification. The Author at the same time recommended particular attention to the selection of seed, not only of that which is foreign, but also of that which is indigenous; and after noticing the principal kinds of cotton cultivated in America, those of India were similarly enumerated. The culture in America was compared with that practised in India, and the results of some of the experiments, which had then been made known on the Indian cultivation of American cottons were referred to. The improvement of the indigenous cottons was recommended, and the parts of the Bengal presi-

Essay on the culture of Cotton.

Over-production of parts of vegetation.

* Published in June 1834, in his "Illustrations of the Botany, &c., of the Himalayan Mountains."

dency best suited to the culture of cotton were pointed out, that is, the banks of the Jumna between Agra and Allahabad, with Bundlecund above the Ghauts and Malwa. He came to the conclusion that there could be "no doubt that by the importation of foreign and the selection of native seed, attention to the peculiarities not only of soil, but also of climate, as regards the course of the seasons, and the temperature, dryness, and moisture of the atmosphere, as well as attention to the mode of cultivation; such as preparing the soil, sowing in lines, so as to facilitate the circulation of air, weeding, ascertaining whether the mixture of other crops with the cotton be injurious or otherwise, pruning, picking the cotton as it ripens and keeping it clean: great improvement must take place in the quality of the cotton."

Parts of N. W. India suited to culture of Cotton.

Conclusion of the author that good Cotton might be cultivated in India.

We have already seen, p. 81, that the attention of the Court of Directors of the East-India Company was turned, at as early a period as 1788, to the improved cultivation of cotton in India, and that measures were adopted, apparently well calculated, to insure the object in view, as these consisted, in the first place, in obtaining reports from India on the state of the culture and commerce of cotton in the different provinces of that country. Subsequently, instructions were sent out for the culture of cotton, as well as seeds of the West-Indian and American cotton, and machines for cleaning it. A cotton farm was established, and rewards offered for improved speci-

Means adopted by the Court of Directors of the East-India Company to improve the culture of cotton.

Reports required.

Instructions sent out.

American seeds.

Cleaning machines.

Measures adopted by the Court of Directors for improving the culture of Cotton in India.

Cotton Farm established in 1794.

mens of cotton. In the "Report of the Proceedings of the East-India Company in regard to the production of Cotton in India," published in 1836, we have a detail of the measures which have been continued to be taken from the above time to the date of the publication; many of these have been and are briefly noticed in the following pages, under the heads of the Presidencies where they were undertaken, consisting, with the repetition of some of the previous measures, in the sending, in 1813, of a person experienced in the cleaning of cotton from America to India, and of the establishment of Cotton farms in 1818.

American cleaner of Cotton sent to India.

Cotton Farms established in 1818.

A general view of the measures adopted is taken in the letter from the Secretary to the Court of Directors, (Reports, p. 117), dated 5th September 1828. Lord Ellenborough, then President of the Board of Control, suggested, on the 7th October 1828, "the cultivation of all the finer sorts of foreign cotton in different and distant parts of India, under very different circumstances of soil and climate, and of transmitting to England, cleaned in the American manner, and with every precaution to protect them from the weather, samples of the cotton so raised, for the purpose of comparison with the cottons of other countries."

Suggestion of Lord Ellenborough.

Propositions of Mr. Tucker.

On the 17th November following, a comprehensive view of the whole question of the supply of cotton from British India was taken by H. St. George Tucker, Esq., a member of the Court of Directors, in which, among other propositions, ten in number, it was suggested, that "two or more plantations, on a large scale, should be established, and that persons acquainted with the mode of cultivating cotton in America should be sent out to India to manage the experimental farms," *v*. p. 29.

Propositions of Mr. Tucker.

Capt. Bayles of the Indian army having carefully considered the subject, offered his services, and was deputed by the Court of Directors, in March 1839, to proceed to America for the purpose of obtaining information, seeds, and machines for cleaning cotton, and of endeavouring to induce persons well acquainted with the culture of cotton to proceed with him to India. Capt. B. having fully effected his mission, has returned with ten American planters of experience: of these, three have already proceeded to Bombay, and three to Madras, and the remaining four are to accompany him by the overland route to the Bengal Presidency.

Capt. Bayles deputed to America; returns with ten experienced planters; to be sent by the Court of Directors to India to cultivate Cotton.

The measure adopted by the Court of Directors of inducing experienced American planters to proceed to India, and to grow cotton in the different parts of that empire, seems the best calculated to insure the experiment being made in the most complete and satisfactory manner. The mechanical part, that of picking, drying, and keeping clean the cotton, and separating it effectually from the seed without injuring the staple, will undoubtedly be perfectly performed. One source of difficulty will thus be

Cleaning will be perfectly performed.

Culture of Cotton in India by American planters

removed—that of forming a correct opinion respecting the natural qualities of the Indian cotton. The culture also being perfectly understood, will no doubt produce the largest return of cotton that is possible, and fineness, strength, and length of staple will be insured, as far as dependent on culture. This especially, wherever the soil and climate are most similar to that in which the planters have been in the habit of adopting a similar mode of culture, with the same kind of seed.

will be perfect wherever practicable.

American culture will require modification in some situations.

But in many situations it will happen that the soil and climate differ considerably from that which characterizes the banks of the Mississippi, or of the Alabama, or the prairies of the latter. The same treatment therefore may not be exactly suitable to the new situations; though these may, with some modification of the culture, be capable of growing as fine cotton as any other part of the world. The modification will depend in some measure on the chemical and physical properties of the soil, the peculiarities of the climate, and the course of the seasons; the effects of all of which may have been ascertained by some of the numerous experiments which have been made for a series of years in the different Presidencies.

Dependent on physical agents.

The influence of physical agents understood by scientific men.

The full influence of physical agents, such as light, heat, air, and moisture, will be clearly understood only by those who are acquainted with the principles of some of the physical sciences; while the information respecting the experimental results is scattered through a variety of European and Indian publications. It is highly desirable however, that the experience of the planters in their own country should be made as available as possible in the country to which they have removed, and this without the loss of valuable time, or the repetition of useless experiments. This will probably be best effected by putting them in communication with gentlemen who are acquainted with the principles of culture, as well as in some measure with the practices adopted in the cultivation of cotton, and who are at the same time not ignorant of the history of what has already been done in India. There are, fortunately, gentlemen with the necessary qualifications in all the three presidencies, whose present appointments require in them the possession of such information, and who from their occupations will take great interest in the successful result of the important experiment which is in course of being tried. These are, Dr. Falconer in the north-western provinces of India, Dr. Wight at Madras, and Dr. Gibson at Bombay.

American culture of Cotton in India.

Desirable that the planters be put in communication with gentlemen of scientific and practical knowledge.

The planters being strangers in a new country, unacquainted with its language, manners, and customs, will, moreover, require some medium of communication, not only with the natives with whom they will constantly have to act, but also in the first instance with the government officers, who will have to institute negotiations respecting the land they are to occupy. The above gen-

Useful also for communicating with natives and Government officers.

Importance of scientific with practical information.

tlemen will be useful for such purposes, as well as in imparting scientific information and the results of the experiments in and the practices of India, without interfering in any way with the management of the farms, or the cultivation of the cotton.

Choice of localities.

In choosing the localities for the farms in each Presidency, attention must be paid not only to its being a favourable site for the growth of cotton, but also one that is not unhealthy, and of which the example will have influence over as large a space as possible. It is next necessary to determine the mode in which the experiment is to be tried, and the kind of cotton which is to be cultivated. In the first place, it is desirable that a small farm should be held by the planter, to whatever extent he thinks he can personally superintend, in which with his own establishment of workmen, horses or bullocks, and tools, he should be able to cultivate cotton in every respect exactly as he desires. In this he might vary the culture, so as to see the effects of earlier or later sowing, more or less open planting, the degree of ploughing and weeding that is requisite, or the extent and times of topping or pruning that are beneficial. The careful system of picking, drying, and cleaning will be equally applicable to all, and the latter will require to be carried on under cover, and by the aid of the perfect machinery which Captain Bayles is conveying to India. But the buildings ought not to be more expensive

Mode of experiment.

Kind of Cotton.

Personal farm.

For experiments.

Picking, &c. and cleaning by saw-gins under cover.

than is absolutely necessary, or, at least, what is essential ought to be distinguished from what is optional, in order that the expense and experience may serve as useful guides for others. In this respect, however, the best advice will be that of the planters themselves.

Buildings for cotton cleaning.

As there will in the first instance necessarily be considerable difficulties to be overcome, and several modifications of culture may be required to meet the varieties of soil, of climate, and of season, so these will probably be best surmounted by mutual consultation. It will, therefore, be advisable that the planters in each Presidency should at first make their experiments in localities so situated that the same saw-gin would answer for them all. When a knowledge of climate and seasons has been acquired, separation might then take place to a greater or less distance, as might be thought advisable, and each planter would then be fully able to adapt his culture to the soil and climate of his own locality.

Desirable that the planters at each Presidency should be together at first.

Might afterwards separate.

The kinds of cotton to be cultivated will depend, in some measure, upon the views of the planters themselves, but in a great degree upon the places where they are located. There is no doubt that some of the kinds, as the Sea-Island, Bourbon, and Pernambuco, succeed best in the south, while the Upland Georgian, and perhaps the Egyptian, flourish best in the northern provinces. The success of these will also depend

Kinds of Cotton to be cultivated.

Kinds of Cotton to be cultivated.

upon the soil, as it is well known that the perennial species have not succeeded in the black cotton soil of India, though this is well adapted to the annual cotton plant of the country. It may perhaps, wherever not too retentive of moisture, be found suitable with improved culture to the Mexican plant, now exclusively cultivated in Louisiana. Independent of the kinds, whether foreign or native, which it may be determined to cultivate most extensively, it will be extremely desirable, nay essential, that a small portion of ground, say a beegah or an acre, should be devoted to each of the principal kinds of cotton which have been enumerated, besides to the Tree and Herbaceous cottons of India. Of the latter, picked seed from the places where the best cotton is now grown, should be tried.

Must depend on soil and climate.

The most suitable extensively.

Every kind in small quantities.

Persons employed under planters to be instructed.

The people employed under the planters should, as many of them as possible, be at first of rather a superior class of labourers or cultivators. It may be also suggested as worthy of consideration, whether some apprentices from the Orphan Schools may not be beneficially placed at each farm, who, as well as the former, might be afterwards useful in more extensively diffusing the benefit of the improved practice, which will no doubt be successfully introduced.

Successful practice to be made known to natives.

When the culture best suited to each part of India has been practically ascertained, it will then be extremely desirable to endeavour to induce the natives of the district to adopt the improved modes, both of cultivating and of cleaning cotton. This, by inviting them to inspect the new culture, sending round the natives who may have been instructed, and by distributing plain instructions in the native languages, describing the processes of culture and of cleaning, as well as, if possible, giving a comparative view of the expenses, quantity of produce, and the prices obtained for the improved cotton. In all these operations, the officer who is supposed to be the medium of communication between the planters and others, will be able to render the most essential service. Specimens of the cotton as grown should be sent to the Presidencies, where they may be submitted by the governments to the several Agricultural societies and commercial men; so that early opinions might be obtained respecting the different kinds of cotton which are produced, and the utmost publicity given to the progress of the experiments. It would be desirable also that the planters should themselves be provided with specimens of the different kinds of cotton which are brought to the English market, and which would serve for comparison with the several kinds of cotton grown on their plantations.

Instructions for culture in native languages to be distributed.

Specimens of Cotton grown to be submitted to examination.

The planters should be furnished with good specimens of all the kinds of Cotton.

Planters in the interior of India complain that they have no encouragement to bestow extra labour, and incur greater expense in growing superior cottons, as these when brought to market at the Presidency bring only the same prices as the ordinary cotton of the country. The cot-

Complaint of Indian planters.

Superior, bring only the prices of ordinary Cottons at Presidency.

Complaint of Indian Planters that extra labour is not repaid by improved prices.

ton Committee of the Agricultural Society of Calcutta admit, that parties there are interested in keeping down the prices of staples, which will not be properly valued until their prices are established in Europe. The Secretary writes to Colonel Skinner, who had planted and sold Georgia cotton, and obtained only the price which good country cotton realized—"It appears to me that you have not given your new cotton a fair trial, and that if you had sent it to England direct, you would have reaped better returns than in Calcutta; and I ground my opinion upon the circumstance, that had your cotton been equal to the first quality American, the result of a sale in this country would have been the same, inasmuch as it was a new article." It is, therefore, necessary that a portion, or the whole, of the produce of each of the new farms should be sent regularly for sale to the markets of London and Liverpool.

The experimental Cottons should be sent to London and Liverpool.

As the object of these extensive experiments is not only to grow superior cotton, but also to obtain accurate information for still more extensive application, so it is desirable to have reports from the planters, however brief, respecting the details of their culture, from the different parts of India in which they may be situated. The scientific officer, who may be in communication with the planters, should furnish, at least, a general annual report, including notices of the soil, climate, and peculiarities of seasons, as by this means some general data will be obtained of

Reports from Planters.

extensive application. The defects will thus be avoided of previous experiments, of the details and particular results of which we know too little to be able to rank them among successful investigations, or as partial or complete failures.

Reports on the experimental culture.

Bengal Presidency.

Extent over which Cotton is cultivated in India.

Cotton is cultivated in the Madras presidency from 8° to 17° of north latitude, in that of Bombay from 16° to 24°, and in the Bengal presidency excellent cotton has been grown in the neighbourhood both of Calcutta and of Dacca, as well as near Delhi, that is, from 23½° to 30° of north latitude. So that there would appear to be favourable sites in India for the culture of cotton over an extent of 22° of latitude.

Cotton of Dacca

The muslins of Dacca, so long celebrated, have always been manufactured from a cotton grown to the eastward and south-east of the city of Dacca, and a few miles inland from the banks of the Burrampooter; the plant has been figured by Dr. Roxburgh in vol. 3, t. 269, of his Coromandel Plants. It has often been doubted whether the superiority of the manufacture was dependent on the skill of the workmen or the goodness of the cotton; but from Mr. Lamb's account it appears to be carefully cultivated. It will probably be found that both have some influence, and it is certain that the workmen prefer the

carefully cultivated.

Cotton preferred as its thread does not swell.

Dacca cotton, because, as Mr. Bebb long ago explained, its thread does not swell in bleaching, as is the case with the cotton grown in North-Western and Central India. (Vide Reports of East-India Company on Cotton, p. 350.)

Cotton of N. W. India.

Of the cotton which is grown further north, Mr. Duncan, as early as 1789, relates, that the greatest part of the cotton produced in Benares (N. lat. 25°) is spun into thread, as the spinners there prefer such cotton to the generality of that imported from foreign countries. Of this, the cotton imported from Nagpore was held in the highest estimation, and considered nearly equal to that from Surat, though that grown near Benares is described as being very little inferior to it. Previous to 1802, we learn, from a report on the cotton trade of India by the Bengal Government, that the average annual quantity of cotton imported into the Honourable East-India Company's provinces on that side of India by the Ganges, had been for many years 450,000 maunds of ninety-six pounds, for the manufacturers of Benares, Bengal, Behar, and Orissa. Of these, 180,000 maunds were the produce of the Deccan, and 270,000 maunds from the northward, principally from the country along the banks of the Jumna. This tract, including the three districts of Currah, Carah, and Etawah, which had always produced a considerable quantity of cotton, subsequently came into

Cotton of N. W. provinces of India, 1802.

the possession of the Honourable East-India Company. The estimated produce at that time was 150 to 175 pounds of clean cotton per acre.

Cotton of the Doab and of Bundlecund, 1832.

The author in proceeding down the Jumna in January 1832, observed that the cotton plants on its banks, especially below Agra, though smaller, were very prolific bearers, the bolls were larger, and the cotton better than he had seen either higher up or lower down the river. Subsequently, he was informed, that the best cotton was grown in Bundlecund, in the neighbourhood of Jalown, not far inland from Calpee; that the next best was that of Raja-Kh era, below Agra. Good cotton is produced all along the banks of the Jumna, as far north as 30°. In the selection of sites and during the experiments, occasional visits by Dr. Falconer would be valuable, in communicating scientific information as well as the results of his experience.

Cotton of the Banks of the Jumna.

Cotton of the Doab; produce per acre.

That the country in northern India is well suited to yield abundant crops of cotton is evident, from Mr. Vincent, of Nudjuffghur, stating that, in the tract of country lying to the north of Allahabad, "the produce of a begah (one-third of an acre) is, on an average, about a maund of cotton, and two maunds of seed, which is as readily sold as the cotton itself, being an excellent food for cattle." This alone is at the rate of 246lbs. per acre, taking the maund as equal to 82lbs., but as the Allahabad maund contains 96 siccas, and is equal to 96lbs., the produce

Crop not subject to failure, and saleable.

obtained will be 294lbs. per acre. Mr. V. further observes, that the cotton crop is not so subject to failure as the grain crop in general, and is preferred, because it is always saleable, which the latter is not." But "the cotton cultivation on the right bank of the river Jumna being so far superior to the Doab cotton, the latter is extensively imported into Bundlecund, for the fraudulent purpose of being mixed up with the Banda and Jalown cotton." This is produced not only of a fine quality, but also in large quantities, as Mr. Bruce of Calpee writes, that though sown broad-cast and with other grains, yet that the average produce is upwards of 350lbs. per acre, and that the best black cotton soils yield as high as 617lbs. of cotton to the acre. Alluding to the crops sown with the cotton, he also states, that "very often these extraneous mixtures more than pay for the land-rent and labour of the whole cultivation." The Cotton Committee of the Agricultural Society of Calcutta, from the accounts of the Akra farm, estimated the profits on the culture of Georgian cotton at about 30 per cent.

Cotton of Bundlecund, quality of, produce per acre, expence of culture and profit.

Cotton of Central India, much esteemed.

The cotton of the interior or Central India, whether we consider the opinions of the native manufacturers on the Madras coast, or those of Benares or Bengal, or the exporters at Bombay, has always been highly esteemed. It was bought also at Dacca, and they paid 19 rupees a maund for the cotton of Sironje in Malwa at the time that their own cotton was selling for about six rupees, which was about the same price, as the former was cleaned and the latter uncleaned cotton.

Soil and climate of Central India.

The soil of Central India is peculiar, consisting in many places of the black cotton soil; the climate also differs from that of the Lower Provinces. It is more than probable, therefore, that the causes are physical and may be discovered, which will account for the superiority as well as the facility of culture of cotton in these districts.

Causes probably physical which favour production of Cotton.

Localities for Cotton Farms.

It would be very desirable, therefore, to establish the first experimental farms near the localities where good cotton, and in abundant enough crops, is already grown. The banks of the Jumna present the most desirable locality, as at no great distance, they afford abundance of the black soil as well as of the ordinary poorer soil of northern India. Localities must be searched for all along this tract; the neighbourhood of Banda is eligible, both on its own account, as from the nearness of the country above the Ghauts, where the soil and climate are nearly identical with that of the cotton districts of Central India. An experiment might at the same time be instituted on the opposite side of the Jumna, that is in the Doab, where cotton has so long been cultivated to a considerable extent, and where, as we have seen, very large returns per acre have in late years been obtained.

Banks of Jumna.

Banda, Eligible localities for Cotton Farms, also above the Ghauts,

in Doab.

As it would be desirable to ascertain the possi-

Desirable to bring the Cotton into earlier bearing.

bility of bringing cotton into earlier bearing, so that the whole crop might be collected before the frosts come on in December, it has been suggested that this might be done by sowing in April, and bringing the plants forward by irrigation. In such a case, the Delhi Canal affords great facilities and eligible situations. Colonel Colvin introduced the culture of the Upland Georgia cotton into upwards of one hundred villages along its banks. The cotton he himself cultivated in a sandy soil, which was useless for every other purpose; the produce, after five years of culture, was thought to be deteriorated; but even then it was 30 per cent. more valuable than the cotton of the country. The culture was necessarily imperfect, and with imperfect culture, cotton deteriorates in America quite as readily as in India.

Cultivating by irrigation.

Cultivated along Delhi Canal, by Col. Colvin.

Deterioration of Cotton if improperly cultivated.

Desirable to establish farms in Central India.

As it is possible that the black cotton soil may be found suitable not only to the cotton indigenous in the country, but also with modified culture to the Upland Georgian or the Mexican, so it will be desirable to introduce the improved and modified culture and the best seed still further into the interior. For such a purpose the tracts above the Ghauts, as round Lohargaon, Jubbulpore, and Saugor, afford numerous favourable sites. The other tracts are near a navigable river, down which the cotton may be conveyed at all seasons of the year. A farm far in the interior may be considered ineligible; but the Cotton Com-

Objections obviated of difficulty of access.

mittee of the Agricultural Society of Calcutta justly observe, "It is obvious that there can be no reasonable objection made to the extension of operations by the Society to those districts, from which private speculators can with profit transport cotton to Calcutta for sale, on the score of difficulty of access, or deficiency of transport, and other similar impediments; but the facilities and the selected stations, it is known to your Committee much exceed any difficulties which may be expected to arise, for Agra and Bundlecund are situated close to the river Jumna, and from Jubbulpore to Mirzapore, on the banks of the Ganges, the great cotton mart of the North-western Provinces, a bridged and metalled road of 269 miles in length, equal to any in England, has been made by Government; and at all the stations the means of transport, namely, to the river, hackeries (carts), camels, and bullocks, and on the river boats of every description, abound." (Vide *Report, Calcutta* 1839.)

Means of access to and from the interior of India.

Road from Mirzapore to Jubbulpore.

The experiments with seed distributed by the Court of Directors of the East-India Company, and by the Agricultural Society of Calcutta, have been carried on over an immense extent of territory, and the information which has been elicited is so varied and valuable, that little doubt remains but that good cotton may be grown in the southern as in the northern parts of the Presidency. The kinds which succeeded in the south are the Sea-Island and the Pernambuco, while the Georgian

Good Cotton has been grown over a great extent.

Experiments to be instituted in the Southern provinces.

is suited to the north, though some of excellent quality has been grown by the Agricultural Society in the Akra farm, as well as by several gentlemen in the neighbourhood of Calcutta. It would be desirable therefore to test the effects of an improved culture and one modified so as to be suited to the climate, in the southern provinces, or on the Tenasserim coast, and in the Muttuck country, as the results would be important and applicable to a vast extent of territory.

Bombay Presidency.

Cotton long exported from Bombay.

The Bombay Presidency has long exported large quantities of cotton both to Europe and to China. Some of this, usually quoted in price-currents under the names of Surat and Broach, brings higher prices than any other cottons cultivated in India by the natives, and the best Surats are often quoted at prices only a little inferior to the great mass of short staple American cotton. Both brokers and manufacturers have frequently given very favourable reports on the quality of this cotton, but much of that exported from Bombay is the produce of Mahratta countries in the interior or Central India.

Surat and Broach Cottons highly valued.

Measures adopted by E. I. Company. Cleaning machine sent in 1794. Farm established. Foreign seed and instructions distributed.

Attempts have long been made by the East-India Company, both in the Madras and Bombay Presidencies, to improve Indian cotton. A cleaning machine was sent out, and a cotton-farm established at Rhaudaterra, as early as 1794. Foreign seeds were dispatched, instructions on the culture of cotton were distributed, and rewards offered for the improved specimens of it. But as the produce of these provinces still continued inferior to what was required by the manufacturers, cotton-farms were directed to be established in 1829; those in Guzerat were placed under the superintendence of Mr. Finey, after his decease under that of Mr. Martin, and the experimental farms in the Deccan, Candeish, and Dharwar, under Dr. Lush. The cotton grown at the several farms having been sent to England, was reported on by experienced brokers, and the results prove that the cotton of these provinces can be much improved; for though these experimental cottons had been injured in the process of cleaning, probably from inexperience in the use of the saw-gin, they are described as being worth from 6¾d. to 9½d. per pound. There is no doubt that in suitable soil, and with the careful culture of the Broach districts, the improved processes of American agriculture would produce still greater improvement, and at all events a greater return of cotton per acre.

Rewards offered.

Cotton Farms established in 1829.

Cotton produced worth from 6¾*d* to 9½*d* per lb.

Probable improvements in Cotton culture.

Keeping in view the principle stated under the head of Bengal, it would be desirable to have the experience of the American planters extended in the Bombay presidency over as wide a surface of country as possible. The best cotton districts are widely separated from each other, and at opposite points of the Bombay territory. These are the southern Mahratta country, about 16° N. lat.,

Localities for experimental culture.

S. Mahratta country.

where the experimental farms were established, because presenting tracts considered by Dr. Lush well suited for the purpose. Guzerat and Cattywar are the districts where the well known superior cottons are already grown by the natives; in consequence of which, these were selected as the sites of the northern experimental farms, and much favourable land for the purpose is found between the latitudes of 21° and 24° North. This part of the country was the site of the experiments of Mr. Assistant Surgeon Gilders in 1816-17, who, having observed the causes which led to the failure in the attempt to introduce the cultivation of Bourbon cotton into the western districts, considered the obstacles to have been exclusively of a physical nature. He at the same time stated, that both the soil and climate of the districts lying between the Subermuttee and the Myhee promised a favourable result. The cotton grown by Mr. Gilders was considered at Bombay fully equal to any produced in Bourbon, and in London as the best specimen that had been imported from Bombay raised from Bourbon seed. It sold for 15d. per lb. With so much sagacity had Mr. Gilders selected the site of his experiments, that fifteen years afterwards Dr. Burns collected seed from trees growing apparently wild. These being sown, produced plants of which the cotton was pronounced equal to the best from New Orleans. The cotton grown at Laberkowa, within two miles of Mongrole, though confined to

Guzerat and Cattywar.

Experiments by Mr. Gilders near Kaira.

Excellent Cotton produced by Mr. Gilders,

by Dr. Burns.

Cotton of Laberkowa.

a space of 200 beegahs, or thereabouts, is so highly valued, that on the spot it will fetch six-sevenths of a rupee per maund more than any other kind in that part of the country; yet the natives say they frequently use seed from Guzerat, or any part of the country. The superiority must therefore depend either upon peculiarity of soil and climate or excellency of culture. One point only of the latter is related, but that is one of great consequence. For instance, the people are in the habit of carefully extracting the cotton alone from the pod in the field; and this is, probably, of considerable importance, as some of the American planters are of opinion, that the staple of Indian cotton is much injured after it is collected, by being allowed to heat when piled up, often for a long time, before it is cleaned.

Cotton of Laberkowa, near Mongrole; produce of careful culture.

As the poorer soils of India have been found to suit the American cottons better than the black soil, and this latter to agree with the indigenous cotton, it is desirable in the Bombay, as in the other Presidencies, to include, in the experiments, both the black and the other soils of the country. Though the cotton is good, and very abundantly produced, the chief difficulty seems to be the shortness of the season for ripening the cotton, conveying it to the outports, and shipping it before the accession of the rains. This might probably be obviated by earlier sowing, perhaps, also, by bringing forward the crop by irrigation, and for this the rivers in the

Different soils to be included in experiments,

Shortness of season for ripening Cotton and picking.

Profits of Cotton culture in Bombay Presidency.

northern parts of Guzerat afford great facilities. The profits attending the culture of cotton appear to be considerable, as Dr. Lush says he is "convinced that the grower and the merchant may get ample profit when the best India cottons are at 5d. per lb." No one is better acquainted than Dr. Gibson with the various localities best suited to the culture of cotton in the Bombay presidency, as well as with the practices of the natives.

Madras Presidency.

Cotton manufactures of Madras coast.

The cotton piece goods which were so extensively exported, and so well known by the name of Madras Long Cloths, would appear to indicate the probability of parts of this presidency being favourable for the production of good cotton; but it has been ascertained that these cloths were chiefly manufactured from cotton brought to the coast from the interior of India.

Attempts to improve Cotton, by Dr. Anderson, by Dr. Roxburgh,

Cotton is, however, extensively cultivated within the limits of the Madras presidency, and attempts have for a long time been made to improve its cultivation. As early as 1790, we find that Dr. Anderson was employed in sending Mauritius cotton seeds, as well as "Brown Cotton Seeds," imported from Malta; to different parts of the peninsula; and Dr. Roxburgh, who left Samulcotta in the Northern Circars and took charge of the Calcutta Botanic Garden in 1793, had already ascertained that the elevated, dry, and less fertile soil of Coromandel was better suited than that of Bengal to the Bourbon cotton. Mr. B. Metcalfe, who had resided several years in Georgia and New Orleans in the capacity of merchant and a cleaner of cotton, was sent, in 1813, by the East-India Company with American machines for cleaning cotton, and directed to be employed at one of the factories in the Ceded Districts in Tinnevelly, or wherever his services might be thought most useful. Cotton farms were directed by the Government, in 1818, to be established at Tinnevelly, Coimbatore, Masulipatam, and Vizagapatam. To Mr. Heath, who was commercial resident at Coimbatore, we are indebted for the publication of the best instructions on the Culture of Cotton in India. These refer to the several subjects of Soil, Climate, Culture, Pruning, and Cleaning. He obtained them from Mr. Hughes, who had for some time been engaged in the culture of cotton in the Tinnevelly district, and whose success was so considerable with the Bourbon cotton, that for twenty years "Hughes's Tinnevelly Cotton" continued to be quoted in the Liverpool market as the best from India, and sold at higher prices than the American short staple cottons, and 3d. per lb. above the best Surats. The fact is important, on account of the latitude of Tinnevelly being only 8½°, and because the success was evidently the result of skill applied to the culture. The produce, though only 100lbs. per acre, was fine in quality and much esteemed.

the Court of Directors send Mr. B. Metcalfe out to India.

Cotton Farms established in 1818.

Cultivated by Mr. Heath,

by Mr. Hughes.

Goodness of Tinnevelly Cotton,

the result of skill applied to the culture.

Dr. Wight appointed to report on Cotton culture in Madras Presidency.

In March 1836, Dr. Wight was appointed by the Madras Government to inquire into the state of agriculture in Southern India, and to report on the best methods of cultivating cotton and the other valuable products of the country. The collectors of districts having been required to send in reports on the statistics and peculiarities of the culture of cotton in their respective collectorates, have furnished materials for a valuable report. From this, we learn that in Vizagapatam, about north latitude 17°, the return is much greater than in any other district, as the produce is said to amount to "forty-six maunds, or 1,150 lbs., of seed cotton per acre, nearly equal to the best, and exceeding the ordinary American crops." The culture here is peculiar, as very liberal pruning is practised. In Trichinopoly, with a fertile soil, 783 lbs. which is the next highest, is the greatest return, which, though so much less than the above, is still more than double the average return from other districts. But no reports had then been received from North Arcot, Bellary, and Cuddapah; the two last are stated by Dr. Wight to be the principal cotton districts of the peninsula.

Produce per acre in Vizagapatam,

in Trichinopoly.

Experiments over a wide space of territory.

As the objects in establishing experimental farms, under the superintendence of experienced American planters, are not only to find the best localities for growing good cotton, but also to ascertain the modifications of culture which may be best suited to different soils and climates, it would be desirable to have these farms established over as wide a space of territory as possible. It is fortunate, therefore, that two of the districts which now yield the largest produce are also the most widely separated, Vizagapatam being in the north, and Trichinopoly in the south; while Bellary or Cuddapah, intermediate in position, may with them be indicated as eligible sites for the farms. The best of these may be selected as that in which the joint experiment should be made in the first year.

Experimental culture of Cotton.

Localities for farms.

Dr. Wight's scientific knowledge and practical acquaintance with the subject would be extremely valuable, as affording information respecting the peculiarities of soil, climate, and culture in each district. He has published a valuable paper and a table, embracing the results of his investigations of the reports sent in by the officers of Government of thirteen districts in the Madras Presidency. This embraces the several items of the kind of cotton cultivated, the times of sowing and of obtaining the produce, produce per acre, charges on the culture, the amount of the assessment or the land-tax, and the profit of the cultivator. Every item differs very considerably in the different districts. In Masulipatam, where the expenses are Rs. 2.11.6, and the assessment Rs. 2.17.7, and the produce of clean cotton 150lbs. per acre, the profit is stated as being only 8 anas and 11 pice, while in Vizagapatam the expenses are Rs. 18.8, the assessment

Rs. 14, the return per acre 290lbs., and the profit is Rs. 12.8.

in different soils.

As the native species of cotton succeeded only in the black cotton soils, and the foreign species in the poorer sandy soil, it would be desirable to make the experiments in a situation where both soils might be tried.

Good Cotton cultivated all over India.

In southern latitudes chiefly from the influence of Europeans;

by natives in northern latitudes.

We perceive that cotton is produced of good quality over vast tracts of Indian territory, by the application of European skill and energy, as far south as Tinnivelly; and in Vizagapatam, eight degrees further north, in large quantities per acre, chiefly through the introduction of American modes of culture. This was one of the sites of the former Cotton Farms, and a part of its effects, as well as of the example of Europeans, is evident in the liberal pruning which is there practised. The fine cottons produced by the unaided efforts of the natives are in the more northern provinces both of the Bombay and Bengal Presidencies.

Causes which favour the production of Cotton.

The cotton of Central India finds its way on the west to Surat, and on the east to Mirzapore, which has long been the great Cotton mart of that side of India. The causes which favour the growth of cotton, esteemed both in India and England, in the tract of country extending from Surat and Ahmedabad, or from about lat. 21° and 23°, in a broad band across Malwa to Banda and Rajakhaira, in about 25° and 27°, near the banks of the Jumna, are no doubt physical. The black cotton soil which is spread over a great portion of this tract has undoubtedly a considerable share in producing the effect; but good crops of cotton are produced in some parts where there is no black soil, as immediately on the banks of the Jumna and in the Doab. It will therefore probably be found, that the comparative dryness of the climate after the plant has got well established in the ground, checks the vegetative vigour, and favours the production of prolific fruit. The native modes of culture are chiefly characterized by close sowing, crowded plantations, and unchecked growth. These and the mixture of crops even, are better suited to a dry soil and climate, than to a rich soil and moist atmosphere. Hence the culture has proved more successful in the hands of the natives in the northern than in the more southern latitudes of India.

Soil and comparative dryness of climate favour growth of Cotton in the north.

Native modes of culture best suited to such situations.

The same effects may, however, be produced by culture in a rich soil and climate. Frequent ploughing and turning up of the ground will produce dryness of the soil; open planting and the free admission of air will equally increase evaporation from the leaves. These, combined with topping the plant and pruning, will check its tendency to run into stalk and leaf, but favour the production of flower-buds, fruit, and abundance of cotton. It may therefore, perhaps, be grown as well in the southern as in the northern parts of India.

The same effects and successful results may be produced every where by careful culture.

Taking into consideration the facts we have

Conclusion. before us respecting the native culture of Cotton, and the results of the numerous experiments which have been made to improve it, there is sufficient satisfactory evidence to justify confidence in the complete and profitable success of the cultivation of very superior kinds of cotton in various parts of India. But the American or European Planters who thoroughly understand the Practice, must also pay sufficient attention to the Principles, so as to be able to modify the former to suit it to the soil and situation in which they are placed. They must also make it their *principal* business to establish the Culture, and to succeed as Cotton Planters. But attention is necessary to soil and climate, and every part of the improved culture of the present day, as well as to careful picking, early drying, and complete cleaning by effective machinery, before Cotton is packed and can be presented to the Merchant for transmission to the Manufacturer.*

* The foregoing observations having been written to accompany documents referring to the important experiment which is in course of being tried, to improve the culture of Cotton in India, the means by which it is to be effected, have rather been referred to, than detailed. This will account also for some of the repetitions of what had been before treated of, and for a few alterations subsequently made, to suit the purposes of this work. It has been seen that various measures have been adopted for a series of years by the Court of Directors and the Indian Governments to improve the culture and cleaning of Cotton. Notwithstanding the success which has attended many of the experiments, no permanent improve-

ment has yet taken place in the Cottons of India; in fact, according to the testimony of practical men, both in Liverpool and Manchester, it has even deteriorated, as they are unable to purchase as good and as clean Cotton now as they used to do fifteen years ago. A more complete experiment than any that had been instituted was yet required, before the question could be considered as finally settled, of the capability of India for producing superior kinds of Cotton. This was determined upon, as related at p. 9, and is so complete in every point as to leave nothing more to be desired for the satisfactory settlement of this important culture.

Captain Bayles, with the ten experienced American planters, has also brought seed of the best kinds, especially of the Mexican Plant, now the most valued in Louisiana and Southern Alabama. Also Saw-gins by several makers, as Brookes, Carver, Idler; but the instrument of Mr. Jones seems best adapted to the Indian cotton seed.

The author has derived much valuable information on the culture of Cotton in America from Mr. Mercer and the other planters, who he has no doubt will succeed in growing it equally well in India.

The opportunity being too favourable not to be taken advantage of, Captain Bayles, with Messrs. Mercer, Finney, Blunt, and Terry, the American Planters for Bengal, accompanied by the Author, visited brokers, spinners, and manufacturers, in London, Liverpool, and Manchester, to make inquiries on various points relating both to Indian and the other Cottons which are imported.

A few preliminary experiments were also made on the powers of the American Machines in cleaning Indian Cotton. All experiments on cleaning cotton are however made here under the most unfavourable circumstances, as the Indian Kupas (that is cotton with the seed) has been imperfectly dried, and this of itself injures the staple. It has also been kept for many years, which has further dried up both the seed and the staple, making the latter more brittle and easily injured by the process of cleaning.

From inquiries made to ascertain what kinds of cotton it is most desirable to cultivate in India, it appears best, as a general rule, to imitate the American short and long staple cottons as nearly as possible. It has by some been thought unadvisable to increase the supply of long staple cottons, such as Sea Island, Pernambuco, &c., to a great degree; but of this there is no fear. If the supply were abundant and regular, the prices might fall, and long staple Cottons would be used for many of those purposes for which short staple cottons are now alone employed. But it will not be easy to increase the supply, if regular, beyond the demand.

With regard to Indian Cotton, satisfactory information was obtained respecting its qualities, and that it is not its cheapness only which causes it to be employed in our cotton manufactures. The objections to it are no doubt great, inasmuch as there is always one-fourth, and often more, of loss from the intermixture of dirt, and yet more from waste in consequence of the very short staple or nap being mixed with the long staple. These, in the process of cleaning by the saw-gin, are separated by the great draught created by the rapid revolution of the cleaning brush. The Indian Cotton is also short in its staple, and liable to break, apparently from the imperfect drying it receives at the time that it is picked. Notwithstanding these imperfections, it is extensively employed in our manufactures, partly no doubt owing to its cheapness, but also in consequence of possessing some positive good qualities, and which distinguish it from the American short staple cottons. The first of these is colour, by which yarn and cloth in which it is employed are much improved in appearance; the second, with which the manufacturers of Dacca* are as well acquainted as those of

* "The general distinction in quality, the natives of Dacca make, is whether the thread made therefrom swells or not in the bleaching."—Bebb on Cotton of Dacca, in Reports, p. 350.—This property, which is not possessed by the Cotton of Dacca, makes this preferable for the fine muslins of that city, but

Manchester, is, the swelling of its thread, which, when the cloth is bleached, enables the intermediate vacancies to be filled up, giving the whole a more substantial appearance. The third good quality is, that in dyeing, it takes the colour more uniformly than the other cottons.

The great importance attached by the Court of Directors of the East-India Company to this great experiment in all its bearings is evident, from the pains which have been taken, and the expense which has been incurred in rendering it complete in every point. As the saw-gins had arrived at Liverpool, it was determined that their powers of cleaning Indian Cotton should be carefully tested before they were dispatched to their destination: the results were reported in the *Liverpool Times*, &c. and in the *London Journal of Commerce*, which says,—"We perceive, by the accounts from Liverpool, that, on Friday the 17th ultimo, the Chairman and Deputy-chairman (W. Butterworth Bayley, Esq., and George Lyall, Esq.) accompanied by Sir Robert Campbell, Sir J. L. Lushington, Sir Richard Jenkins, M. P., and John Loch, Esq., Directors of the East-India Company, James C. Melvill, Esq., Secretary to the Court, Dr. Royle, and Mr. Greene, of the Correspondence Branch, arrived at that time, where the machinery had been previously landed from America, for the purpose of witnessing certain experiments which the Directors had ordered to be made with the saw-gins procured by Captain Bayles. The immediate object being to ascertain whether the action of so powerful an instrument could, without alteration, be made available in cleaning the Cotton of India, which is of a staple somewhat shorter, and possessing less tenacity than that of the United States.

"The experiments were conducted at the manufactory of Messrs. Fawcett and Co., and the result proved to the satisfac-

---

the cotton of northern India, which does possess this property, seems to be valued by the manufacturers of piece goods of Benares, v. p. 19, as it is in the present day by those of Manchester.

tion of the party assembled on the occasion, consisting of the principal manufacturers, brokers, spinners, and mechanics of Liverpool and Manchester, that, with some trifling modifications in the saws and plates, the machines in question may be used in India, under proper superintendence, with complete success.

"We have been favoured with samples of the cotton produced on this interesting occasion. The Surat Kupas selected for the gins is in a dirtier condition than any we have before met with, but when ginned, although evidently cut in the staple, presents a fair sample of "prime Surat;" it appears also to have come freely through the cards. We understand that the average time consumed in ginning eighty-four pounds of the Kupas (equal to an Indian maund), by one gin containing sixty saws, may be taken at twenty-five minutes; the average quantity of clean Cotton produced being 20lbs.; seed, 60lbs.; waste, 3lbs.; and the average price placed by the valuers on the clean cotton, 4½d. per lb.

"We shall most probably have occasion shortly to recur again to this subject; in the mean time, we cannot but sincerely congratulate the public on the fair promise which the liberal measures adopted by the East-India Company hold out, if vigorously prosecuted, of securing to this country a supply of cotton from our own possessions, at a considerably reduced cost, and to an almost unlimited extent."

The success was complete, much more so indeed than would appear from the above quoted average price, as some experienced brokers were of opinion that the cotton cleaned by the gins had been under rather than over-estimated, and that the best might fairly be valued at 5½d. per lb. One sample, sent to a broker, without any notice of the mode of cleaning or any other particulars respecting it, was pronounced worth 6d. a pound, and that several hundred bales might be sold at that price. Of the cotton cleaned by the saw-gins, the staple is, no doubt, slightly injured, but much less so than could have been anticipated from the former accounts of the action of the saw-gin on Indian Cotton. That the injury was then exaggerated, or proceeded from inexperience in the use of the saw-gin, is evident from one of Whitney's machines, which had been returned from India, having been included in the experiments. It must not be omitted, that one of the instruments did not act so well as was expected, in consequence of the newness of the saws. This is always obviated by the planters in America, by making new saws act in the first instance upon seeds mixed with sand, which reduces the rough and fine edges so as to injure the cotton in the least degree. This precaution had been taken with two of the instruments, but not with the third, which will account for the average value of the cotton not being so high as it otherwise would have been. An engineer was heard to observe, that the teeth of the saws should be approximated as nearly as possible to the curved thorn of a rose, which with its sharp point would lay hold of and carry forward without injuring the staple of the cotton.

The benefit of the introduction of such an instrument as the present American saw-gin, will undoubtedly be considerable, as it is easily able to turn out 600 pounds of clean cotton a day. The Indian planter will thus receive the full value of his article, instead of having it depreciated, in consequence of its being mixed up with one-fourth of dirt, upon which he has to pay expenses in packing, conveyance to the sea-port, freight, and insurance, as well as upon the cotton. He will at the same time not lose the sale in India of the waste and short nap, which will be as useful as better cotton for quilting garments, &c. in that country. The demand in England will, at the same time, very considerably increase, as a manufacturer stated, that instead of using it only in small quantities, it would be preferred and employed in millions of pounds, if only brought to them in the state it was turned out before them by the saw-gin.

The satisfactory nature of the result is still further proved by the following documents. The first and second, referring to cotton cleaned at Liverpool; and the third, to the opinion of the Merchants, Manufacturers, and Spinners of Manchester, where the saw-gins had been sent by the Court of Directors to be submitted to a further trial. It is important to notice that a press was at the same time exhibited by Mr. William Laird, of Liverpool, in which 400lbs. of cotton was pressed in twelve minutes by four men to the ordinary size of a Surat bale.

" *To the Directors of the Honourable East-India Company.*

"Honorable Sirs,

"In compliance with the request of the Chairman for my report and opinion on the recent experiments made at Liverpool with the American saw-gins, &c. upon East-India Cotton, I beg respectfully to state, that I concur generally in the Report made at Liverpool, and forwarded to London on Tuesday last, which renders any lengthened one from me. unnecessary. I think the valuations therein given might fairly have been stated ¼d. to ½d. per lb. higher, as the present relative value with American Cotton; in which opinion I am confirmed by several brokers who examined the samples more at leisure than could well be done at the time the experiments were made, and whose valuations were chiefly at 4¾d. to 5¼d. per lb.; but in drawing up the Report, it was deemed best to use great caution, and adopt the first estimate. Had the experiments been tried upon new cotton instead of old, I think the result would have been still more satisfactory.

"I am decidedly of opinion, that the American saw-gins, under the superintendence and management of American planters, are calculated to accomplish the great object contemplated, the obtaining a large supply of a desirable and useful quality of cotton, presuming the gins are to be used in the districts or farms where the cotton is grown, and the cotton there secured from the influence of weather by being packed into bales; judging from the appearances of East-India Cotton there is much injury done by exposure, and bad management. These remarks have more immediate reference to cotton from Bombay, which is of longer staple, and consequently, in much greater demand than cotton from Calcutta and Madras.

"I remain, Honorable Sirs,

"Your most obedient Servant,

(Signed) " Jas. R. Tetley."

" *22d July* 1840."

"*To Capt. Bayles, H.E.I.Co. S., Adelphi Hotel.*

"*Liverpool, 22d July*, 1840.

"Dear Sir,

"Herewith we send you 3 hanks Twist spun from your own Cotton, *viz.*:—One hank No. 12 Throstle Twist; one hank No. 16 Mule Twist; one hank No. 32 Mule Twist.

"Our object is to show you what quality of Twist your Cotton produces on coarse as well as fine numbers; No. 12 Throstle Twist and No. 16 Mule Twist we consider to be very good, and the No. 32 Mule Twist very fair yarn, considering the quality of Cotton.

"The Cotton (yours ginned) when compared with Surats of an ordinary quality, is about ¾d to 1d. per lb. better, owing to its being much cleaner and free from seeds; it cards free, and in general works well. The Cotton is obviously cut and nipt in the ginning to a small extent, which would be a great improvement if obviated. We rate it equal to fair Orleans or prime Surats. If such Cottons could be produced so cleaned, a very great preference would be given it to ordinary East-India and Surats, which is commonly full of sand, seeds, and shell: it would also be preferred to low Americans for its very bright colour.

"We value this ginned Cotton with 5d. Bowd's or Orleans, and 1d. per lb. better than 4d. Surats.

"We are, Sir, your very obedient Servants,

"THE NORTH SHORE MILLS COMPANY.

"We consider this Cotton to lose less weight in spinning than common East-India Surats."

"According to the notice put up in the Exchange room on Thursday, the experiments ordered by the Hon. East India Company to be made on ginning East India Cotton, by means of the American Saw Gin, were exhibited, on Saturday last, at the manufactory of Messrs. Lilly and Sons, Stone-street, Manchester, under the able superintendence of Capt. Bayles, assisted by the American gentlemen who are about to proceed with him to India. The result cannot be better shown than by reference to the annexed letter written on the spot, and signed by most of the first spinners and merchants in Manchester :—

"*Lillys' Engineering Establishment,*

"*Manchester, 1st August,* 1840.

"The Merchants, Manufacturers, Spinners, and others interested in the various branches of the Cotton Trade, having been this day invited to witness experiments by Saw-Gins imported from America, upon the cleaning and ginning of East India Cotton, imported in the natural state of boll or pod, with the view of ascertaining the practical application of the cleaning machinery of the United States, to cotton grown in the East Indies, record with great pleasure their conviction, that the experiments now made, clearly establish the fact, that this machinery has been successfully applied for the purpose desired and intended.

"The national importance of a supply of raw material, to maintain the industry of Great Britain is admitted; and the parties immediately interested in the Cotton Trade hail with extreme satisfaction any attempts made to increase the supply of raw cotton in particular, and the manufacturing community of this town and neighbourhood beg thus to express their approbation of the conduct of the Directory of the Hon. East India Company, and of Capt. Bayles and the gentlemen associated with him, in the attempts they are making to improve the cultivation, and to enlarge the supply of East India Cotton, and it is hoped that every support will be given by the Hon. Company here, and by Lord Auckland and the authorities in India to accomplish this most desirable object.

J. B. SMITH, *President of the Chamber of Commerce.*

H. HOOLE, *Vice President of the Chamber of Commerce.*

HORRICKS, JACSON & CO.
J. MACVICAR.
LAMBERT, HOOLE, JACKSON, & CO.
R. COBDEN & COMPANY.
D. PRICE.
J. P. WESTHEAD.
WOOD & WESTHEADS.
J. LILLIE & SONS.
WATERHOUSE & THOMPSON.
S. RIGGS.
J. MASSEY & SON.
S. M. MOORE & SON.
J. KERSHAW.
GARDNER & BAZLEY.
LANGWORTHY, BRO. & CO.
T. BARTON.
R. ROBERTS, Engineer.
J. POTTER.
KELLY & GILMOOR.
J. NICHOLSON, for Thomas Holdsworth.
W. HIGGINS & SONS.
J. SHAWCROSS.
T. OGDEN & SONS.
N. GOUGH.
MCCONNILS & CO.
J. POOLEY & SON.
C. GIMONY.
T. & R. BARNES.
G. CHEELHAM & SONS, per J. Hill.
T. KAY & SON.
T. BANNERMAN & CO.
M. KENNEDY.
M. ASHTON.
G. SIDBOTTOM.
C. SMITH.
T. FERNLEY, Jun.
T. FERNLEY & SON."

The original information on the Cotton culture of India is contained in the following works: — The Reports on the Proceedings of the East India Company, in regard to the production of Cotton Wool, 1836. Transactions of the Agricultural Society of India. Vol. II—VI. 1836—39. Dr. Lush on the Cultivation and Preservation of Cotton in the districts under the Bombay Presidency, 1837. Dr. Wight on the Cultivation of the Foreign Varieties of Cotton in the Madras Presidency, 1837. Minute of the Govenor-general of India on the Cultivation of Cotton in the East Indies, 1839.

Botanic Garden established at Dapooree in Western India.

Experimental culture of staples of commerce,

In the preceeding notices of the experimental cultures instituted for the improvement of the great staples, not only of Indian commerce, but of that of the world in general, we have seen that with great extent of territory, there is also great diversity of soil and of climate, within the limits of British India. Hence there are great capabilities of successfully cultivating the valued productions of many different parts of the world. The localities which have been chiefly dwelt upon

in Madras Presidency;

are in the Madras presidency; also in the Southern and Northern parts, as well as in the Mountains

in Bengal Presidency;

of the Bengal presidency; but some of the results which have been obtained in Western India, have also been noticed under the heads of Silk and

in Bombay Presidency.

Cotton. But in the Bombay presidency, besides the experiments on Silk and Wool which are in course of being carried on, and the Cotton Farms which have been at different times established, there is also a Botanic garden where experiments are instituted on the introduction of useful plants into that side of India.

Botanic Garden established near Poona.

The house, garden, and grounds of Dapooree, near Poona, were purchased in 1828, by Sir J. Malcolm* for the use of Government. This property

* Sir John Malcolm in proposing its establishment says, "I am anxious for the promotion of liberal science, and I am much

contained 71½ acres of land, of which 11¼ are not arable, and 12½ were occupied by the buildings, &c., and 48 acres of good land, all under irrigation, were left to be formed into a botanic garden. Establishment of a Botanic Garden at Dapooree.

Mr. Williamson was appointed its first superintendent, but died shortly afterwards. Dr. Lush succeeded him. The latter describes the climate as being that of the Deccan. To its variability, and the range of temperature and the moderate monsoons, he ascribes the great extent of vegetable productions of other countries, tropical and temperate, which have succeeded at various times and places in the Deccan, wherever the least attention has been paid to horticultural pursuits. The depth of soil is considerable, and a great portion of it, the coarse black soil of the country. In the immediate vicinity there are beds of limestone in the trap rocks around, together with red chalk

Dapooree Botanic Garden; Climate; Soil.

alive to the expediency and policy of every measure (however trifling it may seem), that can, without unjustifiable expenditure, benefit the country, and add to the peaceable occupation and enjoyment of its inhabitants, of whose habits and character I have sufficient knowledge to be convinced that not example, but every stimulus we can apply, is necessary to rouse them to exertion in the pursuit of objects which are obviously for their own advantage; and I believe the establishment I have proposed, to be quite essential to accelerate their advance in that branch of useful improvement to which it belongs." Sir John relates, that one Mahratta chief, speaking of his success in rearing potatoes, said with truth, "a new vegetable is a trifle to you Europeans, compared to what it is to us Brahmins."

Botanic Garden at Dapooree.

and coarse river sand. The garden contained a number of useful and ornamental, and among them a considerable number of timber trees,

Fruit and Timber trees.

The fruit trees consisted of peaches, guavas, loquats, mangoes, apples, quinces, and apricots; besides the remains of a once celebrated vineyard. There were also specimens of the rose jamon, alligator pear, Indian almond, with others characteristic of the country. That is, we have here, as in other parts of India, the fruit trees of various parts of the world congregated together. It was proposed to pay attention to these as well

Proposed subjects of experiment at Dapooree.

as to Horticultural subjects in general, as also to the culture of pasture and fodder Grasses; the planting of the Mulberry for the Silk culture, together with the cultivation of Medicinal plants. The results of the experiments which were made on the culture of Cotton and the planting of Mulberries, we have already seen under the heads of the former and of Silk.

Dr. Gibson appointed superintendent.

Dr. Gibson having succeeded to the Superintendency of the Dapooree Garden, has zealously prosecuted the objects contemplated in its institu-

Nurseries established.

tion. Two or three small nurseries, as at Hewra, Neergoree, and Sconere, were established in the district in furtherance of the same objects. Such establishments are especially useful, as speaking everywhere to the eyes of the natives, and advantageous to the country, as useful plants are distributed gratis to those who agree to cultivate them. The importance of such introductions will be clearly manifest, when it is considered, as Dr. Gibson says, that the great complaint of the cultivators, is the exceeding cheapness of all the present articles of cultivation, consisting principally of grains, with which the markets are usually overstocked. The necessity, therefore, is proportionately great, of finding other employment for a portion of the people, and of introducing the culture of articles which may meet with a ready sale for exportation. Hence, we see one reason why Cotton is so extensively cultivated, and Opium so rapidly increased in quantity throughout Central India.

Nurseries established. Observations on their utility.

All measures calculated to forward the increased culture of useful objects received the utmost encouragement from the unwearied and enlightened zeal of the Revenue Commissioner, Mr. T. Williamson, who has particularly directed attention to the cultivation of Foreign Cottons and the Mauritius Sugar Cane, Mulberry planting, Coffee, Tobacco, and Tea, (the last he mentions as succeeding at Nuggur,) the Cochineal Insect, Culinary Vegetables, and Fruit-trees. But we cannot avoid remarking that many objects of culture which have long been naturalized in other parts, are only now being introduced into the west of India.

Important objects of culture.

Among the subjects to which Dr. Gibson, as well as others, have been paying attention, is the planting of Mulberries and the Culture of Silk, and it is gratifying to find that the specimens of

Planting of Mulberry and Culture of Silk.

Western India. silk which have been sent home are highly approved of.* Dr. G. has also been introducing the culture of Arrow-root, Tapioca, and of Potatoes. The last he planted in November, and dug up at the end of February, and found them to be of very good quality. He states that they thrive best in the red soil, where the grain crops are comparatively scanty and precarious, and that they would yield a remuneration superior to that afforded by the Rubbee crops, even at one-third of their present price. From his example and advice many of the natives were become as anxious, as they were before averse from potatoe cultivation, and he had consequently supplied seed to a number of cultivators.

Potatoes.

Adopted by Natives.

Olive, Coffee, &c.

Dr. Gibson conceives that many of the hill localities are eminently fitted for the naturalization of the products of the south of Europe, as the Olive, &c; others for the culture of Coffee, and some for many of the useful plants and trees of the New World. He was endeavouring to direct attention to the culture of Linseed, and also to

* But it is mortifying to learn, at the same time, as the Author did, in one of the most extensive silk mills in Manchester, that Bengal silk had fallen off very much in quality in the last few years. By the latest accounts, we learn that "the Calcutta exports of silk are now three thousand maunds less than last year, and are not likely soon to increase. One lot of superior European Filature Cossimbazar has been sold at 15s. 8d. per factory maund; but it was the finest we have ever seen."—Circular of Messrs. Whyte and Holmes. Calcutta, 6th June 1840.

that of Safflower, Lucern, Guinea Grass, &c., which were known in some, but not so common in all the districts as they might easily be made. The Grape Vine, Dr. G. mentions, as common in the easern parts of the Deccan, where it afforded a cheap and delicious article of food, sold in some bazars, and yet that it was uncultivated in many places well suited to it. Into Candeish it had been introduced by the Collector of Revenue, and was quite naturalized, though it had at one time been said that the air of this district was unfavourable to it. The Grape Vine.

The Mauritius Sugar Cane had been introduced into Bombay by the zeal and energy of Mr. Brownrigg, and had been extensively distributed by Mr. Williamson. Dr. Gibson was also employed in cultivating, extensively distributing, and in endeavouring to induce the natives to take an interest in the culture. He had made an agreement with one cultivator, to whom he supplied the ground, and half the seed, on condition of his furnishing labour, and the water for irrigation, and that they were to divide the produce equally. He had succeeded in making sugar after the West-Indian method, and the specimens of sugar which he has sent to this country are excellent in quality. Mauritius Sugar Cane.

He had also turned his attention to the subject of medicinal and other drugs, and mentions that those from the Deccan and Candeish were collected in the Chandore range. The forests which Medicines and other Drugs.

Western India. Forests of Timber. lie close under the ghauts in Candeish and the Deccan, he is of opinion, require being attended to, as on these forests the Deccan is completely dependent for timber. He fears, as destruction, of Teak timber especially, vastly exceeds production, that in a few years considerable deficiency will be experienced.

Dr. Burns on experiments at Kaira in culture of Medicines, Mulberry, and Silk. At the same time that these experiments were carried on by Dr. Gibson in the Deccan, Dr. Burns was paying attention at Kaira, in the northern parts of Guzerat, to the culture of Senna, Scammony, and of Colocynth, the last being indigenous in that part of India; to the planting of the Mulberry and the culture of Silk, where he had succeeded in producing some of the last of very good quality, as well as the Cotton mentioned at p. 339, as being considered equal to New Orleans, from seed obtained from plants which had been planted for more than fifteen years.

Botany of Western India. The Botany of the Bombay presidency is less known than that of the other parts of India; and, therefore, the comparisons which we are able to make with its vegetation and that of other countries, is less definite. Colonel Sykes, however, brought home a collection of plants, of which the Author has engaged to give an account, and which, as it is the first and only one which has been brought to this country from that side of India, will be proportionately valuable when its contents have been compared with the Herbaria in the metropolis, in ascertaining the peculiarities of the Flora of the West of India. This, the more so, as Col. Sykes has already published the results of his observations on the Geology, Meteorology, and Zoology of the tract of country where his plants were collected. We have at present sufficient data for stating, that the botany of the Bombay side of India resembles that which characterizes that of the Peninsula in general, and such as is generally found in the plains and jungles of India.*

Botany of Western India.

The Productive Resources of the Madras Presidency.

In a former part of this work we have seen the early attention which was paid in the Madras Presidency to the improvement of the culture of various staple products. These efforts were not followed by the successful results which might reasonably have been anticipated; as we find the Governor, Sir F. Adam, in an able minute, remarking in 1836 on "the extraordinary disproportion which has been long felt to exist between the state of the trade and agriculture of the provinces under this Presidency, as compared with the

Minute of Sir F. Adam.

Disproportion between Trade and Agriculture, and capabilities of the Presidency.

* A very valuable catalogue of the plants of the West of India has lately been prepared by Messrs. Graham and Nimmo, and published by the Agricultural Society of Western India. Bombay, 1839.

Madras Presidency.

extent and fertility of the soil, and its adaptation for the successful cultivation of many of the most valuable productions." "The able and voluminous reports furnished by the Revenue officers on the results of the exertions made by the Government to introduce the cultivation of American Cotton and Tobacco, and on the means best calculated for improvement of the culture and preparation of these and other articles, adapted to secure to this country a due share in external commerce, which have been elicited by the queries circulated by order of Government, afford much information which will be useful to Government and its officers, in originating and carrying into effect the measures proper to be adopted in future attempts to promote these important objects."

Reports of Government officers on Tobacco and Cotton experiments.

Value of accurate information.

Sir F. Adam further observes, that it will be of great benefit to the public and to individuals to be furnished with accurate information on the circumstances in which the successful prosecution of the cultivation of articles for export and for home consumption must depend. Also, on the advantages and defects of the native processes, and the modifications in the methods of cultivation and preparation which must be adopted to secure a remunerating price in Europe or in India for the country or exotic Cottons, Tobacco, Dyestuffs, and numerous other articles for which the soil and climate of the Peninsula are peculiarly adapted.

It also appears, that the little success that has

hitherto attended the exertions of Government and of individuals, has arisen from the want of the information necessary to enable the latter to pursue the proper course of exertion, and the Government to afford the requisite encouragement to induce and enable the Farmers to cultivate successfully new kinds of produce, or to improve the quality of indigenous productions.

Little success, in consequence of deficient information.

From the extent and variety of the facts and statements contained in these papers, and the paramount importance, that what is to direct the measures of Government and the exertions of individuals, should be subjected to rigid investigation, it was felt necessary that an individual should be selected for the task of their examination and condensation, whose pursuits have rendered him familiarly acquainted with the subject, and who could ascertain and correct, by personal observation and well-directed inquiry, whatever might appear either doubtful or erroneous.

Varied and valuable facts contained in Government Reports.

To do justice to the subject and to the authors of these reports, Dr. Wight, of the Madras Medical Service, a gentleman of distinguished scientific acquirements, and whose pursuits have been directed to these subjects, "was appointed to make a useful condensation of the whole of the documents, and of the replies to such enquiries as he may address to the several revenue officers, who will be directed to afford every information in their power." To this he was expected to add the results of his own observations on the methods

Dr. Wight appointed to condense information in report.

Dr. Wight appointed to condense Reports, &c.

of culture of the great staple products of the country. His attention was in the first instance more particularly directed to the subject of Cotton, Tobacco, Coffee, Pasture Grasses, and Timber Trees, and the selection of sites best fitted for the introduction of many valued products of foreign countries.

Queries prepared by Dr. Malcolmson.

A series of queries were promulgated by order of Sir F. Adam throughout the Madras presidency, which were prepared by Dr. J. G. Malcolmson, now of Bombay, but at that time Secretary of the Medical Board at Madras. Those queries refer particularly to the subjects of Cotton, Tobacco, Senna, Turmeric, Grasses, and Soils. They evince the author's comprehensiveness of view, as they embrace every point calculated to elicit such information as will be valuable in establishing principles, or elucidating the causes, both of successful and of unsuccessful practice.

Papers on various useful products.

Cotton, Nuth Grass, Mudar, Senna, Gamboge.

On the plants which yield the Cassia of Commerce.

Dr. Wight, in prosecution of the duties of his appointment, has published a series of valuable papers, as that already noticed (p. 341), on the cultivation of Cotton in the several districts of the Madras presidency; others on the Nuth Grass of the Ceded districts; on the cultivation of Senna; on the Mudar; on the plant which yields the Gamboge of Ceylon; on the several plants which yield the Cassia of commerce. "The first of these," he states, "is the Malabar Carua of Rheede, the second Nees von Esenbeck's Cinnamomum aromaticum. The list, however, of Cassia-producing plants is not limited to these two, but I firmly believe extends to nearly every species of the genus. A set of specimens, submitted for my examination, of the trees furnishing Cassia on the Malabar Coast, presented no fewer than four distinct species; including among them the genuine Cinnamon plant, the bark of the older branches of which, it would appear, are exported from that coast as Cassia. Three or four more species are natives of Ceylon, exclusive of the Cinnamon proper, all of which greatly resemble the cinnamon plant, and in the woods might easily be mistaken for it, and peeled, though the produce might be inferior. Thus we have from Western India and Ceylon alone, probably not less than six plants producing Cassia; add to these nearly twice as many more species of Cinnamomum, the produce of the more eastern states of Asia and the Islands of the Eastern Archipelgo, all remarkable for their striking family likeness; all I believe endowed with aromatic properties, and probably the greater part, if not the whole, contributing something towards the general result, and we at once see the impossibility of awarding to any one individual species the credit of being the source whence the Cassia Lignea of commerce is derived; and equally the impropriety of applying to any one of them the comprehensive specific appellation of Cassia, since all sorts of Cinnamon-like plants, yielding bark of a quality unfit to bear the designation of Cinnamon in the market, are passed off as Cassia."

Plants yielding Cassia of commerce.

On Flora of Courtallum and Pulney mountains.

Besides several papers denominated Contributions to Indian Botany, Dr. Wight has some extremely interesting observations on the Flora of the Courtallum, as well as on that of the Pulney mountains. In the former much valuable information is given on several of the Natural families of plants found there. On the Pulney mountains he finds European together with tropical forms, and suggests the cultivation of Coffee. The soil is fit for the production of grain of the first quality, if a little more care was bestowed on its culture. "This the inhabitants do not think it worth, because, they say, they cannot sell it, and what is the use of taking so much trouble with what we have to eat ourselves?"

On grafting tropical plants.

A valuable proposition is made in his paper, on an application of grafting so as to render it a means of naturalizing new fruits. Conceiving that, in the introduction of tropical plants, the chances against success depend more on the soil than on local differences of climate, he suggests as one of the means to be tried, that of grafting the trees under experiment, on hardy country stocks that are known to thrive in nearly all kinds of soils. The only precaution to be observed, as indispensibly necessary to success in grafting, is that of always using stocks of the same genus or natural order with the scion to be grafted.

On the Homöothermal method of acclimating plants.

A very ingenious suggestion is that which Dr. Wight calls the homöothermal method of acclimating extra-tropical plants within the tropics, in which by altering entirely the constitution, and thus qualifying the plant, though originally from a cold or temperate climate, to endure, uninjured, the extreme heat of the tropics. This is similar to Mr. Speed's method of germinating, and at first growing such plants with the assistance of artificial heat, until they become accustomed to the natural heat of the climate; and rests on the supposition, that plants raised from seeds, sprouted under a high temperature, have their constitutions so modified, as to better fit them for successful culture in higher temperatures than if raised in the usual manner under shade.

Homöothermal method of acclimating plants.

Dr. Wight has recorded the results of his botanical investigations in a series of works * now in course of publication, which forming valuable contributions to science, are extremely important

Dr. Wight's Works.

---

* Prodromus Floræ Peninsulæ Indiæ Orientalis, by R. Wight, M. D., and by G. A. W. Arnott, A.M. Vol I. London, 1834.

Contributions to the Botany of India, by R. Wight, M.D. London, 1834.

Illustrations of Indian Botany, or Figures Illustrative of each of the Natural Orders of Indian Plants, with observations on their Botanical Relations, Economical Uses, and Medicinal Properties, including descriptions of recently discovered or imperfectly known plants. Madras. Parts I—XI. 1838-39.

Icones Plantarum Indiæ Orientalis, or Figures of Indian Plants. Madras. Parts I—XI. 1838-39.

For this work, Dr. Wight says, "Dr. Wallich, the indefatigable Superintendent of the Calcutta Botanic Garden, has most liberally undertaken to supply me with copies of the rich collection of drawings appertaining to that establishment, left by the late Dr. Roxburgh."

Botany of the Indian Peninsula.

as aids to all who wish to become acquainted with Indian Botany, and who desire to be convinced of the extensive practical applications of the scientific investigations of the present day. In his work, Illustrations of Indian Botany, with coloured plates of various plants, he gives general observations on the geographical distribution, properties, and uses of the plants belonging to the several natural orders. His separate Papers are published in the Madras Journal of Literature and Science.

AGRICULTURAL AND HORTICULTURAL SOCIETY OF INDIA.

Institution of the Society;

In a survey of the means which have been adopted for developing the resources of India, it would be unpardonable to omit noticing a body, of which the Author is proud of having been one of the early members, and which has exerted itself vigorously in directing attention to improvements in the cultivation of the great staples of Indian commerce—that is, the Agricultural and Horticultural Society of India, to whose Transactions he has so frequently referred. This Society was established on the 14th September, 1820, subsequent to the distribution of a prospectus by the venerable Dr. Carey, whose views on the advantages of such an institution we have already mentioned at p. 71. Mr. W. Leycester, of the Civil service, was appointed President, and Dr.

on the proposal of Dr. Carey.

Carey, Secretary, when he prepared a series of queries which were circulated throughout the country, respecting some of the interesting points of Indian Agriculture. On the 21st November 1821, the Governor-general in Council, "to mark, by a public act, the interest which he takes in its progress," granted one thousand rupees to be distributed in prizes, promising that it should be continued annually, subject to the approval of the Court of Directors.

Agricultural and Horticultural Society.

Patronized by the Government.

The Society first directed their attention to, and offered prizes for, improved specimens of Coffee and of Cotton, as also of European and Indian fruits. They imported fruit trees from Liverpool, and seeds from Europe, the Cape of Good Hope, and New South Wales. In 1827, they began distributing medals for the best specimens of European vegetables, if cultivated by natives. We observe that on the 16th January 1828, no less than 109 *malees*, or native gardeners, attended to have prizes awarded. The Society afterwards offered to grant medals for the best essays on a variety of agricultural subjects, such as Indian soils, manures, the acclimating of foreign plants, on the cultivation of indigo, sugar-cane, and coffee.

Objects first attended to by the Society.

The first volume of their Transactions was not published until 1829, and the second in 1836. But since then four more volumes have been published, as well as the monthly proceedings of their Meetings. As it is interesting to know the number of Members, and the classes of society to

Publication of Transactions.

Classes of society to which the Members belong.

which they belong, so in later years we have had an analysis of the whole given. After the Society had been established nine years, we find that there were only 97 members: of these, 34 belonged to the Civil service, 17 were clergymen, lawyers, or medical men, 6 military men, 11 natives of rank, and 29 agents, merchants, planters, &c.; that is, 57 were unconnected with, and 40 were interested in, trade or the produce of the land. In the year 1839, we find there were 460 members; 98 of the Civil service, 69 military, and 40 medical officers, 20 law officers, 9 clergymen, 14 Europeans of no particular profession, 7 honorary members; in all, 257; with merchants and others engaged in commerce, 85; indigo planters, and other tropical agriculturists, 89; Asiatics, 29; in all, 203. The President complains in regard "to the natives of the country, who would ultimately be the greatest gainers by the labours of the Society, that so few had joined it, and that its objects had not met from them a more cordial support."

Attention to Horticultural subjects.

The Society, though they did not at first neglect agricultural subjects, as is evident from their prospectus and queries, and the premiums which they presented for the cultivation of coffee, yet chiefly attended to horticultural objects, including fruit trees, for the furtherance of which they established a garden. This seems to have swallowed up too much of the funds, and to have diverted the attention of the members from the meetings, and the publication of their proceedings. The Society has been blamed for this, but we have seen that all culture must partake at first of the nature of gardening ; but the members generally were then too apathetic to take much interest in the agriculture of the country. It was thought, however, and justly by many, about the beginning of 1829, that the efforts and funds of an Indian Agricultural Society might be better applied—in a word, that the sugar, cotton, coffee, silk, and other great staples of commerce, were far more legitimate objects of its special encouragement, than European fruit trees, &c. A further stimulus was given to the proceedings of the Society in November 1829, when it was intimated, that Government were desirous of co-operating with it, to promote the production of articles of raw produce of an improved description.

Increased attention paid to Agriculture

Co-operation of Government.

The Society, in their reply, recommended the more immediate means of improvement, consisting in the distribution of seeds, plants, useful information, and rewards. The government immediately granted 20,000 rupees for premiums, and in further aid of the Society's efforts, they were authorized to establish an experimental farm, for which the annual sum of 10,000 rupees, exclusive of rent, was allowed, and 4,500 for buildings, and stock for the first year. A special report was delivered to the Society, on the 12th August 1835, on the experiments made at the Akra farm on the cultivation of Cotton, Tobacco, and Sugar cane, which is published at the end of the second vo-

Experimental Farm established ;

Reported on.

Recent Progress of the Society.

lume of their Transactions This has been already referred to, as well as the numerous valuable papers contained in the subsequent volumes on most of the subjects treated of in this work. A portion of the Botanic Garden at Calcutta has been allotted as a nursery, and the members of the Society have continued to prosecute their researches with a vigour,* which cannot but be productive of very beneficial consequences to themselves and to the country. This has been chiefly under the Presidency of Sir Edward Ryan, with the able assistance of the successive secretaries, Mr. Robison, Dr. Wallich, Mr. Bell, and Dr. Spry. Their Transactions are indispensable to all who desire to enter upon any of the great cultures. It is to be wished that increased attention should be generally paid in future communications to the full influence of physical agents, and to the physiology of vegetation.

Other Societies established in different parts of India.

The example of the Calcutta Society has been followed by the institution of several branch Societies in different parts of India, and by the establishment of an Agricultural and Horticultural Society at Madras in 1836, and another at Bombay for the west of India, in 1830. We have only seen the first part of the "Proceedings" of the latter Society, where the same useful subjects attract attention, such as Sugar, Tobacco, Coffee, Cotton, and all kinds of natural products.

---

* As an instance, it may be mentioned, that 34,000 Otaheite sugar canes were distributed during the year 1839.

Recapitulation of the Survey of the History and Prospects of the Productive Resources of India.

Having laid aside, for the present at least, any detailed notice of the treasures of the animal and mineral kingdoms, we have seen how much vegetables contribute to the wealth of nations, and how essential is their careful and extended culture to the comfort and improvement of a country. This as yielding an abundant supply of food both for man and the animals he has domesticated, affording various products which may form articles both of internal and of external commerce, as well as be useful both for home and foreign manufactures, and all be valuable as sources of revenue, and contribute to the necessary expenses of all civilized countries. Importance of the culture of plants.

The culture of vegetables we have traced as connected with civilization itself; at first, limited in extent, and partaking of the nature of garden culture; subsequently extended into the open fields of a country; and at a still later period distinguished into the culture of particular plants, which continue to characterize different countries and nations in modern as in ancient times. Progress of the Arts of Culture.

Attention to, and improvements in, Agriculture we have seen followed by the disappearance of famines, great increase in the numbers of the people, as well as in the prosperity of the country. And yet, though conducing so much to the com- Benefits of improved Agriculture.

Arts of Culture promoted by Sovereigns, fort and riches of the subject, we have observed that, in the first instance, it has in most countries required the interference, and the encouragement of the Sovereign, for the commencement of cultures, which were as much for the advantage of the individual as for the improvement of the country. We had occasion also to notice in the course of our survey that the improvements in agriculture had not usually proceeded from its ordinary cultivators, but from those who with cultivated minds had turned to it as a recreation, or with the desire of improving what was of national importance, and which they saw but imperfectly performed. The want of skill in the earlier cultivators is apparent, from their depreciation of soil which in subsequent times is found well able, when differently cultivated, to produce the very plants with which they could not succeed.

and by non-professional individuals;

by union of men into societies.

This deficiency of skill, and the inability of individuals to contend with all the difficulties incident on improving old, and in introducing new cultures, seem to have been felt in the associating together of men for a common purpose in Societies. Here each might take up, or induce others to take up, different parts of the extensive subject, and the whole be forwarded by mutual consultation and united energies.

Plants, nature of.

Plants being living and organized bodies, fixed in the earth and growing in the air, have their functions dependant in a great measure upon physical agents. And, as the Arts of Culture obtain their principles from the sciences which treat of the several agents of Light, Heat, Air, and Moisture, and the Physiology of Vegetation, so did they improve with the improvement of the several Natural Sciences, and when men began to think of applying the Principles of Science to the Practice of the arts of culture. This we may see in the comparatively recent great improvements in the Horticulture as well as in the Agriculture of Europe.

Arts of Culture improved with progress of Natural Sciences.

Gardening and Agriculture were, no doubt, practised in eastern countries long before they were known in Europe. But once introduced, they have, like many other of the arts, similarly originating in the East, attained a degree of perfection unknown in the countries of their birth. With the characteristic energy of the European character, these have not been confined to the narrow limits of their own respective countries, for we find them spread wherever their influence extends, and especially introduced into their several colonies. Those who see a country teeming with population, and abounding in the cultivated produce of the soil for their subsistence and comfort, seldom think of the slow progress by which the several arts have arrived at the state of civilized perfection: nor how much the country they inhabit is indebted for many of what appear its natural riches to the zeal and energy of its earlier inhabitants. But if we refer to the annals of history, or the records of science, we shall soon be

Great improvement of Arts of Culture among the European race,

and spread wherever their influence extends.

Countries enriched by introduced plants.

convinced that many of the richest districts were, and that at no very remote period, but barren wastes, and their most valued products introduced from far distant countries. Though not more striking, it is yet within the memory of man that great changes have taken place in the Colonies and extra European countries both in the increase and decrease of some great staple products, which Europe had perhaps first received from some older civilized country, and conveyed to its earliest colonies.

Contrast between the neglect and patronage of Arts of Culture.

Those who do not readily perceive the benefits which have been derived, from the successive introduction of new plants, or the improved culture of old ones, have only to observe the stationary state of those European countries, or their Colonies, where these arts are neglected, and contrast them with the progressive improvement of such countries as England, where they are esteemed by the people, and patronized by the great. If we wish still further to be convinced of the importance, or are desirous of tracing the effects, of introducing useful plants into a country of which the soil and climate are suitable, we have only to inquire into the history, and observe the present state of many of the products of different countries, as well as of the principal staples of modern commerce. If we do so, we shall be surprised at finding how many were once strangers in the countries where they are now most abundantly produced.

We have seen that the Romans, and afterwards

Charlemagne, introduced into Europe many of the Vegetables and Fruits of Eastern countries. Since the several kinds of Corn, especially Wheat and Barley, were cultivated by the earliest civilized nations, it is probable that they also were introduced from the same direction, as probably also their Flax and Hemp. We see how much of the riches and commerce of the South of Europe consist in the oil of the Olive, and the dried Fruits, which like the Grape vine were of similar origin; and how much the latter enriches the countries where it flourishes, whether with its Fruit in a fresh or a dried state, fermented into a Wine, or distilled into a Spirit; the Mulberry of China supports there the Silk-worm of the same country. The Corn, Flour, and Fruits of the United States of America were originally received from Europe, and their Rice from India; even their Cotton and Tobacco, though indigenous in the New World, they derived from the more southern parts of their own continent. The West Indies, nursed into prosperity by the labour of slaves, and propped up by discriminative duties, were indebted for Sugar in the first instance, to the cane of the East Indies, and subsequently to that of Otaheite. Their Coffee and Aloes were introduced from Arabia. Rice and Plantains, Ginger, Indigo, once extensively cultivated, Pepper and Ginger, Tamarinds, Mango, Oranges, and Lemons, were all introduced from India, with Cloves, Cinnamon, and Nutmeg from other parts of Asia. The extended and varied

Agriculture and commerce of many countries from introduced plants.

Europe.

North America.

West Indies.

Introduced plants in South America.

territories of South America, abound in a great variety of vegetable products, coveted by other nations; but with the exception of Wheat, Plantains, Coffee, and a few Fruits, they have acclimated few of the plants of the Old World. But notwithstanding their natural riches, their commerce is small. The Cape of Good Hope is indebted to the Grape vine of Asia for the Wine which it exports, and, like New South Wales, to Europe for its Corn and Fruits, and the breed of Sheep, which yield the highly-valued Wool of these countries.

Cape of Good Hope and New South Wales.

Indigenous products of different countries.

Many countries, no doubt, chiefly export the products of their indigenous plants as the North of Europe and North America their Timber, Turpentine, Pitch, Tar, and Potash. The South of Spain, its Barilla. Africa its Gum, Myrrh, Aloes, and Dates. Arabia its Coffee and Senna. Tibet its Rhubarb. China its Tea and Silk. Persia its Gum-resins. Of medicinal substances only such as are indigenous to the soil, are exported from most countries, as Jalap from Mexico, Bark from Peru, Sarsaparilla and Ipecacuanha from South America, and these are all collected as produced by nature. A few of the valuable indigenous products of the New World are alone extensively cultivated; as Cocoa and Tobacco, Vanilla, Allspice, and Arrow-root.

Culture of introduced plants in India.

India, abounding as it does in highly prized natural products, indigenous to its soil, has yet appropriated others, which are hardly less valuable in contributing to the comforts of the people, extending their commerce, and increasing the revenues of the state. It is more than probable, that Wheat and Barley so extensively cultivated, and forming the chief food of the natives of Northern India, were introduced from the Tartarian or Persian region. Flax and the Poppy most likely reached India from the same direction. Hemp is indigenous in the Himalayas, and may therefore have been the source of that found in the plains, though, like the Flax, it seems to have been known to all the civilized nations of antiquity. Tobacco we know was taken from America, as was also Maize, or Indian corn, which is not cultivated to the extent, or with the care it merits, considering the nourishing nature of its grain as food for man, and its straw as fodder for cattle. The Capsicum is so extensively cultivated both in the plains and mountains, and has become such a necessary of life, that few will believe that it was originally introduced from the New World, though it is considered to have been so by all botanists. So many species of Silk-worm and of Mulberry are indigenous in India, it is possible, that the common species may also be a native, though it was most likely introduced at an early time from China.

Introduced plants in India.

Wheat, Barley.

Flax, Poppy.

Tobacco.

Maize.

Capsicum.

Silk-worm.

The indigenous products are, however, numerous and equally valuable, as Rice, and numerous smaller Grains and Pulses, which afford food to the inhabitants, while Sugar has been cultivated from such early times, that we are unable to trace its earliest history. Pepper, Cardamoms, Ginger, and

Indigenous products of the vegetable kingdom.

Indigenous products of the vegetable kingdom in India.

Turmeric furnished them with condiments; their Cotton provided them with clothing; Indigo, Lac, Munjeet, and numerous other Dyes, with colouring matter; many Vegetable Oils, fitted either for food or for affording light; Sun and Jute for cordage; Catechu as an astringent and for tanning leather. These form the principal articles of the modern commerce of India; and they must always have been produced within the limits of its territory. Many of them can be traced as having been known to the Greeks and Romans at very early periods.

Mineral substances produced in India.

The substances which have been noticed, with the exception of Silk and Lac, are from the vegetable kingdom; but several Mineral substances are equally produced in great abundance within the Indian territory, and which are too obvious to have escaped notice. These the Author has already noticed in another work. "As Common and

Salts.

Rock Salt; the former evaporated, as now, from sea water in the Bay of Bengal; the latter abundant in the salt rocks of the Punjab. Borax was probably obtained, in former times, as at the present day, from Tibet. Saltpetre must long before the time of the Arabs have been washed out of the soil, as it is in the present day, and was required for making the fireworks for which the Indians have long been famous. Sulphate of Soda (kharee muttee) they are in the present day well acquainted with, and obtain by similar means. Alum is made in Cutch, from an Alum earth; it is in constant use by the Hindoos in a variety of arts, as well as in medicine; and its Sanscrit name, *phitkara*, begins with a letter which is wanting in the Arabic alphabet. Sal Ammoniac must have been familiar to the Hindoos, ever since they have burnt bricks, as they now do, with the manure of animals, as some may usually be found crystalized at the unburnt extremity of the kilns. The Egyptians obtained it from the soot of the same kind of fuel. The Sanscrit name, *nuosadur*, is that, moreover, under which it is described by Arabian authors. Lime, they have long known how to obtain, by burning, not only limestone, but also shells and corals. Charcoal and Sulphur they were early acquainted with; the former they obtain from a variety of plants, and value that of each according to the purposes for which it is required.

Mineral substances prodused in India.

"The alkalis even must have been known to the Hindoos, as salts from the ashes of several vegetables; and caustics made from them are mentioned in the works to which the Arabs had access. The ashes of the plantain (Musa sapientum), and of the dhak (Butea frondosa) most frequently mentioned for medicinal purposes, must have afforded them a Carbonate of Potash (Pearl-ash), while the incineration of the Salsolas and Salicornias on the coasts of the peninsula, and the shores of the salt lakes of North-western India, must in former, as in the present day, have afforded them a Carbonate of Soda (Barilla), which is also

Alkalis known to the Hindoos.

Alkaline Salts known to Hindoos.

found effloresced on the soil in some parts of their country." Essay on the Antiquity of Hindoo Medicine, p. 40.*

---

* As Hindoo works on medicine make references to the above substances, as well as to the three principal acids, and to nine of the metals, the author conceived that Chemistry originated with the Hindoos, and was borrowed from them by the Arabs, especially as Serapion, Rhazes, and Avicenna quote from Sanscrit works, one of which, the Susruta, has a chapter, the title of which Professor Wilson translates, as "*Rasayana* or Chemistry, or more correctly, Alchemy; as the chief end of the combinations it describes, and which are mostly metallurgic, is the discovery of the universal medicine, or the elixir that was to render health permanent, and life perpetual."—Essay, p. 39.

Professor Dietz (vide Essay, p. 64) had already discovered, though the fact was unknown to the author, that the later Greek physicians were acquainted with the medical works of the Hindoos, and that Hindoo physicians even held appointments at the court of Harun-al-Rashid. Mr. Cureton has since published a paper on the Indian physicians at Bagdad, to which Professor Wilson has appended remarks, identifying many of the names. He comes to the conclusion, as the author had done by another series of proofs, "that the astronomy and medicine of the Hindoos were cultivated anteriorly to those of the Greeks, by the Arabs of the eighth century." Vide Journ. Royal Asiat. Soc. No. XI, p. 105. 1840.

The early attention paid by the sovereigns of India to the culture of trees and of useful plants, and the great attention paid by the natives of India to medicine, and the esteem in which it was held, are proved by the following most important inscription, of the date of about 220 B.C., deciphered by my late friend, the deeply lamented Secretary of the Asiatic Society of Calcutta, Mr. James Prinsep. Journal Asiatic Society, vol. V., p. 158. Calcutta, 1838.

"Everywhere within the conquered provinces of râja Piya-

Commercial articles produced less in their native,

In the preceding very cursory view of the commerce of different countries, we observe that many of the principal articles are not so much exported from the countries where they are indigenous, as from those where they have been introduced by individuals, or the patronage of the government. Also, that these strangers in new countries and climates are better and more productively cultivated in them than in the regions of their birth, in consequence, no doubt, of the zeal and energy of the people, who in the first instance took the trouble to introduce them. But also owing to the increased skill required on the part of the cultivator to overcome the difficulties opposed by nature. These are often apparently so great as to seem insurmountable, while, in fact, all that is required is such modification of the culture as to suit it to the new situation or to the

than in the countries where they are foreign.

Owing to skill and industry of inhabitants.

DASI, the beloved of the gods, as well as in the parts occupied by the faithful, such as *Chola, Pida, Satiyaputra,* and *Ketalaputra,* even as far as *Tambapannì* (*Ceylon*), — and moreover within the dominions of ANTIOCHUS the Greek, (of which ANTIOCHUS' generals are the rulers)—everywhere the heaven-beloved ràja PIYADASIS' double system of medical aid is established; — both medical aid for men, and medical aid for animals; together with medicaments of all sorts, which are suitable for men, and suitable for animals. And wherever there is no (such provision)— in all such places they are to be prepared, and to be planted: both root-drugs and herbs, wheresoever there is not (a provision of them), in all such places they shall be deposited and planted.

" And in the public highways, wells are to be dug, and trees to be planted, for the accommodation of men and animals."

Countries rich in gifts of nature, often neglect Arts of Culture.

product that is required. We have at the same time observed, that the countries which most abound in natural riches are frequently least solicitous about possessing the valuable products of other parts of the world. But they are unfortunately equally careless about their own, which they cultivate but little, or with indifferent skill, relying entirely upon the bounty of nature: this produces apathy and indolence, instead of the requisite degree of energy to benefit to the full extent by the facilities which she bountifully offers.

India rich in natural products, also cultivates extensively.

India, like China, offers a great contrast to both, as fertile in soil, favoured in climate, and rich in natural products, its inhabitants have yet from an early period practised extensive cultivation. They have originated, moreover, some of what are considered even the improved processes of agriculture in Europe. Possessing, as they do naturally, Rice, Sugar, Cotton, and Indigo, they have yet, as we have seen, long cultivated Wheat, Barley, Flax, Poppy, and in later times, Capsicum, Maize, and Tobacco, and still more recently the Potatoe and many of the Fruits of different countries. The early attention paid by the natives of India to such subjects is a proof of their civilization. This is remarkably conspicuous in so many articles of their ancient commerce, being not the spontaneous production of their wilds and forests, though these were not wanting, but the results of careful culture, and of manufacturing skill. This is evident in the Steel which was pre-

Manufactures and Chemical arts early practised by natives of India.

sented to Alexander the Great on his reaching the north of India. Cotton, also, we know, as having formed the clothing of the Indians in the time of Herodotus. It is probable that it was exported to Asiatic countries at still earlier periods, as the word *karpas* is used in the book of Esther, c. i. v. 6 (translated *hangings*): also *karpasos*, by Arrian; both are derived from the Sanscrit *karpasa*, Hindee *kapas*. We see this also in Sugar, which was known to the Greeks: here they must have expressed the juice of the cane and then crystallized it into sugar. Also in the Indigo, respecting which Dr. Bancroft says, "By what circumstance or event the people of Hindoostan alone were led several thousand years ago to discover and adopt means by which the blue colourable matter of the indigo plant might be extracted, oxygenated, and precipitated free from almost all the other matters naturally combined with it, and afterwards brought into the dry solid form in which we now find it, no one can, I believe, conjecture."—(Philosophy of Permanent Colours.) Their early success in so many Chemical arts, can only be explained, as the author has inferred, by their having originated the science of Chemistry, instead of the Arabs, as is generally supposed.

Manufactures and Chemical Arts early practised in India.

Cotton Cloth.

Sugar.

Indigo.

We have stated, that the natural fruitfulness of the country, and the facilities for culture, must early have furnished a superabundance of food, tended to increase the population, and allowed some the leisure to pursue manufactures, com-

Natural fruitfulness allowed leisure for arts and sciences.

India early famed.

merce, literature, and science. Hence the early celebrity and far-extended diffusion of the rich products of the Indian soil, as well as of the prized manufactures of their patient industry. In the present day, though manufacturing both Indigo and Sugar, India must be considered a great agricultural country, because these, as well as its Corn-grasses, Poppy, Cotton, and Mulberry, &c., all require extensive cultivation. Yet, notwithstanding its ancient fruitfulness, we may often hear it mentioned as unfitted to produce Cotton, Tobacco, and Rice equal to America, or Sugar and Coffee, like the West Indies; or Silk, like China or the South of Europe; or Flax like Ancient Egypt, or Hemp like Modern Italy. But we have seen that England was itself thought unfitted even for the growth of vegetables and of those fruits which we now see produced of the finest quality; not from any change in the soil or improvement in the climate, but in consequence of the increase in skill of its cultivators. We have also seen that the Arts of Culture even in Europe have arrived by slow degrees at their present perfection, and that the impulse has been given by sovereigns, remarkable men, and in later times, by the associating together of individuals in societies.

Still manufacturing, but chiefly agricultural; now thought unable to produce some of the great staples of commerce.

Probably owing to inferiority in skill to the western world.

Though we have stated that India was indebted for its ancient celebrity to its superior agricultural and manufacturing skill, yet it does not follow that these can now compete, either with the improved manufactures, or with the agriculture of Europe in the present day, or with that of North America, or of the West-Indies, which are conducted with the energy and skill characteristic of the European race. But by following the course which these have so successfully pursued, the same results may and undoubtedly will be obtained in India.

India now inferior in skill to some other parts of the world.

In the preceding observations we have briefly alluded to the origin of the Arts of Culture, and their slow progress both in Europe, its Colonies, and in Extra-European countries, for the express purpose of comparing with other countries the Natural Resources of India, the Progress which has been made in the Arts of Culture, and the Prospects which may be looked to for the future.

Historical survey of arts of Culture, to compare with their progress in India.

The Soil and Climate are as varied as the British territories in India are extended. Every part is rich in a great variety of Natural Resources, valuable for Food, Commerce, and Manufactures. Much has been done to increase these by the introduction of useful plants of all countries, both in the northern and in the southern provinces. The great variety of useful products yielded by plants generally, p. 13, is shown to be secreted by many of those indigenous in, or introduced into, and cultivated in India. The list of all these might have been very much extended.

The soil and climate being favourable and natural products abundant

The soil is as capable of producing, and the climate as suited to these varied products, as it ever was. Yet that they are not cultivated with

Skill alone required in India.

Skill alone required in India to compete with other parts of the world.

the skill which is desirable, is not to be wondered at, since the Hindoos find their ancient systems of Agriculture sufficient for their purposes, and they are naturally prejudiced in favour of that which has the sanction of antiquity. Few, if any, of the Europeans who have settled as cultivators in the country have been professional farmers. The majority were therefore unacquainted with the practice of the art in Europe, as well as with the details of tropical culture in the New World. Still fewer have been familiar with the Sciences connected with the Arts of Culture, and which in the absence of experience would have given them principles for guidance in their practice.

Extensive results have already been obtained.

The efforts of the Government, we have seen, were commenced at an early period, and have been continued up to the present time, in instituting experiments, often on an extensive scale, for the improvement of the resources of India. In addition to these, plants of all countries have been incessantly introduced into the country by the Government gardens; and many which are useful and important have been naturalized all over the wide extent of British India. Several societies also have now been established. Our object has been to show the course that has been pursued, as well as the results which have been obtained, and by the observations on the failures or the successes, to indicate the course to be followed in future experiments—that is, the necessity of applying scientific principles to insure successful practice.

Thus, in the history of the several experimental cultures of which we have given the details, we see the Poppy cultivated in the cold weather, like other foreign introductions, as Wheat, Barley, and Flax, and acclimated by the natives of India. The opium produced is of as good quality in the territories without, as in those within European influence; because, being simply an inspissated juice, it required only care in the collection. The Flax plant is valued only on account of the oil contained in its seeds, while the Hemp for the intoxicating nature of the secretions of its leaves. Hence both are so planted as to receive the full influence of light, heat, and air. In one, the ligneous fibre is short, and in the other hard and brittle; but a modification of the culture in both, consisting only of the adoption of the European mode of cultivation, or the imitation of that practised by the natives themselves for cordage plants, would, no doubt, secure softness and length of fibre, and the production of probably as good flax and hemp as in any other part of the world. Tobacco imported from the New World is now cultivated all over India, but is not prepared so as to be esteemed in European markets, because, when cut, it is exposed to the full effects of the sun and air, and thus becomes dry and powdery. While in America the greatest care is taken by effects of heating when heaped up, moisture and afterwards by careful drying in the shade (that is, by the process of curing), to bring it to a soft, pliable state, of a brown colour, and with a honey

Instances of successful and unsuccessful culture in India.

Flax.

Hemp.

Tobacco.

Cases of successful and unsuccessful culture.

smell. Hence, therefore, it is too much exposure and dryness which is injurious to the Indian product.

Cotton.

In Cotton, on the contrary, a little exposure and careful drying are absolutely necessary, as if heaped up when fresh picked, the staple is sure to get discoloured as well as weakened. This very injurious process is that actually practised in India, the cotton with the seed being frequently heaped together for some time before it is cleaned. Besides neglect in the cleaning of cotton, the growth of the plant also is in most parts of India neglected, and very different from the careful culture of America; there being no selection of the seed; also close sowing and mixture of crops, by which the growth of the parts of vegetation is favoured, instead of those of fructification.

Sugar and Indigo for their successful production require attention to the culture of the plants, as well as to the Chemistry of the Manufacture.

Indigo,

The colouring matter of the Indigo being stored up in the leaves, and these being produced in the greatest profusion in the rich provinces of Bengal, makes the culture there the most lucrative; while the comparative dryness of the northern provinces and their freedom from inundation are favourable for the production of the seed. This is consequently supplied by the planters of the north, to those of the south, and has probably had considerable effect in preventing deterioration of the plant. India, we have also seen, was deprived of the commerce, when European skill was applied to its manufacture in the New World, and recovered it again by the very means by which it had been deprived, assisted by the continued and powerful support of the East India Company. Cases of successful and unsuccessful culture.

The cultivation of the Sugar Cane, so as to insure the largest secretion of saccharine matter, has been less attended to; but the different physical states on which this is dependant afford a fruitful subject for experiment. We have seen, that when the necessities of Great Britain required it, a trade in sugar was immediately established. The China Sugar Cane was introduced into India nearly at the same time that the Otaheite Cane was taken to the West Indies. This is now spreading all over India, though some doubt whether it be superior to the Cane of China; but there can be no doubt that the sugar of the East Indies has been greatly improved by the application of the skill in manufacture of the West Indies, and that it will be still more improved. Sugar.

The Tea plant, we have seen, was, on scientific grounds, supposed could be grown in the Himalayas: the results of the experiments, as far as they have yet gone, prove the opinions to have been correct. The tea from Assam has been pronounced a good, strong, and very useful description, and that it will probably be classed with good and fine Congou tea. From the accounts which have been received here of the cost of production, with every charge for conveyance, it is likely Tea plant.

Cases of successful and unsuccessful culture.

that the Assam Company will considerably undersell the Chinese. (Lords' Committee on Petition of East-India Company.) Dr. Falconer is also of opinion that the culture will most undoubtedly thrive, and Tea be produced at a cheaper rate than in China.

Coffee

Coffee is becoming cultivated in various parts of India, and produced of very excellent quality. The Fruit trees of various countries are as much at home as in their native sites, and many of the important plants of the New World, as the Mahogany, Logwood, Pimento, are becoming spread over the whole country. There seems no limit to the extent to which the acclimating of the useful plants of other countries may be carried, as there is no reason why we should not be able to do this as easily as many of them have acclimated the indigenous plants of India.

Fruit trees.

Mahogany. Logwood. Pimento.

Animal substances. Cochineal

With regard to animal substances, the experimental culture of Cochineal was as successful as could be expected with the materials at that time obtainable. And sufficient was learnt to satisfy every one that the true Cochineal insect would thrive well in the districts where the wild kind had spread with such amazing rapidity. The Government patronage, though liberal enough to have established the culture even of the true insect, had only a temporary effect upon that which was so inferior, as the increased employment of Lac, and the diminished price of Cochineal, combined their effects in discouraging the culture.

Cases of successful and unsuccessful culture.

Silk.

The Silk culture, though known to India, was only established on a firm basis by the energetic patronage of the East-India Company, and then only by sending Europeans well acquainted with the Italian method of culture to improve the silk of India. The difficulties were altogether great, inasmuch as both the best kinds of Silk-worm and of Mulberry were required, and a climate suited to both. The best mode of culture of the Mulberry and the treatment of silk-worm in the different parts of India have yet to be determined, but it is probable that the culture may be extended over many districts where it is at present unknown.

Wool.

Wool is one of the articles which has most recently become an article of commerce. From the measures which have been adopted by the Government of sending to India the most approved rams both from Europe, the Cape, and New Holland, and from the suitableness of the climate and pastures of many parts of India, there is little doubt that this will also be established as an highly important, and much improved branch of Indian commerce.

Natural products, or Drugs—importance of.

Though we have confined ourselves chiefly to the principal Agricultural objects, and those which form the great Staples of Commerce, it would have been easy, as may be apparent from hints in several passages, to have enlarged on many other substances, as well as on those coming under the head of Natural Products. These employed

Indian Natural Products or Drugs.

by the natives of India in their various arts, might, if better known, be useful also for the manufacturers of England, and thus serve to increase the commerce of both countries. Many of these come under the general denomination of Drugs, and we learn from Mr. Larpent's evidence before the House of Lords' Committee, March 1840, that those coming from India are generally thought in the mercantile world to be inferior to the drugs imported from other parts of the world. That the great object of merchants connected with India is to encourage them in the English market, and to improve their qualities. But to this, there are great difficulties in the high duties which are imposed on their introduction into this country; as Mr. L. informs us, that the answer merchants get when they urge their correspondents to improve their qualities, is, "Your duties are so high that it is of no use to attempt to improve them."

Indian Drugs said to be inferior.

High duties imposed on in England.

Many Indian drugs are inferior, from the carelessness of the natives in preparing and in collecting them ; but a part of their imputed inferiority is ascribable to their being merely different in their constituents from some of those better known, which are imported from other parts of the world. For it is only when the constituents of a natural product are accurately known that we can speak with any confidence of its relative value. Because what is unsuited for one purpose, may be preferred for another, and therefore what one manufacturer

Supposed inferiority of Indian Drugs.

Imputed inferiority of Indian Natural products.

might consider inferior would be considered superior by another. Of the importance of these natural products or drugs, one may be convinced, by the history of the trade of Lac and Shell lac, Safflower, and more recently in that of Rape and Linseed, Cocoa nut oil, and Caoutchouc, and many others which remain in the category of drugs, until becoming known and used, they are imported in large quantities and come to be ranked as staple articles of commerce. Catechu was only employed in tanning after the analysis of Sir H. Davy. The value of many others is evident from some of the Chemical analyses which have recently been made in India by Dr. O'Shaughnessy, and in this country by Mr. E. Solly.

Results of review of experimental cultures.

In the review which we have thus taken of the different experimental cultures, we have seen that several have become established as great Indian staples, and yet the difficulties which, as in almost all new cultures, were encountered in their establishment, and the course by which they arrived at their present state, seem to be forgotten. An attentive perusal of their history is, however, instructive, as showing the measures to be adopted, or those to be avoided, and the results which may be expected, even when first experiments have not been successful, as in the cases of Tobacco and Cotton. In the accounts which are given of the several experiments made, we seldom find any complaints that plants do not grow; for, in fact, those suited to a warm

Probable improvement of Indian products from increased skill in culture.

climate, usually grow too much from the combined warmth and moisture of the climate. To these experimentalists often think it necessary to add richness of soil, though this only increases the usual fault of over-luxuriance. But after a repetition of trials, a modification of treatment, and the application of European science, we find that improvement does eventually take place, and improvements will no doubt continue to take place, when the same means are adopted and the experiments are made in a suitable soil and favourable climate. Superior science and careful culture seem to have been originally the causes of the great celebrity of the products of Ancient India, and they have elsewhere produced similar results in modern times. But as civilization has advanced, the European race have applied their energies and skill to the culture of the same products, and in soils and climates similar to that of India. Hence the productions of India have had to compete with the highly improved products of these countries, and therefore a still further degree of skill is requisite there to produce yet greater improvement.

Nature of skill required.

The skill required for the culture either of the indigenous or exotic plants in India may be distinguished into two kinds:—

1. A practical knowledge of the details of culture in general, or of that peculiar to particular plants

2. A knowledge of the principles which are

applicable to all, and which necessarily influence all the results.

Nature of skill required for cultures in India.

Practical experience or the advice of practical men.

The first can only be acquired by practice, or observation, or by consulting the writings, or taking the advice of practical men. This is, however, generally applicable only to the particular soil and situation to which a planter has been accustomed. But those who have carried on the arts of culture in the varying soils and climates of different districts know that in all some modifications of treatment are required. Therefore, before commencing culture in a new situation, farmers first ascertain by inquiries respecting the soil and climate, what are the modifications of treatment necessary to insure success. By combining a knowledge of the practical details of culture in different places, and seeing how they correspond with the principles of the science, it is possible so to arrange the instructions for culture as to be applicable to a new soil and situation. This would save many mistakes; and at all events, point out the sources of error and the means of obviating them.

A knowledge of the principles of culture.

A knowledge of the principles on which depend the successful practice of the arts of culture, can only be thoroughly acquired by those who are acquainted with, at least the general principles of several sciences. Though a knowledge of these is not essential for successful practice, it is yet difficult without them to understand the full operation of physical agents or the modifications

Sciences connected with the Arts of culture.

which may be required in different cultures to suit them to new situations.

Rock formations as forming earths.

Though an acquaintance with rock formations may not be essentially necessary to a knowledge of soils, yet earths are formed from the disintegration of rocks exposed on the surface, and these often extend over a considerable extent of country. Hence we are often able, without examination, to say that such and such mineral constituents will predominate in the soil and subsoil of another, perhaps distant district, and to which the same culture will therefore often be applicable.

Chemical analysis of soils.

Chemical analysis will reveal to us, indeed, the constituents of a soil, and show us whether those are such as are best suited to the culture we wish to attempt; also enable us to judge what are the constituents it has in excess, and what in deficiency, and therefore on the mineral additions which require to be made.

Physical properties of soils.

These are as material as the organized additions which it requires, as manure for the plant. For on them, in a great measure, depend the physical properties, which are quite as important as the chemical, as on them depend the firmness and consistency of the soil, its power of retaining water, or of becoming dry, its capacity of absorbing humidity, or oxygen from the atmosphere, or of becoming more or less warm by exposure to the sun.

Geology of India.

Few of the varied soils of India have had their chemical or physical properties carefully examined, but we have now a very fair general idea of the rock formations of different parts of India, and may infer that, of much of the intermediate tracts. Thus commencing with the south, Drs. Buchanan Hamilton and Heyne, Mr. Turnbull Christie, Drs. Benza and Malcolmson, and Mr. Cole, have described that of the Peninsula. Col. Sykes has elucidated the trap formation of the Deccan; Dr. Thomson the geology of Bombay; and Capt. Grant of Cutch. Dr. Voysey, when attached to the Trigonometrical Survey, published some of the earliest papers on the geology of Central India; this has been since described by Dr. Malcolmson and by Capt. Jenkins. Meywar and the valley of Oudeypore have been described by Mr. Hardie; Malwa by Capt. Dangerfield; Saugur by Capt. Coulthurd and Dr. Spry; Bundlecund by Capt. Franklin; the series of rock formations on the great military road from Calcutta to Benares, and the sandstone formation of N. West India, by the Rev. Mr. Everest. Much valuable information is also contained in the works of Dr. B. Hamilton. The Himalayas, which bound the great Gangetic plains, have been described by Mr. Colebrooke, Dr. Gerard, Capts. Herbert and Cautley, Mr. McClelland, and Dr. Falconer, as well as by the Author.* Immense deposits of

Sciences connected with the Arts of Culture.

Geology of different parts of India described.

* Mr. McClelland has furnished a valuable report on the Coal and Mineral resources of India. Dr. B. Hamilton has described the Minerals of the Rajmuhl Hills; Capt. Herbert those of the Himalayas; Drs. Anderson and Heyne those of the Peninsula. The Author has enumerated most of the Mineral Productions: *v.* Essay on the Antiquity of Hindoo Medicine, p. 97, &c.

Sciences connected with the Arts of Culture.

fossil remains have been found, both along the Nerbudda and the Jumna, as well as in the Himalayas, but not having immediate reference to our subject, we need not further notice.

Meteorology in reference to plants.

The necessity of attending to the climate of a country, when attempting a new culture, is generally acknowledged. Few, however, pay attention to the details which are absolutely necessary to be known, before we can be assured that the climate of a place is suited to the plant we wish to cultivate. Observation could alone have informed us what peculiarities of climate are suited to particular plants. The illustrious Humboldt has shown how different cultures are, in consequence, restrained within certain limits. As the temperatures of different countries which correspond in latitude have a general correspondence, so it has been inferred that the plants of one will grow in the other. This is often found to be the case, but still exceptions are frequently observed. These can usually be accounted for, from some difference in the climate, or want of suitableness between the soil and climate. Observations of the thermometer, which are so generally made, are seldom taken with all the precautions necessary for ascertaining the true climate of the open country of a place. They are sometimes observed in the house, and frequently at such hours and under such circumstances as to prevent us knowing the true extremes, and therefore the means of temperature. The first is essentially necessary, as a very short

Sciences connected with the Arts of Culture.

frost, or a very little exposure to the hot winds, may be injurious to many plants. For perennials we require to know the annual temperature, but for annuals only that of the season of cultivation. This in India being very different at different periods of the year, we require the extremes and mean temperature of the rainy as well as of the cold season. Temperature, however, is not sufficient; the dryness and moisture of the atmosphere are equally essential; also the effects of absorption of the solar rays, by which we ascertain the heat to which plants are exposed during the day at the surface of the earth; likewise those of radiation, which will give us information regarding the cold to which they are exposed during night. Also the quantity and times of rain, as well as the force, temperature and dryness, or moisture of the wind; as on these will depend the rate of evaporation, which will influence the growth of plants, and therefore the mode in which we should grow them. For instance, cotton requires to be planted at such distances as to allow of the free circulation of air, and thus a certain loss of space is caused, but this should not be more than is necessary. As the distances depend on the soil and climate, the drier air of the northern provinces will admit of the plants being placed much closer to each other than in the moister soil and air of Bengal. The importance of such investigations has been pointed out in the several specific subjects which have been treated of.

Meteorology as connected with vegetation.

Sciences connected with the Arts of Culture.

The Meteorology, like the Geology of India, is known in a general way, and we have very good series of observations at several stations all along the extent of British India, and may for the present infer that of intermediate places. At these, precise observations are, however, also required, and will form a fruitful subject of interesting observation. Many important papers are contained in the Transactions of the Royal and Asiatic Societies, and in the invaluable Journal of the Asiatic Society of Bengal, edited by the late highly-talented and deeply-lamented Secretary, Mr. James Prinsep; also in that of the Madras Society of Literature and Science.

Magnetic Observatories, having also Meteorological instruments, ordered to be established in India.

Precise information will also be afforded by the Magnetic Observatories, which, in conjunction with her Majesty's Government in different parts of the world and with the naval expedition under Capt. James Ross, the Court of Directors of the East India Company have, on the application of the Royal Society, directed to be established at Simla, in the Himalayas, Singapore, Madras, and if possible at Aden. The best instruments both for Magnetic and Meteorological observations have been provided, and placed under Engineer officers, who have been instructed in their use by Professor Lloyd, of Dublin.*

* To those desirous of making observations, it may be suggested, that they could not confer a greater benefit on Indian Meteorology, than by making simultaneous observations with

As the Arts of Culture are employed upon Plants, it would appear necessary that a cultivator should be acquainted with the science of vegetation. This, however, is seldom the case, though a general knowledge of the subject is essential to a right understanding, even of the operations of agriculture; or of the effects produced on the plant or its products by the more or less exposure to the influence of physical agents, or by the several labours on the soil or plants which constitute agriculture. Though it is not requisite that a cultivator should be acquainted with what is generally considered Botany, but which is only the systematic department of that extensive science; yet it is essential that he should know the plant he wishes to cultivate, that he may not mistake it for some other variety, or perhaps species of the same genus, as has often been done. Sometimes even one plant has been cultivated for another, when they had no other similarity than that of being employed for the same purpose.

Sciences connected with the Arts of Culture.

Botany, or the knowledge of plants.

One department of the science which treats of Vegetation, namely, that of the vital actions, called the Physiology of Plants, is so interesting, and at the same time so important, that a knowledge of its principles would form an agreeable pur-

Physiology of Plants.

---

those made at the Magnetic Observatories, &c., at as many and at such hours as are convenient to the individual, and suited to attain the object in view, conformably to the instructions drawn up by the Meteorological Committee of the Royal Society.

Sciences connected with the Arts of Culture.

suit, and is at the same time essential towards conducting a scientific, and it might almost be said a successful, cultivation in a new situation. By it we may understand the process of germination and the growth of the plant, as well as the functions of the root, stem, and leaves, and the processes which favour the appearance of flowers and the production of fruit. The Author has frequently endeavoured to direct attention to the influence of external agents on the growth of the different parts, and consequently on the products of plants, so as to alter the quality and the productiveness of some of the great staples of Indian agriculture. To this subject he hopes to return on some future occasion, and to elucidate it, with the details applicable to Indian culture and climate; feeling that when principles are understood, sources of error will readily be discovered, and modifications of treatment easily be made. The importance of this subject is strongly evinced by the appearance, while the present work has been passing through the press, of one by Dr. Lindley, called the "Theory of Horticulture," elucidating the practice of gardening by the principles of vegetable physiology. Much of this is necessarily applicable to culture of all kinds.

Physiology of Plants.

Action of external agents.

Geography of Plants.

Another important branch of the science of botany of the present day is one which has been already alluded to at p. 244, that is, the Geography of Plants. Almost every one knows, that particular sets of plants are found growing in hot and tropical parts of the world, which, when transferred to European latitudes, require the climate of our hot-houses, while those from more temperate climates are suited to green-houses, and those from colder parts of the world to the shrubberies and forests of the country.

Sciences connected with the Arts of Culture.

Geography of Plants.

The Natural Classification of Plants, which has also been alluded to, *vide* p. 242, affords peculiar advantages in studying their geographical distribution. Because we soon perceive, though there are exceptions, yet that the great majority of the families of plants are found flourishing in the greatest numbers in some particular country or climate, and existing only in small numbers, or as single species, in other countries, but where there is usually some similarity in climate. The Indian flora, as at present ascertained, consists of about twelve thousand species of plants, which are distributed in upwards of two hundred natural families. Among these, there are representatives of almost all the principal families of plants, and certainly of all those which contain useful or important plants.

Natural classification of Plant.

It has therefore been inferred that many of these useful plants of other countries, or their congeners, or those belonging to the same family, and which so generally flourish in a similar soil and climate, might be successfully cultivated within the wide-spreading limits and elevated mountains of the British dominions in India.

Transmission of Seeds to and from India by the Overland Route.

Transmission of Seeds to and from India.

The advantages being undoubted, and the prospects of success great, the Court of Directors of the East-India Company determined on not allowing the opportunity, offered by the speedy communication with India, to escape, of sending to that country the materials for growing there the plants suited to its varied soils and climate, and such as are likely to conduce to the improvement of the country, and the benefit of the people; obtaining also from its mountains such as are suited to the climate of Great Britain. The subject was brought under the notice of the Court of Directors by a despatch from the Governor-general, dated Simla, the 16th Aug. 1838, intimating that his lordship had addressed an order to the officers in charge of such districts in the north-western provinces as are either within, or which border on, the Himalayan range, instructing them to collect in the autumn, suitable seeds, bulbs, and roots, for transmission overland to England.

The Governor-general, adverting to the facilities afforded by the steam communication, and referring to the interest known to be taken by the Court in increasing the Vegetable riches of the two countries, expresses a hope that such useful seeds and plants may be sent out to India as may gradually be naturalized in that country, and recommends inquiry being made in this country for advice on the subject.

Advantages of the Transmission of the Seeds of Useful Plants to India.

On the importance of the object contemplated by Lord Auckland, and sanctioned by the Court of Directors, it is scarcely necessary to offer any remarks. So large a share of the wealth of every country is composed of its vegetable productions, and those productions in such a variety of ways minister to supply the wants of man, that to increase their number or improve their quality cannot fail to be regarded as a benefaction to the country thus enriched. Indebted as man is to the vegetable kingdom for food, shelter, and clothing, for the means of restoring health and assuaging pains, the propriety of Governments promoting the introduction of valuable plants into the countries over which they rule can scarcely be questioned. In India, particularly, the duty of acting upon these views is enjoined by peculiar reasons. The productive powers of the soil will give every advantage to the attempt of those disposed to call them forth, and the people being accustomed so generally to a vegetable diet, renders it important to secure to them as large a supply and as great a variety of such diet as possible. The occurrence of those severe visitations of Providence, by which the happiness of the people is for the time destroyed, and even the preservation of existence rendered almost impossible, calls imperatively for the adoption of any measures, such as the introduction of plants less dependant on rain, which might tend to avert such calamities, or alleviate their effects. The commercial position of India requires a large amount of exchangeable productions, and these must be raised from the soil, for it is to agriculture that India must look for the means of engaging in commerce.

Great extent to which the introduction of Plants may be carried.

Carried to its legitimate extent, the plan for the enrichment of India by such vegetable productions as are adapted to the country would be a most extensive one; for, as is observed by Dr. Lindley, "from the great extent of the British possessions in India, and the infinite modifications and combinations of soil and climate to be found within them, there can be no doubt whatever that almost every production of every climate, except the Arctic, may be so completely naturalized, that where they are of any importance as objects of cultivation, they may be brought to all the perfection of which they are susceptible in other countries."

Recommended to be undertaken.

It has accordingly been recommended that the gradual introduction, from every part of the world, into India, of every variety of tree and plant adapted to its climate, should be an object steadily kept in view. Also that such measures should immediately be taken as may be necessary to secure a supply of seeds for future seasons in such quantities as seem desirable, with reference to the means that may exist for their cultivation.

Despatch of the Court of Directors on the subject.

In the Proceedings of the Agricultural and Horticultural Society of India, of the 12th of June 1839, we find that the Governor-general had forwarded to the Society the despatch of the Court of Directors to the Governor-general of India, of the 13th of February 1839, together with the letters which had been written by Dr. Lindley and the Author in reference to this subject. The Court say, "We are sensible of the importance of the subject to which, in the letter under reply, you have directed our attention, and we have resolved on gradually furnishing you with the means of carrying on extensively experiments for naturalizing in India useful and desirable plants, indigenous in other countries." "We have forwarded some varieties of seeds, &c., highly important either as affording articles of food, or possessing medical virtues, and they will deserve all the attention that can be afforded them." "We shall continue at the proper seasons to send supplies of other varieties, and it is our wish that the greatest care should be bestowed, with a view to their naturalization, for the benefit of the country."

Despatch respecting the Transmission of Seeds to India;

"With regard to the collection of seeds for transmission to this country, we are of opinion, that the expediency of bearing in mind the nature of the climate to which they are to be exposed should be impressed upon those to whom the task is to be committed."

from India.

The Society, after the reading of the despatch and its enclosures, determined, in furtherance of so "useful and philanthropic an object, — that in reference to the communication now read from the Honourable the Court of Directors of the

Resolution of the Agricultural Society of India.

Resolution of the Agricultural Society of India.

East India Company, and with the view of aiding as far as possible, the intentions therein expressed, and the labours of those scientific gentlemen at home, who have so kindly interested themselves in the subject — a committee be formed for the purpose of suggesting such plants and trees as may be thought desirable for introduction into India, and those that can be furnished in return, and that the committee be instructed to obtain communications from the Branch Societies and other available sources throughout India."

The measures which were adopted here in consequence of the resolution of the Court it is unnecessary to particularize, as more fitting occasions may occur for entering into the necessary details.

Times when seeds should arrive in India.

Keeping in view the necessity of obtaining the seeds of plants of different countries suitable to the different parts of India, the principle exhibited in the tables at p. 246 may serve as a guide. To obtain complete success will require only perseverance, and a systematic arrangement of the means adapted to the ends in view. The roots and seeds requiring tropical culture should be in India by the middle of June; that is, at the beginning of the rainy season. Those intended for cultivation in the plains during the cold weather, should arrive in October and November, while such as are to be sown in the Himalayas need not be there before March, or even April.

The seeds obtained from various sources may be sent in separate parcels as intended for warm or for cool climates, as for Bombay, Madras, Calcutta, and Saharunpore, or for the Hills of Mahabhaleshwur, Neilgherries, Darjeeling, Mussooree, and Simla. Wherever practicable, the Botanic Gardens or their nurseries seem the most suitable situations for the first cultivation of the various seeds or plants which may be introduced, but the Gardens of the several Horticultural Societies at the Presidencies might be equally advantageous wherever they are desirous of joining in the experiment. Whenever a plant has become established, or its seed has ripened in one garden, these should be distributed to the others which have been enumerated, or to the several branch Horticultural Societies which have been established, or to individuals who are inclined to pay the requisite attention to such pursuits. The several gardens in different parts of India ought also to interchange their several products, even their indigenous and long-established cultures, more freely and systematically than has hitherto been the case. Gardeners and Farmers in Europe seldom continue to cultivate from the seed constantly ripened in their own grounds, but interchange with, or purchase from others, what these again are ready to do with theirs. **Measures advisable for adoption in India.**

The seeds of a great variety of plants have been sent by the monthly mail at different times to the several Botanic Gardens which have been enumerated, and latterly to the Agricultural Societies of Calcutta and Bombay. Of the measures adopted, an instance may suffice in the extract of the following letter from Monsieur A. De **Seeds sent to India; and Bombay.**

Candolle, of Geneva, who is following the course of the distinguished Botanist, his father.

Letter from M. A. De Candolle.

"Mon cher Monsieur,

"Je viens d'adresser à Mr. Bentham une caisse qui contient différens objets pour vous. Ce sont d'abord des graines, d'espèces cultivées dans notre jardin, et de plantes cultivées en grand dans ce pays. Je ne suis pas parvenu encore à me procurer les Céréales cultivées dans les plus hautes parties de la Suisse, mais j'ai pensé que les variétés usitées dans nos plaines réussiraient peut être mieux dans l'Inde que les semences venues d'Angleterre. On estime en agriculture qu'il faut croïser les semences, c'est-à-dire semer dans un pays des blés venant d'un autre, afin qu'ils aient des qualités différéntes de celles que le climat du pays a pu donner. C'est dans cette idée que je vous ai envoyé des céréales et des légumes communs de ce pays. D'ailleurs nos légumes du continent sont préférables à ceux de l'Angleterre, et leurs graines sont plus mures. Une autre fois je pourrai probablement vous donner des espèces alpines et des céréales des hautes régions."

Arrival of the Seeds in India.

With regard to the time and state of the arrival of the seeds in India, Dr. Wallich, expressing his grateful thanks to the Court of Directors, wrote on the 24th August 1839, that the noble packet of seeds dispatched on the 11th of May had arrived there on the 12th July. The seeds having been immediately sown, several had already vegetated; of these, the highly interesting Sea Island Cotton germinated in four days. Of the moderate supply of the latter, he had furnished small quantities to a number of practical men, as Capt. Jenkins and Dr. Wight. He particularly requests that assortments of seeds may be continued to be sent, especially those from South

America and the West Indies, as they succeed, in general, remarkably well, and that on his part he would do his utmost to reciprocate, by endeavouring to obtain the sort of temperate zone seeds that are so much desired in England. Arrival of the Seeds in India.

Dr. Falconer, to whom the first supplies had been sent, complains of the packing not having been sufficient to keep out the wet, as some Mahogany seeds and others had arrived in a damp and rotten state. India rubber cloth having been adopted for the packing of all the subsequent despatches, he writes, "Your August and September despatches have arrived in excellent order. The double India rubber mode of packing is admirable—it could not be better." The seeds he describes as excellent of their kind, and the supply of vegetable seeds as exceedingly valuable. He requests a fresh supply, so as to reach him in February for sowing in the hills, also as many flower seeds as possible both for sowing in the hills and plains.

The seeds collected in India, as is evident from the diversified nature of the country, will require very different kinds of climate. The kinds most valued here are such as are suited to the climate of the country, and therefore can only be obtained in the mountains, at such elevations as the region of Oaks. Those first sent, having been collected by the zeal of several officers, were more promiscuous in nature than is esteemed by the generality of horticulturists. But the later collections have been excellent in selection, and packed Seeds from India.

Transmission of Seeds from India.

so perfectly well, as to arrive here in as fresh a state as possible. This is evident from the following documents of the vegetation of seeds which hardly ever vegetated here before.

Speaking generally, it may be said that it is desirable to send a selection rather than a great variety of seeds. At first, from being collected in different localities, and by different individuals, many duplicate parcels were sent. It seems advisable, therefore, that seeds collected for transmission to this country should be forwarded to the Superintendents of the Botanic Gardens in the different presidencies, who should, with as little delay as possible, inspect, select, and if possible name such as it was deemed necessary to send, and to separate the few from the plains and vallies requiring a hot climate from those suited to the open culture of this country. The kinds of seed most valued here are those of ornamental or useful flowering plants and shrubs, or such as are likely to be useful as timber trees, or otherwise. By this means, though the bulk and number of the packages would be curtailed, their value would remain undiminished.

Distributed in this country and on the Continent.

The seeds received have been distributed to public gardens, and to distinguished individuals, both in Great Britain and on the Continent, keeping in view the interchange of seeds. The majority of those to whom seeds have been sent have expressed their intention of sending others in return, and many have already done so. I may instance Count Woronzow and M.A.De Candolle, as having already done so from the Continent. The opinions of Dr. Lindley and Messrs. Loddiges are subjoined, as showing the success attending the new mode of transmission with seeds, received chiefly from Dr. Falconer.

Growth of Himalayan seeds in England.

"*Horticultural Society of London,*

"My Dear Sir, "August 24, 1840.

"I have great pleasure in informing you that the result of the seeds, for which we have so repeatedly been indebted to the liberality of the Honourable Court of Directors, has been most satisfactory. A very considerable number of fruit trees, shrubs, and handsome herbaceous plants have already been secured to the country. Among the former are the Deodar in abundance, as well as other Himalayan Coniferæ and Betula Bhojpattra, which would alone render the exertions of the Company in the introduction of new plants of national importance, especially since the large quantity of such things which is imported renders it practicable at once to disperse them through the country.

"Should you desire to have a detailed return of the plants of all kinds that have been raised in the Society's Garden, it shall be provided without loss of time.

"Yours faithfully,

"JOHN LINDLEY."

"Professor Royle."

"Dear Sir, "Hackney, June 23, 1840.

"We are happy to be able to inform you, that the seeds of Pinus Deodara which you were kind enough to send us, have grown perfectly well, scarcely one failing. Also Pinus Webbiana, excelsa, and Khutrow. The advantages of getting seeds overland are most decided; we have had great quantities of Deodara sent by sea from time to time, and hardly ever got one to grow, whereas these quite surpassed all our expectations.

"We remain, dear Sir, yours very truly,

"To Dr. Royle." "C. LODDIGES & SONS."

Resources of India.

From the enumeration of a few only of the vegetable resources of India, and the success which has attended the introduction of many not indigenous to its soil, we may, with no undue confidence, anticipate the most successful results. Of this any one may be convinced, if they consider, as the Author has already said elsewhere, that the southern part of the Indian peninsula, like Ceylon, is suited to the cultivation of Cinnamon, Coco, Nutmegs, and other Spices, and the coast of Malabar for Pepper, Cardamoms, Coffee, and Teak. But they are not more so than are Bengal and the lower provinces of that presidency, for their rich cultivation of Rice, Indigo, and Silk, with Ginger, Turmeric, Long Pepper, and Betlel leaf, luxuriant Bamboos, bread-like Plantains, ever useful Cocoa nut, and slender Areca. The northern provinces having a less rich soil and drier climate, may boast of their Wheat, Barley, and Potatoe culture, at one season of the year, with Rice, Sorghum, &c., at another; as well as of their fitness, together with Malwa, Bundlecund, the West of India, and other parts of the Peninsula, for the production of Cotton, Tobacco, and Opium, while Sugar, numerous Oil seeds, and substitutes for Hemp and Flax are produced in nearly every part. Almost every jungle is occupied by the Lac insect, and Kino is yielded by the Dhak (Butea). The most barren hills afford Olibanum, and the most arid looking plains will nourish the gum-secreting Acacias, and the Mouhwa or

Bassia, of which the flowers are fermented into a spirit, the seeds expressed for their oil, and the wood valued as excellent timber. Even in the western desert, the lakes yield Salt, and their shores are lined with plants, which are burned for Barilla. The mountains, though their bases are covered with a tropical and unhealthy jungle, abounding in valuable timber, have at certain elevations, a delightful climate, and productions analogous to European countries. There we may soon hope to see the Tea plant a thriving culture, and the Hemp turned to useful account. Also, though the cold and bleak tops of these mountains, and the plains on their northern face, appear barren and unproductive, their lakes abound with Borax, and their vallies with Vines; and we have in addition, Spikenard and Rhubarb from the vegetable, with Musk from the animal kingdom. Resources of India.

The multiplicity of subjects which such an investigation embraces, renders it, perhaps, difficult to determine which is the most important, and with which, therefore, it would be most proper to commence: whether with the mineral, the vegetable, or the animal kingdom; whether with such products as are the result of art, or with those which are the spontaneous production of nature. But as we have displayed the advantages derivable from the vegetable kingdom, and as the revenue in India is derived chiefly from the land, the culture of this, and the improvement of Agri- Conclusion.

Conclusion. culture, certainly claim the first place, and most prominent attention, whether we consider the improvement of the present, or the introduction of new cultures. The more so, as in such a course we can include all the vegetable with some animal products. The improvement of Agriculture may naturally be followed or accompanied by the means to be adopted for the investigation and making known the Natural Products of the country, whether of the Animal, the Vegetable, or the Mineral kingdom; and which may be valuable for Manufactures and Commerce. To comprehend the diversities of so wide a field, to evolve its various natural resources, and to display its manifold capabilities, is a task of no ordinary magnitude; but the benefits which may be insured are more than commensurate to the difficulties to be overcome; and if we take only ordinary precaution in suiting our measures to the objects we have in view, every fresh step will afford an advanced position from which to make further conquests, for affording facilities to the Government, and benefit to the People.

APPENDIX.

NOTES ON THE INTRODUCTION OF USEFUL PLANTS INTO INDIA.

*Written at the request of the Governer-General, Lord Auckland, previous to his departure for India, by the Author.**

THE introduction of Plants, both useful and ornamental, into India from other countries, though carried to some extent, has not yet been effected to the degree which is advisable, considering the benefits to be derived, and the great probability of success, if proper principles be attended to, in the selection of plants and the places into which they are introduced.

Of these, climate is the principal, and that of the provinces of the Bengal Presidency may be considered under the three heads: first, that of the Southern parts, or Bengal proper; secondly, that of the Northern; and thirdly, that of the Hill Provinces. The climate of Central India is different from all, but may be considered a modification, in some measure, of the first and second, combining the temperature of Bengal with the dryness of the north-western provinces.

In introducing the seeds of annuals into any part of the Bengal Presidency, except the Hills,

* Read 9th April 1836, and published in the Trans. of the Agricultural and Horticultural Society of India. Vol. iii. p. 37.

it should be borne in mind, that having a cold, a warm, and a rainy season, in the first, that is, from October to March, they are able to grow the products of European latitudes, and in the others those which are peculiar to Tropical countries.

Hence, in proceeding from Europe, it is advisable, and always acceptable, to take fresh seeds of kitchen-garden vegetables, though these in India are now very good; the different kinds of "sweet herbs" might also be taken, as less common, and likely to be established easily in the northern provinces. With respect to plants cultivated as "flowers," many of those which are found in English gardens, with the exception of the spring flowers, will grow in Indian gardens in the cold weather: especially such as require the high summer temperature to bring them to perfection, as many plants, common in Indian gardens, are to be seen in the heighth of the summer in those of England. Many of the late introductions, therefore, from South America and California, would be desirable in India and likely to succeed, especially as the Botanic Gardens of Calcutta and Saharunpore, separated by one thousand miles of intervening country, allow of experiments being made in almost the extreme points of the Bengal Presidency. Fruit trees have frequently been introduced from Liverpool, by the Horticultural Society of India, though the climate of the lower provinces is not well suited for them; but if plants can be conveyed safe to the hills, grafts to any extent might be distributed to the gardens in the plains.

But if it be desired to introduce plants which may be permanently useful, it is requisite to attend more particularly to the climate of the countries where the plants are indigenous, as well as to that of the different parts of India; for there is no doubt that, by a little care, we may find something analogous to whatever may be required.

Bengal, though just beyond the Tropics, may be considered as, in a great measure, participating in a tropical climate; as there is considerable uniformity of temperature and of moisture throughout the year, and the cold of winter is never so considerable as to kill many of the tropical productions of the vegetable kingdom. Here, therefore, may be most fitly introduced many of the productions which form the riches of the Indian Archipelago, though parts of the Indian and Malayan Peninsulas are better suited for the subsequent cultivation. Many also of the plants of Brazil, of the northern parts of South America, as well as of the West Indies, would succeed well in Bengal and most parts of India. Indeed many have already been introduced by means of the Calcutta Botanic Garden, and are distributing throughout the country, as the Log-wood, and Mahogany, Coco, Arrow Root, Avocado Pear, Pimento, Annotto. Others, previously introduced, are common in every part of India, as the Pine-apple, Guava, Papaya, Capsicum, and Tobacco. The success attending these is our best guarantee for that which may attend all subsequent endeavours.

The Cotton and Tobacco of America, it is well known, are far superior in quality to that produced in India, and even the Rice of the former brings double the price of that from the latter country. The Company have for some time adopted measures for importing Cotton and Tobacco Seed from America into India; but with Rice, it seems worthy of inquiry whether it be owing to inferiority of production, or to badness of selection, that so indifferent an article is sent to England. So impressed was a Liverpool merchant of the benefit likely to attend an improvement in the Rice imported into England from India, that he actually sent some bags of American Rice to his correspondents in Calcutta, which in cleaning had been deprived of the embryo, as well as of the husk, and of which consequently there was as little possibility of vegetating as of kiln-dried hops, which have likewise been sent to India by *practical* people. The *Pernambuco* Cotton seems particularly desirable, as Koster, in his account of Brazil, states that it improves in quality the farther the cultivation recedes from the sea. The Martaban and Persian Tobaccos are of so superior a quality, that it seems as advisable to attempt their extended cultivation, as the introduction of the seed of the tobacco of the Havannah or of the Caraccas.

Among the plants which appear worthy of introduction from America into India, the *Cinchonas* are particularly desirable, and would, no doubt, succeed on the Neilgheries; the different kinds of *Ipecacuanha*, as Cephaëlis Ipecacuanha affording the best, and Pyschotria emetica and herbacea, Richardsonia brasiliensis, rosea, and scabra, which give inferior kinds; *Sarsaparilla, Jalap, Quassia, Guaiacum, Cusparia, Cascarilla;* Copaifera yielding *Balsam* of *Copaiba; Balsams* of *Tolu* and *Peru* Trees; Polygala Senega, Krameria triandra; Coutarea speciosa, a substitute for *Peruvian Bark,* and Baccharis genistelloides is another; Dipterix odorata yielding the *Tonquin Bean; Brazil Wood,* Cæsalpinia braziliensis; *Rosewood*, Jacaranda ovalifolia; Hevea guianensis yielding *Caoutchouc*, as well as the Lobelia yielding the same substance; Schinus molle; *Gum elemi* tree; Bertholletia excelsa, or *Brazil nut* tree, are all worthy of introduction, as well as others—as the *Cabbage Palm;* Araucaria imbricata; Orchideæ, and among them the *Vanilla;* Passion Flowers and Fuchsias, as ornamental plants; Ilex Paraguensis, affording the *Mate Tea*, might also be introduced, and from the East of Africa the *Calumba* plant and Telfairia volubilis.

The northern, or rather the north-western, provinces of India, are hot and parched up during the hot weather months, but water is always near the surface. In the rainy season a great equability of temperature, owing to the moisture, is produced all over India, so that in the northern as in the southern parts, Rice is cultivated with the other tropical grains. But in the winter the cold is so considerable, that the thermometer frequently falls below the freezing point; but the general fall and rise are so gradual, as to allow of five months of very fine weather, during which wheat and barley are cultivated in the fields, and European kitchen-garden vegetables in gardens, while the natural vegetation approximates in many respects to that which characterizes what is called the Oriental Region.

Here it would be advisable to introduce, for the sake of experiment, superior kinds of *wheat* and *barley*, to see if they be more productive than those at present cultivated in the north of India. *Flax* also, which is only cultivated as an oil seed, might afford fibre for rope-making, if cultivated from Europe seed. The ***Persian Tobacco*** might here find a suitable locality as well as that from Latakia. Some of the central parts, as Malwa, and some of the northern, appear also the best suited for the cultivation of *cotton*. Many of the Cruciferæ are cultivated as oil seeds: it is worthy of experiment whether those cultivated in Europe for the same purpose, as Brassica napus and campestris, are more productive than the Indian species. *Black* and *white Mustard* might, without doubt, be successfully cultivated, if introduced. *Vines* of a superior kind would be a great acquisition in northern India, and at the foot of the hills the *Hop* would succeed. The *Carob* tree is particularly desirable. The *Olive*, there is great probability, would succeed, as also the *Cork*-tree, with the *Ilex*, *Kermes*, *Dyer's* and *Barbary Oaks*. The *Laurel* and *Sweet Bay*, *Manna Ash*, *Pistachio*, *Mastich*, and *Venice Turpentine*-trees; the species of Cistus yielding *ladanum*. Styrax officinalis yielding *Storax;* the species of Astragalus affording *tragacanth*. *Sumach*, *Savine*, *Scammony*, and *Colocynth*, might all be grown, as well as in the cold weather some of the drugs of colder climates, as *Foxglove*, *Belladonna*, *Hemlock*, and many others. The *Caper Bush* and *Prickly Pear* would undoubtedly thrive. With these also some African plants, as Zizyphus Lotus; *Dragon's Blood Tree;* Acacia vera, nilotica and Seyal; and from Persia, *Gum Ammoniac* and *Galbanum*, with the *Myrrh* from Arabia. As India also stretches nearly as far north, as Africa and New Holland do south, we might also grow in northern India, the Heaths, Proteas, Mesembryanthemums, Aloes and Diosmas of the Cape, with the Eucalypti of New Holland. It would be unreasonable to expect success with all, but the reasons for calculating on it are so strong, that there is no doubt it might be insured for many, and the situation of the Saharunpore Botanic Garden in

30° of N. latitude, enables experiments to be made with facility and with cheapness.

The Hill Provinces, with the exception of being under the influence of the rains, have the climate and seasons of European countries, and as they have the vegetation, they might cultivate all their useful and ornamental products, with the exception of such fruits as require a long summer for coming to maturity.

Here, as Wheat and Barley are cultivated, experiments might be made with *Wheat*, *Barley*, *Bere*, *Bigg*, *Oats* and *Rye*. Fruit trees introduced for affording grafts for the plains, as *Apples*, *Pears*, *Plums*, *Nectarines*, *Apricots*, *Cherries*, *Cranberries*, and *Bilberries*, might be introduced. The *Spanish Chesnut* and *Sugar Maple*. American and European *Oaks* and *Pines* of superior kinds, as well as the *Beech*, *Ash*, and *Lime*-tree. American Magnolias and the Tulip tree ; Drimys Winteri, Rhododendrons, Azaleas, Kalmias, Heaths and the Strawberry tree, would all thrive, and the *Hop* might be successfully cultivated in the vallies and in the mountains, and would be a desirable acquisition as they have begun to brew beer. *Hemp* grows wild, and is abundant, both in the plains of Northern India and in the hills, but it has never been employed for rope-making, though experiments have been made to find a substitute for it.

ON THE TRANSMISSION OF SEEDS TO AND FROM INDIA.

LETTER* FROM PROFESSOR LINDLEY TO J. C. MELVILL, ESQ.

Horticultural Society of London, Jan. 16, 1839.

Sir,—With reference to your letter of the 20th ult., and my acknowledgment of it of the 22d, I beg now to state that I have very carefully examined the seeds which have been received by the Honourable Court of Directors by the overland conveyance from Bombay, and that I shall with pleasure undertake the duty of distributing them, provided the Court approves of the manner in which I propose to do it.

The collection in question consists of about fifty packets of various sizes, containing seeds of plants inhabiting the hot plains of India: a part of these are species of no importance whatever, *viz.* Bixa Orellana, Amaranthus, Lantana, Gypsophila perfoliata, Stachytarpheta mutabilis; a few are Medicinal plants, *viz.* Butea frondosa, Cassia fistula, Cinchona excelsa, Mimosa Arabica, Swietenia febrifuga, Sterculia urens, Mimosa Catechu. The remainder, with the exception of a bag of seeds of the Teak, are hot-house plants, of no known use, but some of which are objects of ornament, and all of which have, I believe, been long since introduced from India to the

---

* Published in the Proceedings of the Agricultural and Horticultural Society of India, 12th June 1839.

gardens of this country. The whole appear to be in good condition. The quantity of each kind of seed is generally small, and in some instances will not bear to be divided: in others there is sufficient for several persons. But as there is little in the collection sufficiently rare or curious to interest those private individuals who are cultivators of stove plants for the sake of their beauty, it does not appear to me desirable to offer them to any except Public Botanical Institutions. I would therefore advise the Honourable Court to direct the distribution to be made as follows:

The seed of medicinal plants to the garden of the Society of Apothecaries of Chelsea:

Duplicates of the foregoing, where any can be divided, and the remainder of the collection, to be sent to the Botanic Gardens of Kew, Edinburgh, Glasgow, Cambridge, and Oxford. After these institutions have been supplied, there will still remain a small quantity of several kinds. Those might be useful in some of the British Colonies in the West Indies; and as a society has lately been established in the Bermudas, for the express purpose of improving the resources of those islands, it might be adviseable to place them in the hands of Lieut. Colonel Reid, of the Royal Engineers, who is now about to proceed to the Bermudas as Governor. In the event of a further surplus, a small supply might be forwarded to the Bahamas, where the Government is also anxious to obtain the plants of other countries.

It will be obvious from the statement already made, that no part of the present collection is of that degree of importance which could justify my recommending to the Honourable Court a further despatch of such seeds by the overland conveyance to this country. It appears to me, that the introduction of plants which are mere objects of curiosity, or only useful in distant colonies, should be left to the ordinary and private modes of communication, unless they are made a subject of special requisition. And as the species found in the tropical climates of India are all of this description, the general rule might be adopted of excluding all such plants from the overland despatch. There is no hope of their being naturalized, or made in any way to conduce to public advantage in this country, for they are without exception uncultivatable, except in hot-houses. It is the more desirable to limit the supplies of seeds from India, to those which come from the cold provinces, because in those districts there is a great abundance of species, the introduction of which is an object of national importance. The similarity of the climate of Great Britain, and of many parts of the Himalayas, is well known, and has been very particularly illustrated by Professor Royle, late Superintendent of the Honourable Company's Botanic Garden, at Saharunpore, in the "Illustrations of the Botany of the Himalaya Mountains;" and consequently it has always been expected that the noble vegetation of the North of India might be successfully transferred to this country. That this opinion was well grounded has lately been proved by the effects of the severe winter, 1837-38, when a large proportion of all the Himalayan trees, and other plants now in this country, exposed suddenly and under very unfavourable circumstances to a temperature of from 4½ to 12½ Fahr. resisted the intensity of the frost as well as our native species. The Deodar, and other Himalayan Coniferous plants, in particular, are evidently as hardy as the Larch, and the Spruce Firs; I would therefore advise that the authorities in India be directed to confine themselves to the transmission by the overland despatch, of the ornamental and useful trees and other plants inhabiting the districts in which the climate resembles that of England.

It is difficult at this distance to define with any precision the limits of such districts, but perhaps a good, and certainly a very simple, guide may be found in the Coniferous tribe, of the habits of all, which we have sufficient information. The Deodar Cedar is hardy, the Pinus longifolia not. It therefore might be directed, that all those districts in which the Deodar* occurs, or which have a colder climate, should generally furnish the supplies to be forwarded by the overland conveyance, that the species belonging to the Pinus longifolia regions should be either excluded, or at least form a subordinate object, and that all plants from yet warmer districts should be entirely excluded.

* Dr. Falconer suggests the region of Oaks.

In the Deodar region and colder localities are numerous species of Birch, Alder, Chesnut, Pyrus, Sycamore, Oak, &c. &c., valuable as timber trees; and a profusion of herbaceous plants, and bushes of striking beauty. Of course, there is also an abundance of plants of no beauty, nor any known use, all which should be omitted, as they are only interesting to systematical botanists, who may be safely left to discover for themselves the best method of procuring them. It is unnecessary to give any more precise direction than this, except in the following cases:—The Prangos Hay Plant, which furnishes valuable food for sheep in cold and barren situations, should be a special object of importation. The Rhubarbs called Rheum Webbianum, spicatum and Moorcroftianum, are also much wanted; and it is most desirable that constant supplies should be forwarded of the seed of the Deodar Cedar, of the Khutrow and Pindrow firs, and of the Neoza Pine; none of which can be expected to bear cones in this country for a great many years, and which must therefore remain confined to the possession of a few persons, unless supplies of seeds are forwarded in abundance from their native places. The nurserymen contrive, indeed, to multiply such species by grafting; but the plants so procured will probably be shortlived, and are not suited to the purpose of forming woods.

With regard to the Seeds which can be transmitted with the best hopes of success from England to India, for distribution to public officers and other residents in the Himalayan range of Mountains, it is impossible for one who is personally unacquainted with the country to advise the Honourable Company with so much confidence as another person might, who has himself resided in the provinces referred to; I would therefore take the liberty of suggesting to the Honourable Court the propriety of obtaining a report upon the subject from Professor Royle, who was so long in the Himalayas, and who must be intimately acquainted with the wants and wishes of the residents there. In the mean while, as the Governor-General has been pleased to do me the honour of signifying his wish that I should be consulted upon the subject, I beg leave to lay before the Court the following general Memoranda.

There can be no doubt that the fine varieties of European fruit trees of all descriptions are desirable objects of export; but the varieties cannot be propagated with certainty by seeds, and as trees are too bulky for the overland route, it is necessary to ascertain whether cuttings will travel with any prospect of success. This experiment is now in course of trial, a packet of small Gooseberry, Currant, and Raspberry plants having been sent some weeks since to Simla at the particular desire of Lord Auckland, and the overland route having been used by permission of the Right Honourable the President of the Board of

Commissioners for the Affairs of India. Should this experiment have, as I expect it will, a good result, there will then be no doubt that all our European fruit trees may be readily conveyed to the Himalaya Mountains. But it will be previously necessary that the Saharunpore Garden should be provided with stocks on which to bud or graft them; if such stocks do not already exist there, they should be provided: the wild pears, plums, quinces, and crabs, of the country, will answer this purpose, as well as those of Europe.

European Vegetable seeds are, in general, objects of importance in India, where many of the races soon degenerate; but they would probably be thought too bulky for an overland despatch, except in a few cases.

England can, I fear, contribute in no great degree to the introduction of other plants to India, unless it were thought advantageous to procure our forest trees and natural shrubs—what seem the most desirable are those which inhabit countries warmer than our own, and which are too impatient of a Northern winter to produce seeds with us. In order to procure them, it would be necessary to communicate specially with persons stationed in many different places; perhaps the British Consular Agents could be employed for the purpose. Supposing that the Honourable Court thought fit to take such measures, it is difficult to estimate too highly the advantages that would accrue to the Natives of India. Among the plants of which seeds should be procured, I would particularly name the following :

The Carob tree, Ceratonia Siliqua, a native of Syria, and the hottest parts of the South of Europe. This forms a large tree, which bears in abundance pods filled with a nutritious substance. It is tenacious of life in a singular degree, and seeks its nourishment far from the surface of the ground, on which account it suffers little from the long continuance of drought. The pods are a common article of food in the countries where the tree is found, and are by some supposed to be the "locusts" on which St. John fed in the Wilderness; they are sometimes sold in the fruiterers' shops of London. During the Peninsular War the pods were found of great value as food for Cavalry horses, and I entertain no doubt that if the tree could be extensively introduced into the drier parts of Northern India, it would render the famines we read of almost impossible. Seeds of this might be obtained conveniently in Egypt.

From the same country at the same time the Egyptian wheat, which succeeds in dry and sterile soil, and the Cassia acutifolia or Alexandrian Senna, might be procured.

Scammony is a drug which is consumed in large quantities in medicine. All that comes to the market is obtained from Smyrna and Aleppo and is so much adulterated as to be materially diminished in value; seeds of this plant could be procured from either place, along with the seeds of the valuable tobacco of Latakia.

Colonel Chesney found at Suvadia, at the mouth of the Orontes, Silk Mulberries of a finer quality than any which he had seen elsewhere; these could be easily procured: Cotton seeds should be procured from every country where the cotton of the West is of superior quality. Botanists know that the varieties of this plant are extremely numerous; and it is hardly to be doubted that, however great the influence of climate may be upon the quality of this substance, special peculiarities in particular varieties are also deserving of the most careful investigation. The Honourable Company's Botanical officers in India have, I presume, already made numerous reports of their experiments upon this subject; but still it is one of such great commercial importance, that further investigation is most desirable on an extensive and varied scale.

The Olive, for which there is not a sufficient substitute in India, must be obtained from the Olive districts of Italy, rather than from those of Spain.

From North America the Magnoliaceous plants are well worth introduction, not only for their beauty, but because of their medicinal importance. The same part of the world might be made to supply the Hickories, Black Walnuts, and other valuable Forest Trees, and most especially the seeds of Acer saccharinum or Sugar Maple, the sugar of which is of good quality, and which Dr. Royle thinks "might be a valuable gift to the people of the hills, who are too poor to buy sugar." These and all other North American seeds should be bought at New York as early in the season as possible, and forwarded by a steamer. Upon their arrival in England they should be opened and carefully repacked according to their several natures, and immediately afterwards dispatched to India. Such precautions are necessary, because in most cases the seeds of North American trees retain their vegetating principle for but a short time, and die very early as well as quickly.

With regard to the introduction to India of American and African Medicinal Plants, it would be necessary to make a special report upon that subject, in case the Honourable Court should be of opinion that it deserves to be considered; and it would embrace a large range of details, which some of the officers of the Company will readily furnish.

I believe I have nothing further to add, except that from the great extent of the British possessions in India, and the infinite modifications and combinations of soil and climate to be found within them, there can be no doubt whatever that almost every production of every climate, except the Arctic, may be so completely naturalized, that where they are of any importance as objects of cultivation, they may be brought to all the perfection of which they are susceptible in other countries, provided proper skill and care are shown in the selection of their situations.

I have the honour to be, Sir,
Your very obedient servant,
(Signed) JOHN LINDLEY, *Vice Sec.*

LETTER FROM PROFESSOR ROYLE,
To J. C. MELVILL, ESQ., *Secretary to the Honourable the Court of Directors of the East-India Company.*

SIR, — In acknowledging the receipt of your letter of the 20th ultimo, informing me that the Governor General of India, with a view to the introduction of the "useful and ornamental plants of England into India," had suggested to the Honourable the Court of Directors the propriety of my being consulted on the subject, allow me to express my gratification at the honour that has been done me. The subject is one upon which I have frequently expressed and published my opinions, and feel well assured that great benefit would accrue to India by the judicious introduction into it of the various useful plants, and even animals of different countries, which are suited to its various climates and wide-spread territories.

Engaged as is the Committee of Commerce and Agriculture of the Royal Asiatic Society in making some of the Natural Products of India known to the manufacturers of Europe, it will be highly gratifying to those interested in the prosperity of India to know, that the other great branch of the subject included in the attempt to improve the resources of India is to be prosecuted under the auspices of the Honourable the Court of Directors and of the Governor General of India. With the necessary attention to principles as well as to details, success in a great variety of instances is as certain, as will be the eventual benefit, and the expence need be but small with two such establishments as the Honourable Company's Botanic Gardens at Calcutta and Saharunpore, situated at opposite extremities of the Great Gangetic Plains, with one thousand miles of intervening territory, and with considerable difference of climate.

The subject is not a new one, though it does not appear in recent times to have been prosecuted with the zeal it merits. But numerous useful Plants have been introduced into India by the Calcutta Botanic Garden, and others by that at Saharunpore. More might have been introduced into the former from the new world, had there been more frequent direct communication with different parts of South America, Africa and the West Indies. The Northern Garden might have acclimated many South of Europe and North American plants, had it not been remote, both from Calcutta and Bombay.

But as different ages of the world have been

memorable for the different routes of commerce, as well as for the interchange of the useful plants of different countries, so may the present time be distinguished by the more numerous introduction into India of useful plants, in consequence of the facilities afforded by Steam Navigation. The Romans, we know, introduced into Europe many of our fruit trees from Armenia and Persia, as the Peach, Apricot, Nectarine, Quince, Cherry, &c., while the Turks introduced plants into Constantinople, which thence spread over Europe, as the Lombardy Poplar, Thorn Apple, Hyacinth and others—so the discovery of America, and of the passage round the Cape of Good Hope, introduced into India many of the productions of the new world, as the Tobacco, Capsicum, Indian Corn, and more recently the Potato, now all so universally diffused, together with such fruits as the Custard and Pine Apples, Guava and Papaya. But few plants have been introduced from the North into India. The Peach and Pomegranate must, no doubt, however, have travelled South, as probably did also the Poppy, now so extensive an object of culture in the cold season of India. In the North of India, therefore, much may be done, and here Steam Navigation proceeding from the South of Europe to Bombay, and thence overland for seeds, or up the Indus for plants, affords every desirable facility.

I, therefore, confine myself in the following observations to "the introduction into India of the useful and ornamental plants of England," begging leave, however, to substitute Europe for the latter, and to include in my summary some of the plants of North America. On account, however, of the peculiarity of the climate of the North of India, it is hardly possible to mention these without some notice of the Tropical plants which may be, and are, cultivated with them.

The Southern Provinces of India, including Bengal, and the Lower Provinces, with much of the Peninsula, being of a tropical nature in climate, with little cold weather, are chiefly suited for the cultivation of the plants, whether annuals or perennials, of the intra-tropical islands, and of the warm parts of America and Africa. As the tropic-like rainy season, however, extends over all India, its peculiarities of a tropical climate, heat and moisture, with considerable uniformity of both, prevail over a great extent of territory for a few months in the year; and, therefore, in the most Northern parts we have the cultivation of Rice, Sorghum, Indian Corn, and other tropical grains, in the very same fields where in the cold weather months we have Wheat and Barley, with Peas and Beans. This double climate and double culture it is necessary to notice, in order to have a complete view of the nature of the country and climate of Northern India.

The mean temperature of the year at Saharunpore, in 30° of N. latitude, is about 73°; and of the months of Jan. 52°, Feb. 55°, March 67°,

April 78°, May 85°, June 90°, July 85°, Aug. 83°, Sept. 79°, Oct. 74°, Nov. 64°, and Dec. 55°. From the middle of October to the middle of April, the various useful and ornamental plants of European climates may be successfully cultivated. The minimum of temperature has been 25° Fahr. in January, and the maximum 105° in June.

The nursery which I established at Mussooree in the Himalayas, at 6,500 feet of elevation, though fifty miles distant, is very convenient for the introduction of European plants. Mussooree has a minimum of only 27°, and a maximum of 80° of Fahr., showing that the equability is greater than in the neighbouring plains. The mean temperature is about 57°, and of the months of Jan. 42°, Feb. 45°, March 53°, April 59°, May 66°, June 67°, July 67°, Aug. 66°, Sept. 64°, Oct. 57°, Nov. 50°, Dec. 45°.

The season for cultivation in the Mussooree climate is from March to October; but between the Saharunpore Garden and Mussooree Nursery, a complete year of moderate climate may be obtained for the germination of seeds of temperate climates, as the mean temperature of the several months is, at Saharunpore, in Nov. 64°, Dec. 55°, Jan. 52°, Feb. 55°, March 57°; and at Mussooree, in April 59°, May 66°, June 67°, July 67°, Aug. 66°, Sept. 64°, Oct. 57°.

The climate having been proved favourable, little difficulty will be experienced with the soil or with the irrigation, as far as the experiments are concerned. The subsequent distribution of plants which have succeeded in the Depôt Gardens must be determined by various circumstances; but the first should only be sent to favourable localities, as failure is apt to discourage further attempts.

The next and principal subject of attention, for which the preceding observations are only preparatory, is the kind of plants best suited to the Northern parts of India, and the Himalaya mountains. Here we must be guided not only by the nature of the plants with respect to vicissitudes of temperature, but also their usefulness—their annual or perennial nature, and in noticing the climate into which we wish to introduce them, take care to compare it with that from which they are to be introduced. The plants to be introduced may be considered with respect to their usefulness, or to their fitness for different kinds of climate. In the former case, we should arrange them under the heads of Food for the inhabitants, or Fodder for their Cattle; such as are likely to be useful in any of the ordinary arts of life, or those which may afford products likely to become articles of commerce. Merely ornamental plants should not be neglected, nor those remarkable for their odour, as both gratify the senses, and offer inducements to many to pay attention to gardening, when other more useful plants are necessarily introduced, and with little additional expense. Fruit trees might appear to many as not included among useful plants, but independent of their increasing the proportion of esculent matter in a country, they might become sources of considerable commerce between the plains and mountains of India, as is now the case with Cashmere.

There is another class of plants to which I paid considerable attention when in India, and which form the chief objects of my present duties—that is, Medicinal plants. I was first requested to do so by the Medical Board of Bengal, and I cultivated many articles which were pronounced, after trial in the General Hospital at Calcutta, to be of the best quality. Dr. Falconer, the present able Superintendent of the Saharunpore Botanic Garden, writes me that Extract of Henbane, which I first cultivated and manufactured, still continues to be supplied from the Saharunpore Garden to the Hospital Depôts. In the same situation, and in the Hill Nursery, many other medicinal plants, now sent from this country, might be successfully cultivated, and thus be not only more cheaply produced, but also prescribed in a fresher state.

Keeping these several objects in view, I have thought it preferable for practical purposes, that is, the operations of horticulture and the selection of sites for the experiments, to arrange those plants I have as yet been able to think of, in three separate lists, according to the situation for which they are suited.

1. Annuals fit for cultivation in the Plains of

India in the cold weather and in the summer of the Himalayas.

2. Perennials probably suited to the Plains of North-west India.

3. Perennials suitable to the Himalayas.

Besides the plants mentioned in the respective lists, I have long thought it a very interesting subject of inquiry to ascertain by experiment whether the grains the people of India possess in common with Europe are of an equal degree of goodness and equally prolific, as for instance their Wheat, Barley, Rape, Mustard seeds, &c. Some of the plants which I have included in my lists are intended to be useful for their products, which may become objects of commerce; but this involves another subject of inquiry, and that is, whether the analogous substances which India naturally possesses are superior or inferior in quality to those cultivated in other parts of the world.

It is probable that some of those enumerated in the accompanying lists may not be suited to the localities indicated, and a still greater number that might be suited to them are, I am well aware, entirely omitted. This has occurred from want of time to give the subject the full consideration it deserves; but as the plan, to be successful to any great degree, must necessarily be carried on for a few years, I shall be happy to return to the subject if required, and point out the plants suited for cultivation in different parts of India.

Though failure may attend some, I am well satisfied that success will attend the majority of instances, and feel the utmost confidence in stating, that, if the subject of the Introduction of Useful Plants suited to the different parts of India be continued, and the Principles be not neglected which should guide these attempts, very beneficial results will in a few years be evident to all. Also, that if this be combined with an Investigation of and Publication to the Manufacturing world of the very varied Natural Products of India; an increase of the Commerce and Resources of that empire will ensue to an extent anticipated by few, but of which, after long attention to the subject, I feel well assured and hope to be able to prove to the sceptical.

I have the honour to be, Sir, your most obedient humble servant,

(Signed) J. FORBES ROYLE, M.D.

London, 31st Dec. 1838.

LIST OF PLANTS,

SUITED FOR INTRODUCTION INTO DIFFERENT PARTS OF INDIA.

Annuals fit for Cultivation in the Plains of India during the cold Weather, and in the Himalayas during the Summer Months.*

Europe Corn Grasses
——— Vegetables
——— Sweet Herbs
Most Annuals of English Flower Gardens
Wheat and Egyptian Wheat
Barley
Bere
Bigg
Oats
Rye
Buckwheat
Mustard, Black and White
Rape, Colza
Flax
Tobacco, Virginia
——— Havanna
Tobacco, Persian
——— Latakia
Peas, Beans
Vetches, Tares
Edible Lupin
Clover, Red and White
Lucern
Alexandrine Clover
Turnips, Carrots
Beet-root
Mangel Wurzel
Skirret, Parsnip
Carraway, Fennel
Dill, Parsley
Aniseed
Hemlock, Foxglove
Belladonna, &c.

* The Annuals suited to the rainy season of every part of the plains, and even of some of the mountains of India, are already very numerous; consisting both of commercial articles, and of such as are fitted for food. Among the former we have Indigo, Cotton, Sugar Cane and Tobacco, even with Rice, Maize, Sorghum, several species of Phaseolus and Dolichos, Paspalum, Panicum, Arum, Sesamum, Sun and Sunnee, and many others. During this season Senna, &c. may be cultivated. Many introductions may be made from the West Indies and South America of new plants, or of varieties of the best kinds of those already cultivated in India.

Perennials suited to the drier and more northern parts of India.

Liriodendron tulipifera
Capparis spinosa
Acacia vera
——— Verek
——— Seyal
Olive tree
Carob tree
Manna Ash
Laurel
Sweet Bay
Mastich tree
Chian Turpentine
Pistachio Nut tree
Myrrh tree
Sassafras tree
Sumach tree
Astragalus—yielding Tragacanth
Cistus—yielding Laudanum
Styrax officinalis
Scammony
Cork tree
Oak Ilex
—— Kermes
—— Dyer's
—— Barbary
Quercus tinctoria
Quercus Ægilops
Quercus Ballota
Cactus opuntia
——— Tuna
——— cochenillifer
Morus alba
——— multicaulis
Savine
Juniper
New Zealand Flax
Poterium spinosum
Liquorice plant
Aloe soccotrina
—— Barbadensis
Euphorbia plant
Assafœtida
Galbanum
Ammoniacum
Sagapenum
Artemisia Abrotanum
——— Santonica
Phœnix dactylifera
Diosmæ sp.
Eucalypti
Heaths
Proteas
Mesembryanthemums
Pelargoniums

Perennials suited to the Summer and able to withstand the cold of the Himalayan Winter.

Almond, Peach
Apricot, Nectarine
Plum, Cherry
Apple, Pear, Quince
Spanish Chesnut
Filberts, Hazle nut

Gooseberry, Currants
Raspberry
Rhubarb, all the kinds
Gentian, Jalap
Seneka
Juniper, Savine
Bilberries, Cranberries
Costus of the Ancients
Saffron
Europe and North America Timber Trees
Sugar-Maple, Hickories, and Black Walnuts
Oaks and Pines
Beech, Ash
Lime tree
American Magnolias
Tulip tree
Drimys Winteri
Rhododendrons, Azaleas
Kalmias, Heaths
Strawberry tree
Rhamnus infectoria
——— saxatilis, &c.
Lavender, Rosemary

Tropical Perennials suited to the Plains, and some to the Mountains, of the southern parts of India.

Coffee, Cacao
Pimento, Papaya
Nutmeg, Cloves
Cinnamon, Camphor
Cocculus palmatus
(Columba plant)
Telfairia volubilis
Pterocarpus erinaceus
(African Kino)
Elæis guineensis (Oil Palm)
Bix a orellana (Annotto)
Persea gratissima
Maranta arundinacea
Canna coccinea
Copaifera, yielding Balsam of Copaiba
Balsams of Peru and Tolu trees
Krameria triandra
Coutarea speciosa
Arenga saccharifera (Gomuto)
Cabbage Palm
Ceroxylon andicola
Vanilla and Tropical Orchideæ
Passion Flowers
Fuchsias
Ilex paraguayensis
Raphis vinifera
Sterculia acuminata
Sarcocephalus esculentus
Anona senegalensis
Chrysobalanus Icaco
Logwood, Mahogany
Nicaragua Wood
Quassia, Simaruba
Cinchonas, all the species
Cephælis Ipecacuanha
Psychotria emetica
——— herbacea

Smilax officinalis
——— medica, &c.
Guaiacum tree
Cusparia tree
Cascarilla plant
Croton Tiglium
Hymenæa Courbaril
Stillingia sebifera (Tallow tree)
Elæococca verrucosa (Oil tree)
——— vernicia (Varnish tree)
Agave, species of
Sanseviera guineensis
Baccharis genistelloides
Dipterix odorata (Tonquin Bean)
Cæsalpinia braziliensis, &c. (Brazil Wood)
Jacaranda ovalifolia (Rose Wood)
Hevea guianensis
Schinus molle
Bertholletia excelsa (Brazil Nut tree)

The foregoing lists having been referred to in the preceding pages (p. 248 and 445), are published as memoranda, nearly, as originally prepared. They might easily be rendered more copious, by an examination of the notices of the useful plants of different countries, but these are scattered, like the accounts of those of India, in a variety of publications, some Botanical, others Medical. A few are found in the lists of the Commerce of different countries, and others are mentioned by Travellers, of whom, however, but few are copious and exact in the relations, like Humboldt, or Spix and Martius. The names, to be fully useful to practical men, ought to be accompanied with a short account of the nature and uses of the different plants, their peculiar habits and culture, and the parts of India to which they appear best suited. This, it is evident, would require much time, in fact, constitute a work of itself. By referring to the Index, most of them will be found in the "Illustrations of Himalayan Botany," and generally with notices respecting the parts of India to which they are suited.

THE END.